At last! With this new addition to the Daily Routines series, elementary teachers can rejoice. For a long time, geometry, measurement, and data have taken a back seat in terms of priority in the elementary math curriculum. This resource provides teachers with practical tasks, strategies, and guidance on how to integrate these math topics intentionally and purposefully, support students' sense making, and allow students to build foundational understanding of this content.

Latrenda Knighten
President (2024–2026), National Council of Teachers of Mathematics
Retired Mathematics Supervisor
Baton Rouge, LA

John SanGiovanni and Dennis McDonald have delivered another essential resource for math educators! *Daily Routines to Jump-Start Geometry, Measurement, and Data* revitalizes often-overlooked concepts with engaging, practical routines. Designed to spark thinking and build excitement, these strategies can be used anytime in math class to inspire meaningful learning and mathematical success. This book is a game-changer for ensuring students connect with geometry, measurement, and data in powerful ways!

Georgina Rivera
Principal, West Hartford Public Schools
Vice President (2021–2023), NCSM
West Hartford, CT

Seeking a quick read about what is important related to teaching K–5 geometry, measurement, and data—that includes engaging routines to support that learning all year? This book is for you! Part 1 lays out big ideas in geometry, measurement, and data across K–5, Part 2 equips us with 20 engaging routines to support those big ideas (with many variations!), and Part 3 challenges us to effectively implement those routines. An excellent resource!

Jennifer Bay-Williams
Professor, Mathematics Education and Author
Louisville, KY

As a mathematics education consultant and coach for 24 years, I highly recommend this low-prep, high-impact resource. It ensures that geometry, measurement, and data are embedded with number concepts, giving math real context. These short, rich tasks make math meaningful and relatable, helping students connect ideas. With editable PowerPoint slides, it's a time-saver for busy teachers. Take the leap—your students will grow!

Jackie Ratkovic
Mathematics Education Consultant and Coach
Alberta, Canada

These authors understand the struggles of today's teachers without placing guilt and shame. They share the truths that every math teacher encounters daily. The book's ideas are shared in a step-by-step approach that can be incorporated into daily classroom instruction seamlessly and are not overwhelming, yet they provide an overwhelming amount of rigor in a short period. The routines allow for flexible thinking, reasoning, and engagement—behaviors that enhance the learning process, and stimulate active learning.

Kim West
Fifth Grade Classroom Teacher
Columbia, MD

This book is a must-have for any K–5 teacher! John SanGiovanni and Dennis McDonald have crafted 20 powerful measurement, data, and geometry routines—each packed with variations that can be implemented immediately. These often-overlooked content areas come to life with practical, engaging strategies that bring meaningful measurement, data, and geometry experiences into your classroom right away.

Zak Champagne
Chief Content Officer, Flynn Education
Olympia, WA

Daily Routines to Jump-Start Geometry, Measurement, and Data serves as an excellent resource for teachers to incorporate practical routines that promote both student engagement and discussion, and are easy to implement. Geometry, measurement, and data are often topics that are disconnected from number sense and hurried through at year end. These routines provide high-quality practice and foster connections that will deepen student understanding.

Cheryl Gray
Division Mathematics Coordinator, Louisa County Public Schools
Louisa, VA

Do you feel as if ideas related to geometry, measurement, and data often get put on the back burner? SanGiovanni and McDonald provide guidance for using a steady diet of routines throughout the school year to engage students in thinking deeply about these concepts. They are easy to implement, and your students will absolutely love them!!!

Susie Katt
K–2 Mathematics Coordinator, Lincoln Public Schools
Lincoln, NE

Daily Routines to Jump-Start Geometry, Measurement, and Data is perfect for any elementary math classroom, offering engaging and easy-to-implement number routines that reinforce key concepts. The embedded professional learning makes it a valuable resource for all educators!

Katie DiMartino
Elementary Math Coach
West Friendship, MD

This user-friendly resource is a must-have for any educator looking to make math both meaningful and fun. It highlights how K–5 math concepts can be taught effectively through geometry, measurement, and data throughout the year rather than left to the final units of study. This resource not only strengthens content knowledge but also sparks students' mathematical reasoning. This book provides clear strategies for implementing engaging routines and linking them to key math concepts.

Rosa Serratore
Past Regional Director, NCSM
CMC Board Member
CA Mathematics Framework Panel
Santa Monica, CA

These routines are designed to complement teachers' efforts and alleviate the stress of covering all concepts before state assessments. By focusing on building students' math agency, particularly with supporting standards, the book highlights how proficiency can be achieved through frequent experiences with geometry, measurement, and data.

Marissa Giangrosso
Math Instructional Coach
Blue Springs, MO

Daily Routines to Jump-Start Geometry, Measurement, and Data, Grades K-5

THE BOOK AT-A-GLANCE

A quick-reference table provides you with a brief description of each task, along with the corresponding task purpose.

JUMP-START ROUTINES FOR GEOMETRY, MEASUREMENT, AND DATA AT-A-GLANCE

TITLE (FOCUS CONTENT)	BRIEF	INCLUDED CONTENT	PAGE
#1 See It, Build It (Geometry)	Students practice recreating arrangements and shapes.	• Shape attributes • Area • Perimeter • 3D figures • Time • Money • Elapsed time	26
#2 Sorts (Geometry)	Students practice sorting shapes based on their attributes.	• Shape attributes • Polygons • Quadrilaterals • Time	33
#3 Venns (Geometry)	Students use Venn diagrams to compare and contrast shapes, figures, and other concepts.	• Shape attributes • Polygons • Quadrilaterals • Angles • Time	40
#4 Find It (Geometry)	Students look for shapes within composite figures.	• Shape attributes • Quadrilaterals	48
#5 Dots (Geometry)	Figures connect dots to make shapes and solve puzzles.	• Shape attributes • Polygons • Quadrilaterals • Angles • Perimeter • Area	54
#6 The Truth (Geometry)	Students consider three statements about geometric figures determining which are true and which are false.	• Shape attributes • Polygons • Quadrilaterals • 3D figures • Perimeter • Measurement conversions • Symmetry	61
#7 On the Move (Geometry)	Students reason about how shapes and figures move through space.	• Shape attributes • Transformations (translations, rotations, reflections) • Counting and skip counting	68

An **About the Routine** section provides an overview of what the routine entails.

ROUTINE 1

SEE IT, BUILD IT

ABOUT THE ROUTINE

In a "quick image" activity, you display or flash an image for a few seconds and then students talk about what they see. This routine borrows from that idea, but students first build an example of the image you flash before talking about how their "build" compares to your flash. This routine is perfect for developing skill with memory, shape recognition, spatial awareness, and vocabulary. It is a good precursor for the routine Find It (Routine #4) or Views (Routine #8). This routine is perfect for any grade as you can easily change the number of shapes and the complexity of the image to increase the challenge. But don't expect that simple images will be easy for all students regardless of their age. At every grade level, you'll find students with refined spatial awareness and memory as well as students who need more time and practice to develop both.

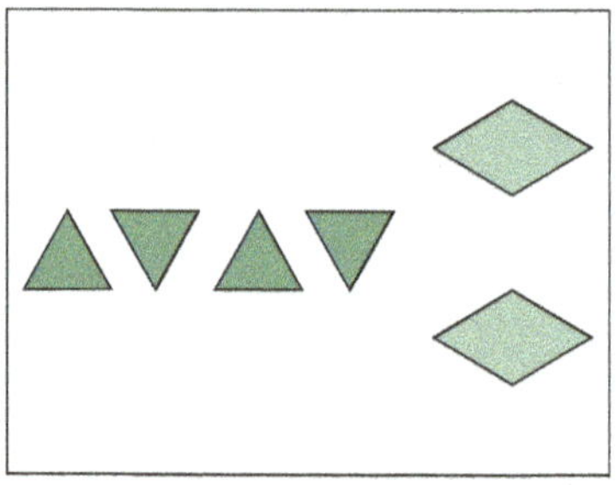

This routine is also a great way to practice vocabulary. Vocabulary in math can be avoided because adults misjudge how capable young students are with language. Terms are replaced with "kid-friendly" language. For example, in first grade, the commutative property might be called the "flip flop" property. This also happens with geometry when shapes are misnamed, or their definitions are completely misrepresented. Take for example the rhombus shown in the image at the start of the routine. It should be called a rhombus. It isn't a diamond or stretched square. Standards require students to learn and use vocabulary with accuracy and precision when talking or writing about math. So then, it is essential that students are introduced to the correct vocabulary from the start and use it during routines like this and others. Plus, if a kindergartener can recognize and name dinosaurs, like brontosaurus, they can surely handle rhombus.

It's critically important that teachers use vocabulary with precision and accuracy as well. But it's OK to make a mistake or speak informally. If you ask, "What's the answer?" just pause and correct yourself by saying, "Sorry, I meant to ask, what is the sum?" In this routine, you might say, "the blue one." If you do, stop and say, "Sorry, I mean the blue rhombus." Doing this shows students that people misspeak occasionally. It also shows them how to correct a statement. Most importantly, it sets the expectation for precise vocabulary use while also providing a brief dose of practice.

As you use this routine with your students, model the use of language and vocabulary. Provide

online resources — All routines can be downloaded for your use at **https://companion.corwin.com/courses/jumpstartroutines-geometry**

Online Resources icons signal the availability of downloadable tasks.

How This Routine Helps sections explain what students will gain from the routine at hand.

What to Do sections break down exactly how to use the routine in your classroom, step by step.

an anchor chart or vocabulary cards nearby so that students can access them when they don't remember a word. Remind students from time to time why precise language matters. Invite them to politely correct incorrect use of language or vocabulary. This invitation may even increase how well they listen to what you and their classmates say about the content.

HOW THIS ROUTINE HELPS

This routine deepens understanding of geometry by providing opportunities for students to

- identify shapes regardless of orientation;
- decompose and compose shapes;
- use precise vocabulary as they discuss designs (MP6);
- define shapes by their attributes;
- look for patterns in designs and builds (MP7);
- identify shapes regardless of orientation; and
- develop perseverance (MP1).

WHAT TO DO

1. Provide a collection of pattern blocks to small groups of students and a white board or something similar to each individual student. They will use this for their workspace.
2. Prepare an arrangement of shapes on a slide or to display with a document camera.
3. Present the arrangement to students for a few seconds. To do this with slides, put a blank slide before the image. Display the blank slide. Advance to the image for a few seconds and then go back to the blank slide. With a document camera, put something over the image like a binder or cardstock. Move it to show the image and then cover it back up.
4. Have students independently build or re-create the image they saw with pattern blocks.
5. Have partners compare their images with each other then have the class come together to share some of the builds they thought they saw.
6. Have students describe their images. For example, they might say, "I think I saw two blue rhombuses and three green triangles." Another might say, "I think I saw two blue rhombuses and four green triangles."
7. Show your image again and have students describe how their builds are different if they don't match your image.
8. You can repeat the activity once or twice in a short routine.

SOMETHING TO THINK ABOUT: SPATIAL AWARENESS

Spatial awareness describes one's ability to understand, analyze, and interpret the relationships between objects and spaces. This could be reasoning about how objects are positioned relative to one another or how an object or objects move. Humans rely on spatial awareness every day as they move through hallways, stairwells, or any other space. It also includes understanding diagrams, maps, or puzzles. Spatial awareness includes mental manipulation of objects. It also connects with pattern seeking and recognition. This routine practices pattern recognition, shape relationships through space, and visualizing. Other routines, like Views (Routine #8), practice visualization and perspective. Playing games like Memory or Blokus, working with puzzles, building figures with blocks or LEGO bricks, and performing body movements are just some of the many ways you can help elementary

Something to Think About sections describe unique considerations for routines.

Variations on each routine are provided to further deepen student understanding and provide ways to meet the varied needs of your learners.

students develop their spatial awareness. And the work may benefit more than just geometry. For example, number lines are spatial representations of number and quantity. They are used in the real world and mentally. Using number lines, or thinking about number relationships in general, is an extension of one's spatial awareness (Krasa, 2010). So, in a way, you might think of this routine and some of the other spatial experiences as number or number sense experiences too.

SEE IT, BUILD IT (VARIATIONS): USING TEMPLATES

This book is stuffed with examples of routines. For many, if not all of them, you don't need slides or any technology whatsoever to engage your students. Yet, having an electronic copy that you can share with colleagues or save for future use certainly has value. The many different routines come with templates for you to create your own examples. In this routine, we have provided a master slide with basic pattern block shapes for you to copy and manipulate. There are also templates baked in for pentominoes (Variation E) and cubes (Variation F). If you come up with your own variations, create a template of shapes or objects so that you can easily build new prompts and tasks for your students.

Variation A: Clues to Build It

Even the most engaging routines can lose luster over time. Simple variations can keep them fresh. One way to do that with this routine is to stop flashing images and start giving clues for students to interpret and build. For the example, you might say, "the build has four shapes." Students would build something and compare. Then, you might offer a new clue like, "one of the four shapes is a hexagon." At that point, students would rebuild their image to include a hexagon if their original idea didn't include one. A third clue is given. It could be something like, "the other three shapes are all the same." Again, students would have to rebuild, swapping out the other three shapes for something that's the same. You can continue to give clues or show the "answer" build at any point. In this case, assume you ended after the third build and displayed this image. Then, have students compare and contrast their builds with the image. Someone may have even built it or at least had the same shapes. It's unlikely that the exact image would be built without a fourth clue like, "the same three shapes are in a row above the hexagon." Don't feel pressure to get this experience right the first time. It will take some practice giving clues. Remember to build your own image first to use as source material for the clues, and keep the early builds somewhat simple with just a few shapes.

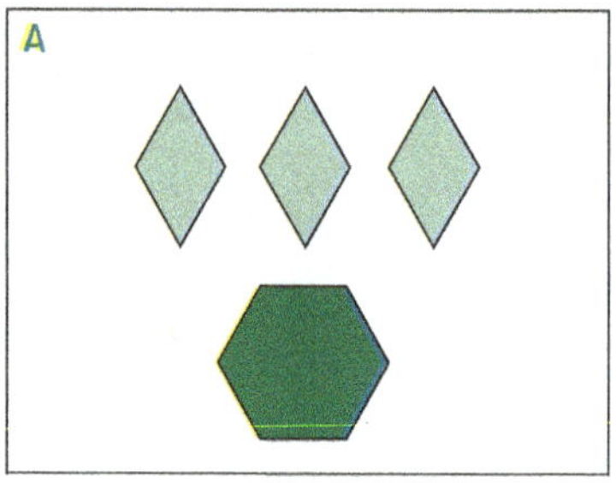

GRADES K–5

DAILY ROUTINES to JUMP-START GEOMETRY, MEASUREMENT, AND DATA

GRADES K–5

DAILY ROUTINES to JUMP-START GEOMETRY, MEASUREMENT, AND DATA

JOHN J. SANGIOVANNI
DENNIS MCDONALD

CORWIN Mathematics

CORWIN

For information:

Corwin
A SAGE Company
2455 Teller Road
Thousand Oaks, California 91320
(800) 233–9936
www.corwin.com

SAGE Publications Ltd.
1 Oliver's Yard
55 City Road
London, EC1Y 1SP
United Kingdom

SAGE Publications India Pvt. Ltd.
Unit No 323–333, Third Floor, F-Block
International Trade Tower Nehru Place
New Delhi – 110 019
India

SAGE Publications Asia-Pacific Pte. Ltd.
18 Cross Street #10–10/11/12
China Square Central
Singapore 048423

Associate Director and Publisher, STEM: Erin Null
Senior Editorial Assistant: Nyle De Leon
Production Editor: Nicole Burns-Ascue
Copy Editor: Heather Kerrigan
Typesetter: Integra
Proofreader: Dennis Webb
Indexer: Integra
Cover and Interior Designer: Scott Van Atta
Marketing Manager: Margaret O'Connor

ISBN: 978-1-0719-7107-9

CONTENTS

online resources Visit the companion website at https://companion.corwin.com/courses/jumpstartroutines-geometry for downloadable resources.

ACKNOWLEDGMENTS

As an author team, we know that every project is a collaborative effort with so many to thank. We thank the Corwin team for making this book a reality. There is no better publishing team to work with than the Corwin Mathematics team. We are lucky to be a part of that team.

From John: I must first thank Erin Null personally for a decade of support, guidance, partnership, and real friendship. Cheers. Thank you to the many mathematics educator colleagues for your support, perspective, and friendship. I am lucky to have so many. You make me better. Thank you (again), Skip Fennell and Kay Sammons, for opportunity and mentorship through the years. Thank you, Dennis, for bringing creativity, insight, and "can do" to this project. Thank you to Oscar and Deryn, you're both in "here" as always. Most importantly, thank you to my wife, Kristen. There are no words.

From Dennis: Thank you to my colleagues, past and present, who have helped me grow as an educator and coach. Thank you to Kay Sammons for your recognition and support of me from the start. Thank you, John and Heather, for your years of trust and confidence, as well as for providing me endless opportunities to grow, learn, and have fun. Thank you to my parents and my siblings, without whom I would be a different person. Finally, an enormous thank you to Valerie for being the best person I know.

PUBLISHER'S ACKNOWLEDGMENTS

Karen Brooks
Math Academic Coach, Chandler Unified School District
Chandler, AZ

Shelley Gartner
Vice Principal, Calgary Catholic School District
Alberta, Canada

Terina Legge
Program Specialist K–6 Mathematics
Mount Pearl, Canada

ABOUT THE AUTHORS

John J. SanGiovanni is a mathematics coordinator in Howard County, Maryland. There, he leads mathematics curriculum development, digital learning, assessment, and professional development. John is passionate about growing new mathematics leaders in the district and through McDaniel College. In addition to the Daily Routines to Jump-Start Math and Figuring Out Fluency series, some of his many Corwin books include *Daily Routines to Jump-Start Problem Solving, Grades K–8*; *Answers to Your Biggest Questions About Teaching Elementary Math*; and *Productive Math Struggle: A 6-Point Action Plan for Fostering Perseverance*. John is a national mathematics curriculum and professional learning consultant who also speaks frequently at national conferences and institutes. He is active in state and national professional organizations, recently serving on the board of directors for the National Council of Teachers of Mathematics and on the board of directors for NCSM.

Dennis McDonald is a mathematics coach in the Howard County Public School System where he supports teachers in grades preK through 5 to implement high-quality instruction, bringing 20+ years of experience teaching in elementary school to his work as an instructional coach. Dennis is a lead developer of curriculum, assessment, and online learning resources. He also works with new and aspiring mathematics leaders at McDaniel College in Maryland, teaching courses in assessment and instruction, with a specific emphasis on geometry in elementary grades.

PART 1

WHY JUMP-START ROUTINES FOR GEOMETRY, MEASUREMENT, AND DATA?

Does a broken ruler still work?

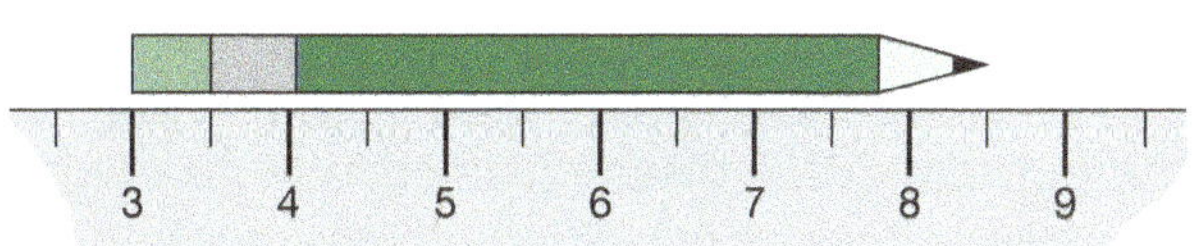

Years ago, standardized tests weren't given on computers. Tests came with scripts for teachers to read and explicit directions that were to be followed exactly. Sometimes students had tests with separate bubble sheets and other times they marked their answers directly in the test booklet. In both of those cases, there were items that called for calculators and teachers would pass them out. In some grades, students would need compasses, protractors, or rulers and those materials would also be passed out. But one year, sometime around 1999, the test booklet was different.

That year, the rulers weren't "real." They weren't passed out. Instead, the ruler was printed on the inside cover of the test booklet. When needed, students were to "carefully" tear it out. You can imagine how well that went with a bunch of second graders. This leads us to the point of this story. As expected, some rulers came out cleanly, some had frayed edges but were serviceable, and some were completely mangled. But test directions were clear and restrictive—students were to use the rulers in the book and *only* the rulers from the book. So, what were that team of teachers to do?

Three of the teachers on that team had nothing to worry about whatsoever. They hadn't felt pressure to cram in certain topics before the test. They had started those ideas early in the year and connected them throughout. For example, they connected rulers with number lines (this wasn't a common thing in 1999). They also taught the content fully avoiding shortcuts and potential pitfalls. With rulers, they taught their students that a ruler measures the difference between two points. In other words, an 8-inch pencil is 8 inches regardless of where it is on a ruler (e.g., 0 to 8, 1 to 9, or 3 to 11). These teachers also practiced measuring throughout the year with center activities, occasional measuring games, and a homework problem now and then.

The other two teachers on the team hadn't done the same. They moved through their curriculum as is. Like most everyone, they fell behind from time to time but found ways to catch up. Even then they found themselves short on time with the test on the horizon. The topics they hadn't covered, like measurement, got minimal treatment. And for the sake of efficiency, they simply showed students how to use a ruler and made sure that their students lined up the object with the 0 on the ruler because doing so would always tell them the answer.

One of us (the authors) was on this team. We remember the conversations with our teammates after the test that day. We're reminded of the value of teaching something fully and then providing bursts of really good practice over and over again for well understood concepts and skills that are sharp and easy to use. And though we *think* the misstep of just lining things up on a ruler has gone away, we know the challenge of teaching everything before an assessment hasn't.

WHY JUMP-START ROUTINES FOR GEOMETRY, MEASUREMENT, AND DATA?

Geometry, measurement, and data concepts are important. They play a major role in everyday life—even for children—from differentiating how big or small something is, to how to best organize different items into a box, to understanding information about the world through data. But these concepts can be overshadowed by other content, like number concepts, computation, or fractions in elementary grades. In short, they aren't typically thought of as major content in various grade levels. The other content takes precedence and, understandably, a majority of the instructional time. Geometry, measurement, and data often takes a backseat right up until weeks before a state assessment. At that point, they are as important as everything else but little time remains. Time constraints trigger mini-lessons on the most basic of these concepts. Time savers and shortcuts, like lining up the ruler, are introduced. Quality practice is impossible.

But what if these concepts were taught earlier in the year? What if ideas about measurement and data were connected to number, computation, and problem-solving so that they weren't seen as separate topics? What if one good lesson was followed with ongoing bursts of practice regularly, throughout the year? It stands to reason that students would have better proficiency and competency with these skills and concepts. The question is how do you do it? The good lessons are likely included in your instructional materials. The high-quality practice might not be.

What if helping students develop spatial awareness through geometry content could spill over into other aspects of learning mathematics? Spatial awareness is the ability to understand and perceive the relationship between objects and oneself in space. It is about orientation, proximity awareness, directional awareness, mental manipulation of figures, and more. Spatial awareness is a foundation for learning mathematics and other content (Metoyer et al., 2015). Spatial awareness makes unique contributions to understanding of number concepts and number relationships (Krasa, 2010). Many people view spatial awareness through a fixed mindset lens assuming one has it or they don't. But spatial awareness can be refined and advanced through exploration and practice.

That's where these routines come into play. They are a source of good practice, engagement, and discussion. They promote thinking and reasoning. We will unpack them more later in this part of the book. First, we want to go over some big ideas about geometry, measurement, and data. Knowing what your students have learned in previous grades as well as where they are going can help you better understand what they really need to get from your instruction and practice. So, take a few moments to get familiar with how these concepts progress. Then, read on for how to get the most out of these routines.

BIG IDEAS IN GEOMETRY, MEASUREMENT, AND DATA ACROSS GRADES K–5

Thinking about that team of teachers in the opening, you're sure to recognize that the value for understanding of measurement concepts wasn't equal among them. Or if it was, it wasn't pursued equally. Three teachers taught the true meaning of measurement and how a ruler works. Two teachers taught a shortcut to get through things quickly. Their tactics may be understandable regarding time pressures and other challenges. Making matters worse, teachers get very little support in developing their own content knowledge and how to teach these specific subjects both in preservice training and while teaching. The small amount of math professional learning time they do get is often focused on standards in major topics such as number concepts, computation, fractions, or word problems, which are somehow often viewed and treated in pacing guides and curricular resources as separate from data, measurement, and geometry. With this in mind, we want to briefly unpack big ideas about geometry, measurement, and data so that you are better armed to teach the content and to practice it well through the routines in this book.

Big Ideas in Elementary Geometry

Geometry instruction worldwide is heavily influenced by a system of thought developed in the 1960s by Dutch educators Dina van Hiele-Geldof and Pierre Marie van Hiele. The van Hiele model is a framework for thinking about the development of geometric thinking. It consists of five developmental levels, with learners of any age beginning at Level 0 and progressing to the next level through learning and practice experiences about specific geometric ideas (Table 1.1).

Table 1.1 Van Hiele Model of Geometric Thinking

VAN HIELE LEVEL	TYPICAL GRADE RANGE	CHARACTERISTICS
Level 0: Visualization	preK–2	Students focus on merely the "look" of a shape, e.g., pointy, looks like a house.
Level 1: Analysis	2–5	Students can group shapes and see how all of a certain figure (e.g., triangles) are similar.
Level 2: Abstraction	5–8	Students can see how groups of shapes relate, such as how squares are all special rectangles.
Level 3: Deduction	8–12	Students can use deductive arguments to develop a proof for a given statement.
Level 4: Rigor	12+	Students can compare various axiomatic systems within geometry.

Source: Adapted from Van de Walle et al., 2023.

The chart shows the typical grades associated with each level, as well as typical characteristics of students whose thinking is at a given level. Two key aspects of the van Hiele framework are that these levels are sequential and experience dependent (Van de Walle et al., 2023). For students to be at Level 2, they had to have moved from Level 0 to Level 1, and then again from Level 1 to Level 2. Levels of thinking can't be skipped over. Movement from one level to another is a result of experiences, not simply the imparting and memorization of geometric statements.

Levels are also age independent. There are no set ages or grades at which students will progress through or work at specific levels (Van de Walle et al., 2023). A typical third grader, who has had rich experiences with geometric concepts, should be working at Level 1. However, any given third-grade class will likely contain students working at Level 0 through (possibly)—depending on each students' prior experience—2. Additionally, a student may reason differently with different content. For instance, a student may show Level 1 thinking with two-dimensional figures, but Level 0 thinking with three-dimensional figures (Clements, 2003).

It is helpful to understand the van Hiele model and the characteristics of student thinking at each level so that you can better plan and implement geometry activities with your students. Students working at Level 0 will have great difficulty working through activities that require the level of abstraction shown by Level 2 thinkers. Moreover, students working at different levels can have difficulty communicating with each other because they are basically speaking different languages (Vojkuvkova, 2012). Intentional planning, however, can promote success regardless of level. The key to this planning is knowing the concepts taught at different grade levels and how students working at different van Hiele levels may think about or understand those concepts. Figure 1.1 shows how geometry concepts typically progress through elementary grades.

Figure 1.1 Big Ideas in Elementary Geometry

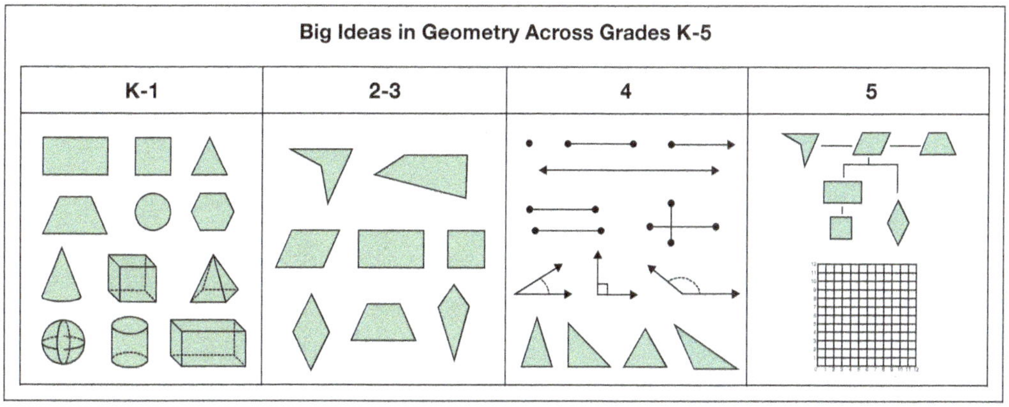

Source: Common Core Standards Writing Team, 2013.

In kindergarten and first grade, the main focus is on two-dimensional and three-dimensional shapes and their attributes. One of the big ideas that students in these early grades work with is distinguishing between defining (e.g., number of sides) and nondefining attributes (e.g., color). They are introduced to the idea that figures can be composed and decomposed, which is one way that geometry connects with number (see Figure 1.2). Even measurement concepts, like area and volume, apply understanding of composing and decomposing.

Figure 1.2 Decomposing Across Mathematics Content

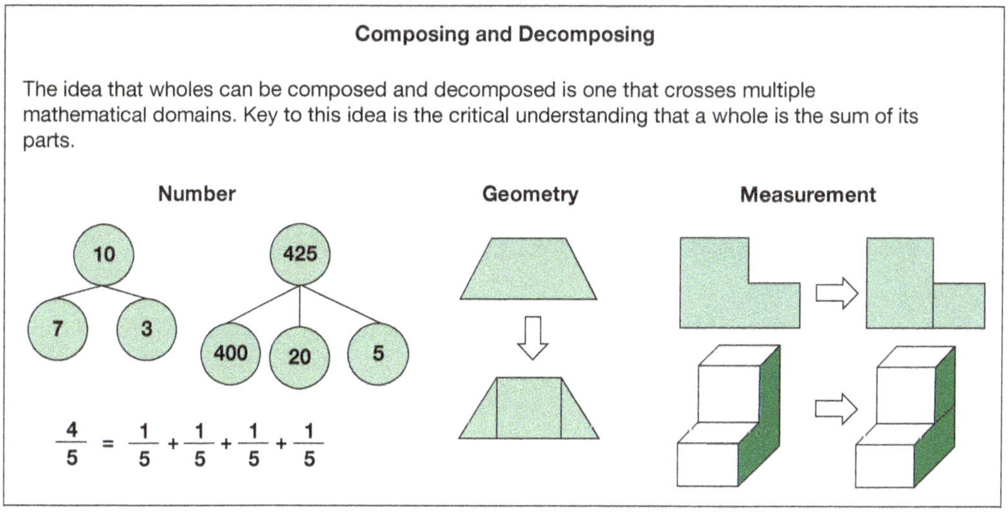

Students in kindergarten and first grade are generally working at what van Hiele identifies as the Visualization stage. Their thinking at this level tends to focus on the "look" of figures rather than their attributes. They often compare new figures to their idea of a shape's "prototype" and can struggle to name figures that don't match their prototype. They are challenged to recognize a shape in a different orientation than their prototypical image (Tall & Vinner, 1981). A student at this stage might say, "This would be a square if you turned it." Students in this stage can also struggle to visualize what they cannot see, as shown in Figure 1.3.

Figure 1.3 Level 0 Example

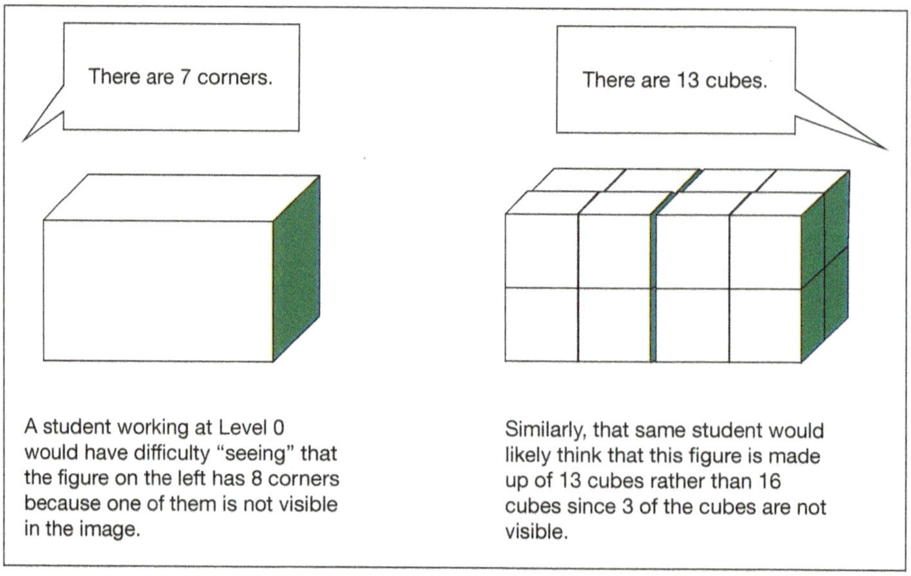

Source: van Hiele Model of Geometric Thinking, 2024.

In second and third grades, more shapes are added to the roster of figures that students must know. At this point, students begin to generalize (e.g., all trapezoids are alike) shapes as well as classify and categorize them (e.g., quadrilateral) based on analysis. They must move from visualizing a trapezoid to analyzing a shape to consider if it *is* a trapezoid. Lots of experiences are needed to develop this level of thinking. Simply, it can't be done in one or two lessons but rather many, many experiences over time (hence geometry routines). Through these experiences, students will begin to naturally use transformations to manipulate figures by flipping or turning them to match a desired orientation. However, they may still struggle to visualize the results of the transformations without physically performing them (Kandaga et al., 2022) (Figure 1.4).

Figure 1.4 Comparing Level 0 and Level 1

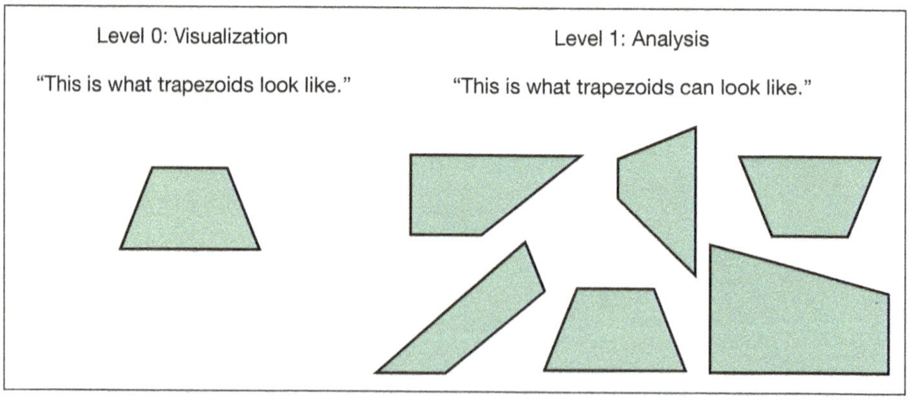

A more sophisticated level of thinking is expected of fourth and fifth graders. They learn about the building blocks of 2D figures like points and line segments. They learn about parallel or perpendicular segments. They explore angles and how to categorize them. These students are also asked to apply these ideas to figures they have known about since kindergarten (e.g., rectangles have two pairs of parallel sides and four right angles). These students now use relationships to organize shapes into a hierarchy. To do this, students must be at the Abstraction stage to form meaningful definitions based on defining attributes and properties. This may be impossible for students still functioning in the Visualization or Analysis stages.

Big Ideas in Elementary Measurement

Measurement is a domain of mathematics that has obvious real-life connections. Virtually every activity humans engage in (e.g., cooking, sports, shopping, traveling) involves some type of measurement. As such, students must learn to measure! They also need to estimate, calculate, and convert measurements within and between measurement systems (e.g., standard and metric). Figure 1.5 gives a snapshot of measurement concept progressions.

Figure 1.5 Big Ideas in Measurement Across Grades 1–5

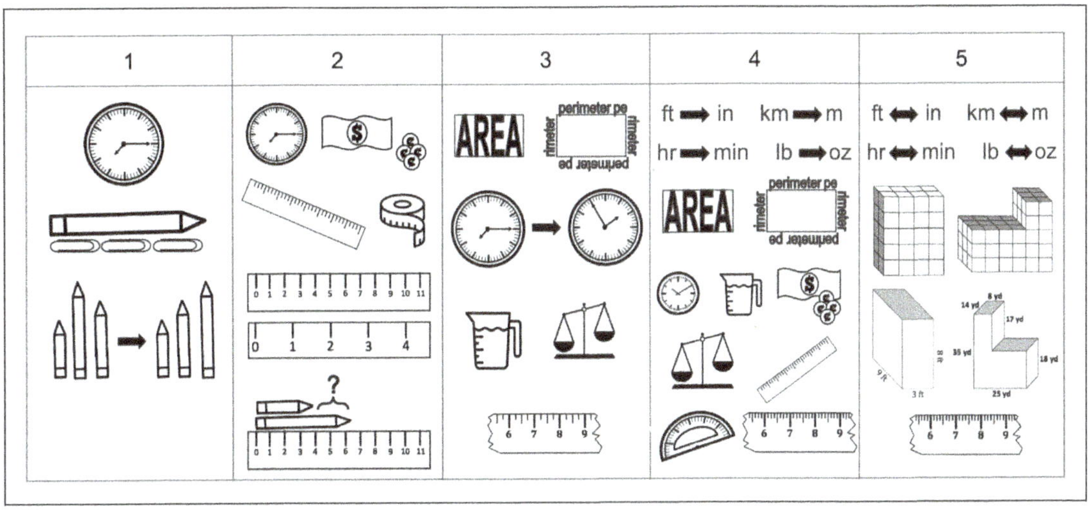

Source: Common Core Standards Writing Team, 2013.

Tape measure credit: istockphoto.com /kadirkaba

Measuring cup credit: istockphoto.com/ Naveed Anjum

The concept of a "unit" is critical in measurement connecting it to other mathematics content, like fractions. Early fraction work focuses on unit fractions to build larger quantities. Similarly, students use units throughout their study of measurement. They learn about standard and nonstandard units, metric and customary units, unit angles, square units (area), and cubic units (volume). In each, the measurement of an object is determined by the number of units needed to equal the measurable attribute (e.g., length, weight, capacity).

Measuring begins with tiling where a copy of a unit, like a paper clip, is used, and copies of that object are laid end to end, with no gaps and overlaps, to match the span of the object being measured (Figure 1.6). Students move from tiling to iterating by moving the unit (e.g., paper clip) along the length of the object and counting the number of units to find the length of the object (Dietiker et al., 2011). While "iteration" may be unfamiliar, it is something we do regularly in life. For example, without a ruler, you might use your fingers to approximate an inch, and then move that span along the length of an object to estimate its length. That's iteration!

Figure 1.6 Examples of Units

Primary students begin to explore the concept of measurement, identifying attributes of objects that can be measured, such as how heavy they are (mass), how tall they are (height), or how much they can hold (volume). They compare objects, gauging which is heavier or longer through direct comparisons. Students move on to using nonstandard units (e.g., paper clips) to make measurements of length, width, or height. They learn that when measuring they must use identical units along a path without gaps or overlaps (Dietiker et al., 2011). In time, students learn that measuring with different units (e.g., large paper clips and small paper clips) will yield different results, which leads to measuring with standard units, selecting measurement tools (e.g., rulers), and determining appropriate units of measure. Work with linear measurement extends to measuring fractional parts of a unit in later grades.

Nonlinear measurement, including mass and liquid volume, starts in primary grades and builds through the years. In those later grades, area is introduced following a similar progression to those other concepts. Learning about area begins with counting squares one by one before using repeated addition and multiplication to find the area of rectangular figures. Learning moves to decomposing irregular area figures and learning the area formula. Volume evolves in a similar way, through exploration of cubic units, to counting cubes, to using multiplication to find volume. As with area, students learn to decompose rectilinear prisms to find the volume of a larger figure.

Two other measurement topics begin in primary grades. The first is time, where analog and digital clocks are read—to-the-hour in kindergarten and to exact minutes by second or third grade. By third grade, students learn about elapsed time and solving problems with it before learning to convert between units of time (e.g., minutes to seconds or minutes to hours). Cost (i.e., money) is occasionally overlooked as a concept of measurement. It follows progression from learning the names and values of coins and bills to solving problems with money, including the act of making change.

Teaching the concept of a clock and how to read it is one thing; doing it with skill and little effort is another. Learning the names of coins and their values is also somewhat straightforward, but skill with counting money can be elusive. Both are great examples of the measurement concepts that need lots of practice. Both are embedded throughout the routines in this book.

Another topic that calls for abundant practice is conversion within and between units of measure. That is, finding how many inches are in 5 feet or how many cups are in 6 pints. This occurs in late elementary school and it is often complicated by students' developing fluency distracting them from unit relationships (e.g., inches to feet) and compromising accuracy leading to frustration and disengagement. Fortunately, conversions are also featured in many of these routines.

Big Ideas in Elementary Data

Each spring, with standardized testing underway, teachers walk around the room and think, "I forgot to get to ________!" For us, that blank often had something to do with data concepts like bar graphs, line plots, or picture graphs. Like geometry and measurement, data (and statistics) is another domain that has traditionally been treated as an extra something to be taught the last few weeks of school after covering all the "important" math. However, data displays provide a rich, relevant context for mathematical problem-solving that can (and should) be done all year long. Most importantly, data literacy—the ability to read, understand, interpret, and communicate data effectively—is increasingly vital in our world. Yet a gap exists between the concepts taught in math and the data skills needed by other disciplines. Every student must have opportunities to develop data literacy (NCTM, 2024).

Being data literate requires a strong conceptual understanding of statistics and data displays. It includes asking questions, collecting data, analyzing data, and interpreting the result (Bargagliotti et al., 2020). It is similar to other kinds of mathematical problem-solving. However, doing statistics is fundamentally different from doing mathematics (Van de Walle et al., 2023). Students in middle and high school delve deeply into statistical processes including things like examining the shape of data with measures of central tendency, such as mean and median. That important learning is built on concepts of data that start in elementary school.

In kindergarten, data is simply about sorting and categorizing. Categorical data is information that can be sorted into groups like the number of red, blue, and yellow teddy bear counters in a bin. Kindergarten students would sort the bears and might even organize their bears by rows on a mat, or perhaps on a number path creating a rudimentary graph. In Grades 1 and 2, students begin to collect data and organize it in a chart to create data displays or graphs. These students begin to analyze different data within graphs having single-unit scales and few categories (e.g., different colors). They answer questions about the total number of data points, how many are in a given category, and how categories compare.

In third grade and beyond, students work with data displays that are increasingly more complex. Graphs no longer use a single-unit scale, counting instead by 2s, 5s, 10s, and so on. Students work with new display types like line plots with data first displayed by whole numbers before fractional amounts appear by Grades 4 or 5. Questions in later elementary grades are similarly more complex, often including more than one step. By fifth grade, coordinate grids, plotting ordered pairs, and examining patterns on these grids emerges before middle school students learn to use grids with line graphs and scatter plots.

Geometry, Measurement, and Data Hazards

Just as students can have misconceptions about number and operations that hinder their computational fluency, students also can develop misunderstandings about geometry, measurement, and data. Sometimes these misconceptions arise because of seemingly good intentions to help students "get the right answer." One example is in the opening of this book where second-grade teachers told students to line up objects with the 0 on a ruler. Other examples include the use of "student-friendly" definitions (see Routine #1), or explanations that aim to make things easier but ultimately create roadblocks for deeper understanding.

Consider the case of rectangles. When kindergarten students first learn about rectangles, they are often told that rectangles are shapes with two long sides and two short sides. While it is true that some rectangles have two long sides and two short sides, not all rectangles have those attributes. If that "definition" of rectangle is learned and practiced, it is highly likely that those students will have great difficulty later understanding why a square is a kind of rectangle, even though it doesn't have long sides and short sides.

Other misunderstandings about shapes and figures occur when students are exposed to only the most prototypical examples of shapes, oriented in a particular way. This creates narrow ideas about what shapes are and what they look like. It doesn't help students advance out of van Hiele's Level 0. For example, if students only see equilateral triangles, like those in sets of pattern blocks, they might not recognize a scalene triangle or an isosceles triangle as also being triangles. Similarly, students whose only exposure to trapezoids is a red pattern block will not understand how the other shape is also a trapezoid (Figure 1.7). You might hear them say, "It *would* be a trapezoid if you just made that side (right side) look like this side (left slanted side)." They need the shape to conform to what they think a trapezoid should be—the red pattern block (i.e., short top, long bottom, and two slanted sides).

Figure 1.7 Level 0 Example With Triangle and Trapezoid

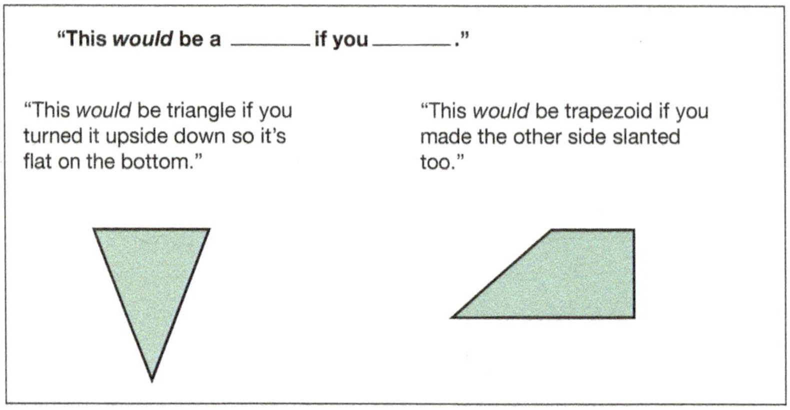

Hazards with measurement aren't only about rulers. Frequently, area and perimeter are confused. Having students memorize that "perimeter means add and area means multiply" can be tempting. But that tip ignores the fact that you can multiply to find the perimeter of figures and that finding the area of irregular figures involves decomposing and adding the smaller parts. Much like teaching key words to solve word problems, quick fixes with measurement concepts may help in the short term but tend to cause more harm than good in the long run.

And as you might suspect, data comes with hazards too. Be wary of the same "helping" pitfall that makes things as simple as possible. While the complexity of the data should be relative to the developing needs of students, oversimplifying data displays and the questions about them can mislead you to think they understand better than they do. It also compromises critical thinking, deep understanding, productive struggle, and potentially their data literacy. For instance, using bar graphs where all bars neatly line up with a number on the scale, such as Graph A in Figure 1.8, is an oversimplification. It's easy for students to trace their finger along the line from the bar to the scale and identify the quantity the bar represents. They can likely do this without any real understanding of the graph. Using Graph B, however, forces sense making, and opens the door to a better conversation about whether Abby is 20½, 25, 30, or something else and why.

Figure 1.8 Bar Graph Comparison

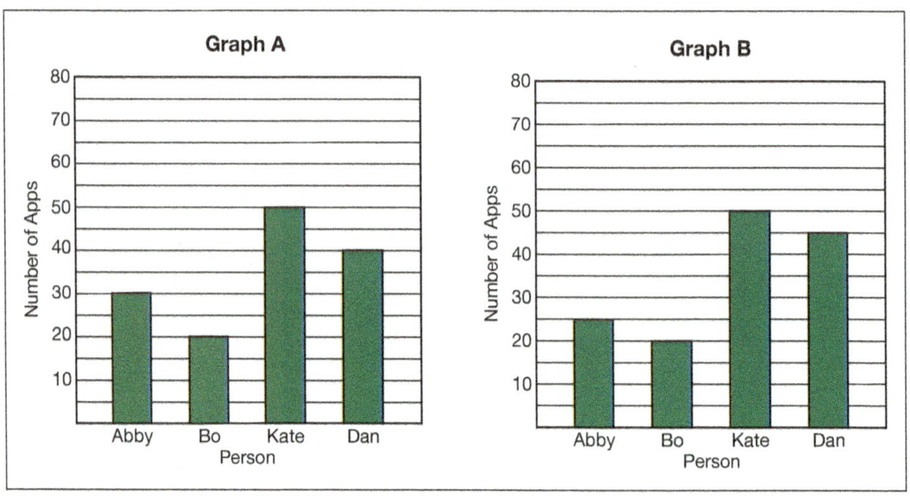

ROUTINES FOR CAPABILITY AND RETENTION WITH GEOMETRY, MEASUREMENT, AND DATA

You have now read about a few of the more familiar hazards with geometry, measurement, and data. When those hazards mingle with fragile number sense, damaged dispositions toward math, lack of experiences outside of the classroom, and the aforementioned instructional time crunch, it's little wonder why students have great difficulty with these seemingly easy topics. But possibly the biggest issue with those hazards is that they circumvent deep understanding while failing to develop 21st-century skills. Those skills are needed for success in the information age (Stauffer, 2022) and include critical thinking and discussion as explaining, justifying, and critiquing others' reasoning. Geometry, measurement, and data activities must incorporate these instead of relying on low-level recall. Experiences should be rich, discussion-laden, problem-solving experiences that expose students to new ideas to stimulate ingenuity and creativity.

The idea of teaching all of this *and* addressing all of the hazards or misunderstandings seems daunting. It probably feels like there isn't enough time to do it, let alone do it well. But what if you practiced them, chipped away at them, little by little? What if you were able to rehabilitate faulty approaches, undo learned shortcuts, and rehabilitate unproductive dispositions using short bursts of rich problem-solving? What if brief activities flush with engagement and discussion were a routine feature of your mathematics instruction?

What Is Meant by a Routine?

A routine is an activity that is done, well, routinely. It is familiar to students once established, and it is adaptable to practice different skills and concepts, or in this case different types of problems (Bay-Williams & SanGiovanni, 2021). Routines aid classroom management while fostering positive relationships within a mathematics community (Berry, 2018). Routines become an instructional habit, maximizing precious time for greater learning opportunity. Teachers can use a variety of routines including those to develop language, number sense, and fluency.

You may be familiar with Number Talks (Parrish, 2010), number routines (SanGiovanni, 2020), or fluency routines (Bay-Williams & SanGiovanni, 2021). In some schools or districts, routines may be recognized as "math talks." Those routines are used for developing number sense and computational fluency and give students an opportunity to play with and discuss numbers. The routines in *this* book go after geometry, measurement, and data. They target specific concepts within these domains. Like other routines, these intend to engage students in reasoning and discussion. They are meaningful, high-quality practice.

The Design of Routines for Geometry, Measurement, and Data

The routines in this book are designed to "jump-start" geometry, measurement, and data. They are engaging opportunities for students to work with and discuss their understanding. Routines are designed to develop reasoning, critical thinking, and sense making. They provide quality practice at the beginning of class or any other time during the math block. They can repair or instill mathematics confidence in your students, shaping productive dispositions and positive mathematics identities. These routines are also exceptional opportunities for building student agency with thinking, reasoning, and doing mathematics in general.

These routines are

- practical and easy for teachers to implement,
- meant for quick engagements (less than 10 minutes),
- thinking exercises meant to ignite thinking and reasoning skills, and
- modifiable to work with most any content.

These routines create an environment in which the Standards for Mathematical Practice (MP; National Governors Association Center for Best Practices & Council of Chief State School Officers, 2010) come to life. Though specific practices are linked to each routine throughout the book, in general students will have opportunity to

- make sense of problems and persevere (MP1),
- reason abstractly and quantitatively (MP2),
- construct viable arguments and critique the reasoning of others (MP3),
- model with mathematics (MP4),
- use appropriate tools strategically (MP5),
- attend to precision (MP6),
- look for and make use of structure (MP7), and
- look for and express regularity in repeated reasoning (MP8).

Designed for Student Engagement and Discussion

These routines are quick bursts of quality practice. You provide a prompt. Students have a few moments to think about it. They talk with partners about their ideas. You bring the class together for students to share ideas and ask questions. You facilitate the discussion, poking at their ideas with questions, probing their reasoning, connecting statements to the problem or to others' ideas. You want to withhold how you think about the prompt or how you would solve it until they have had ample opportunities to share their thinking first. And again, these are quick bursts typically lasting less than 10 minutes at most.

Designed to Build Capability

Geometry, measurement, and data are clearly important. But they aren't topics that can be fully realized in a single lesson or even a handful of lessons over the course of a year. Proficiency and retention come about over long periods, through frequent experience, exposure to different ideas, and application in varied situations. Daily routines provide opportunities for these to grow throughout the year.

In his book *Outliers*, Malcolm Gladwell (2008) suggests that a person needs 10,000 hours of deliberate practice to master something. Though one might argue the exact amount of time, it is logical that the more people do something—the more they practice and experience something—the better they can understand and apply it. Consider playing an instrument. Passing a written test about the parts of the instrument, the way to hold it, and the meaning of recorded notes doesn't mean someone is proficient with the instrument. Instead, it shows that they understand how the instrument works and the basics of how music is recorded on paper. Their ability to play the instrument, and to play it well, is realized and improved as they play it more and more.

This analogy could be applied to geometry, measurement, and data. The theory here is that skill begins with foundational understanding from a lesson and through frequent and plentiful opportunities to practice, students can increase their sense of these concepts along with reasoning and justification skills. You might note that 10,000 hours seems impossible with limited instructional time and the other "more important" concepts already in your curriculum. However, with these routines, students can achieve a great amount of *hours on the road* in just a few minutes a day. Consider this: Through a daily, five-minute routine, students could access 900 minutes of practice in one academic year (180 days).

Designed to Complement Number Routines

Of course, geometry, measurement, and data aren't the only topics taught in elementary mathematics. And as mentioned, these topics aren't even considered major topics in many grade levels. Understandably, they cannot be the only topic featured in your daily routine. They should complement your Number Talk, number sense, or fluency routines. Granted that mingling routines means that you have less time with the content which seems to contradict the notion of 10,000 hours or lots of practice. Keep in mind that the idea is over the course of years. There is no way you can provide 10,000 hours of anything. But you *can* provide quality practice for everything!

Designed for Quality Practice

Quality practice is not defined by the number of problems students complete, the speed at which they complete them, or the number of hours they spend doing mathematics. Quality practice is defined by what students do and how they are engaged. It should engage students in thinking. Quality practice focuses on a skill, varies how students engage, gives opportunity for processing, and highlights connections (Bay-Williams & SanGiovanni, 2021). The routines in this book provide quality practice. They are unique, engaging, and diverse experiences that will help students develop their skills. They are not repetitive, mundane, or mindless drills. They are the quality practice that can help students perform better in class, outside the mathematics classroom, and even better on standardized tests.

Designed to Frame a Growth Mindset and Build Confidence

The idea of consistent, engaging practice promotes other prominent ideas about teaching and learning mathematics like growth mindset. A growth mindset is an approach to teaching and learning mathematics that emphasizes that mindset is more important than initial ability in determining the progress students can make in their mathematical understanding (Dweck, 2006). Students with a growth mindset find agency in doing mathematics. For them, learning with a growth mindset means

- believing that skill can be developed and that great abilities can be built over time,
- viewing mistakes as an opportunity to develop understanding how to solve new problems,
- being resilient by finding ways to get unstuck and work through a problem when the solution path isn't clearly apparent,
- believing that effort builds skill and creates success, and
- reflecting about how one approaches new concepts and problems in order to learn, do, and solve.

Carol Dweck's work establishes that a growth mindset benefits students by empowering them to develop skills through engagement and effort. It positively shapes both their mathematics identity and agency. To realize this, teachers must provide worthwhile opportunities to participate in and discuss mathematics. Regular experience with interesting activities naturally complements the facets of a growth mindset. Routines reinforce that students' ability can be developed through continued practice and effort. They can undercut any students' notion that their mathematical ability is fixed.

A Way to Launch Building Thinking Classrooms

Routines are microcosms of instruction designed to build thinking classrooms (Liljedahl, 2020). They are rich, though brief, tasks that require students to draw on a range of mathematical content necessitating real thinking (Liljedahl, 2016). Topics within geometry, measurement, and data offer context and relevance while provoking curiosity and thinking for students in all grades. Consider the statements shown from the routine That's a Fact (Routine #10) asking students to consider reasonable measures (Figure 1.9). It's nothing complicated but just enough to jump-start a rich mathematical discussion grounded in understanding, experience, insight, and thinking.

Figure 1.9 Example From That's a Fact—Routine #10

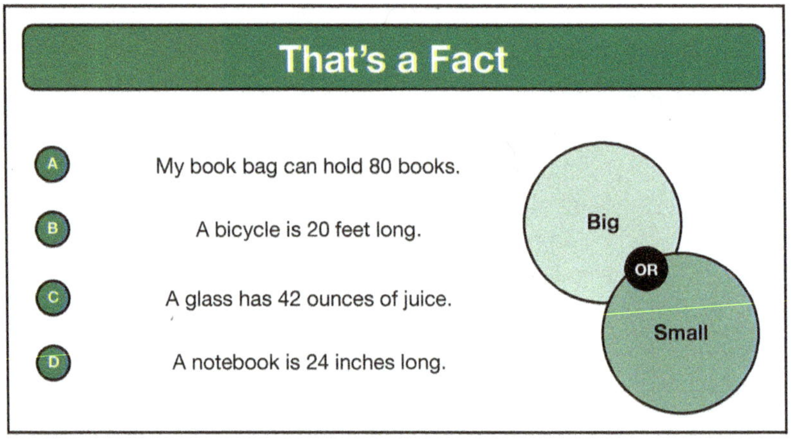

The interesting, accessible prompts of routines set the stage for a math class that has no room for student slacking, stalling, faking, or mimicry. During the routine, students will have to do their own thinking, engage in discussion, explain, justify, and listen. The beginning of the math block is prime time for this because within 3 to 5 minutes, student focus or interest begins to deteriorate. Unless you grab their attention and get them doing something interesting right away. A routine does just that, allowing you to seize those first few minutes effectively using them to reinforce while setting expectations for engagement and discourse for the rest of the lesson.

Designed for Use With Your Existing Resources

Quality practice must be prefaced by high-quality first instruction. Close, Far, Between, and More (Routine #12) is a great way to review and reinforce relationships between measurement units. However, it is not a replacement for a hands-on lesson where students fill different containers and pour from one container to another in order to compare measurements. Concrete experiences better develop abstract understanding of concepts, where students transfer from using physical objects to representations of those objects (Dinsmoor, 2022). The routine should complement that instruction, not take the place of it. Attempting to use it only, or in place of lessons, simply serves to *cover* the content, not develop long-lasting understanding and utility of it.

It may be hard to determine how to use a routine when your instructional block and curriculum resources are already jam packed. We offer a simple suggestion. Identify which components aren't working or what endeavors take time yet yield little results. Swap those things out for a routine. For example, starting class by going over homework causes many issues (SanGiovanni et al., 2023). You can replace that with an opening routine. Another example is the warm-up or "bell ringer" provided in your program. While review is necessary, doing it to start class often hijacks your lesson. Replace that low-level practice with a routine.

While routines are intended to be brief bursts of practice, they can also be source material for designing your own lessons to complement, extend, or replace lessons in your resources. Consider the variation of What's the Order? (Routine #9) that's shown in Figure 1.10. It prompts students to find the length of a pencil in the middle of a ruler and then find the beginning or end of that same pencil when placed on different parts of the ruler. It is a great task that could be practiced as a routine or turned into a lesson where students use real pencils and rulers to determine how shifting placement doesn't change length.

Figure 1.10 Example From What's the Order?—Routine #9

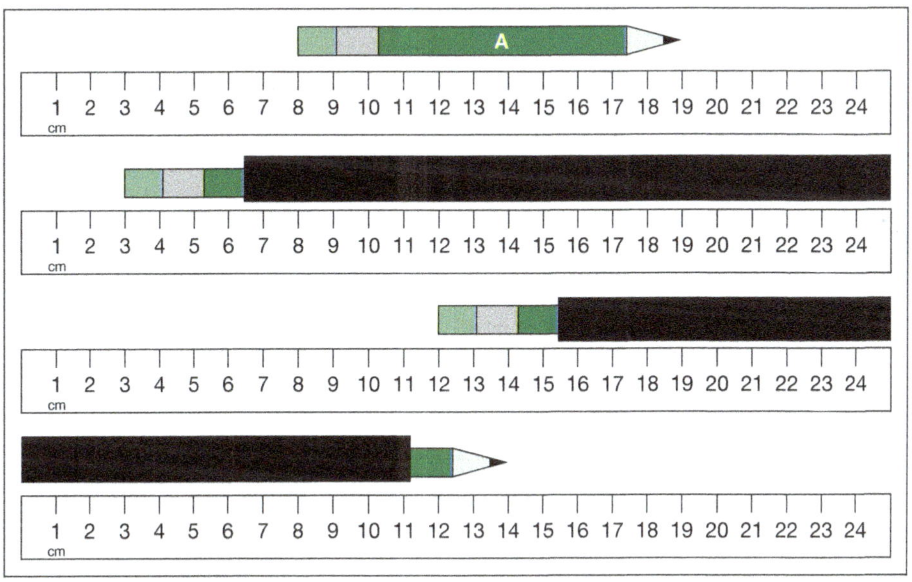

IMPLEMENTING JUMP-START ROUTINES FOR GEOMETRY, MEASUREMENT, AND DATA

Routines in this book are practical, doable ideas for jump-starting geometry, measurement, and data instruction. They support high-quality mathematics instruction. They can complement any curriculum or textbook program that you use. With each routine, you'll find an anchor or introductory example with a specific topic and prompts. Directions for using the routine are provided followed by variations of the routine. Each routine is available as a downloadable, editable set of PowerPoint slides including templates for making your own examples. Ideas for modifying how the routine works or the content it is focused on is also provided.

online resources All routines can be downloaded for your use at **https://companion.corwin.com/courses/jumpstartroutines-geometry**

You can (and should) modify these routines in all sorts of ways. You can adjust the number of prompts. You don't need to use all of the routines. They don't need to be done in a specific order. Adjust them to fit the amount of time allocated for them but know that the first few times you use a new routine will likely take a bit longer until students understand the process.

Timing of Routines: How Long? When?

You can manage how long routines last by adjusting the number of questions you ask or the number of student strategies you investigate. In some cases, you can limit the number of problems or prompts that students encounter. You can modify the complexity of the mathematics. You can cut or extend the amount of time students have to share their thinking with partners. Essentially, *you* control the amount of time allocated to your routine. Directions for specific routines are described in that section of the book. The general shape of a routine is that

- students work with the prompt independently (about a minute or so).
- students discuss their reasoning with a partner or triad (about 2 minutes).
- teachers facilitate class discussion about strategies and reasoning (about 5 minutes).

That said, here are a couple of basic guidelines:

1. Routines are intended to be quick, engaging activities that foster understanding, reasoning, and retention. Typically, they should be no more than a few minutes. Most days they should last about 5 to 7 minutes. Other days, they may be a bit more than 5 minutes. Occasionally, the discussion may be so vibrant and engaging that you find your class spending 10 minutes with the routine. This isn't ideal but note that it may happen from time to time. Also note that these rich discussions are exactly what you want for your students and so spending a few minutes more with them shouldn't be thought of as time lost or wasted.
2. Routines are likely best situated at the beginning of the mathematics class. You can establish protocols for students to enter class and prepare for the opening routine. In this way, they naturally replace mundane warm-ups or review of homework. However, you can flexibly position routines throughout the class as well. In longer classes (75 minutes or more), you may decide that they are best used in the middle of the block as an opportunity for rekindling students' energy and engagement. In other cases, you may find that routines can be useful when offered at the end of the class. If you select the end of class, you must be sure to close instruction for the period early enough for the routine to take place because running out of time is highly likely.
3. Routines may take longer at first. For some students, this may be the first time they are consistently challenged to think about mathematics in their own way. For others, discussing their reasoning may be problematic. For you, facilitating and investigating without lingering too long will take some practice. A routine will become more fluid the more you use it. You might experience a *time bump* when you introduce a new routine. Remember, you control the first minutes of mathematics class. Extend or limit prompts and discussion to help fit the routine in the timelines of the lesson.

Which Routines to Use?

Obviously, you need to know how to facilitate the routine and the basic tenets of it. You must also select the content that is appropriate for your students. Your experience with your students will help. Take cues from class discussion, student work, observation, or test results about the topics and ideas that need to be developed.

There is no suggestion of which to use, when to use it, or how to order the routines in this collection. There is no requirement for how long to use any routine or how many times you should use it during a unit, quarter, or semester. These routines are about geometry, measurement, and data. You might decide to sprinkle them in with your number routines doing those 3 days a week and these the other 2 days. Use the routines that are most comfortable to facilitate and most interesting for your students. Pick the ones that develop what your students need to practice. Select a routine and use it for a few days or weeks before moving to another. Circle back to a routine during the year as you see fit. Remember that any routine can become stale with too much use. Make subtle adjustments to a routine to keep it fresh. Even then, it will be wise to change out routines as needed.

The At-A-Glance section at the end of Part 1 offers a table of routines that includes a brief description of the routine and its focus. Regardless of the focus or purpose, there are complementary skills every routine incorporates. And as mentioned, you can adjust a routine to alter the purpose as needed.

Plan for the Routine

You should focus most of your planning energy on core skills and concepts of the main lesson. Incorporating routines should be pretty easy because they are designed for low-intensity planning. You can use them repeatedly by simply changing out the shapes, images, displays, or prompts. You should be able to change them out with little effort. However, there are some things to keep in mind when selecting and planning the routine.

You might be wondering about how you'll ever find enough shapes, things to measure, or data to create different routines. First, know that every example and variation in this book works for you! All you need to do is make some minor edits by changing shapes, measurement units, or data displays. Adjust prompts. You have templates baked into the online resources to help you make your own examples. And, if you still need more, you can use content, like data displays, in your textbook series or curriculum resources as source material to import into your routines. You'll also notice that there are ideas throughout about how you can enlist your students and their creativity for generating more problems.

Provide Scaffolding That Supports Routines

Most number routines are intended to be mental math activities. Geometry, measurement, and data routines can be mental exercises but occasionally students might need to write something or build models of something. Provide tools to support students as needed. At the least, you and your students can use tools to support discussion and confirm accuracy of calculations and reasoning. Tools you might consider providing include

- pattern blocks and attribute blocks so that students can build models;
- inch cubes or connecting cubes for building 3D figures;

- calculators or number charts for students to confirm accurate calculations and explore patterns;
- fact charts for students to make accurate calculations when recall isn't fully established;
- anchor charts for students to access to help them remember vocabulary, concepts, or conversions; or
- personal dry erase boards, sticky notes, or journals for students to sketch images, record their thinking, and use to support them when communicating ideas.

Support Language and Discussion

Student reasoning and conversation can be buoyed by anchor references during routines. These charts help them organize their thinking and frame their arguments. Most routines come with suggested questions. You might add those to anchor charts so students can think about them before the whole group discussion.

Anchor charts can also capture vocabulary and sentence starters to help students make arguments or rebut classmates. Vocabulary anchor charts might be situated near the projection of the routine so that statements can be made with precise mathematical language. Keep in mind that posting the charts alone will not ensure that students use the language. When vocabulary is overlooked, point out the accurate vocabulary while referring to the chart.

Sentence starters are familiar tools that help elementary students make clear statements. They complement vocabulary charts well. These starters help students begin their declarations. They also help students respond to statements of classmates and their teachers. No one set of starters is better than another. Here are some helpful examples:

> I think that ____ because ...
>
> I decided that ...
>
> I chose ____ because ...
>
> I agree with ___ because ...
>
> I disagree with ___ because ...
>
> I think ___'s idea will always work because ...
>
> The pattern I noticed was ...
>
> My thinking will always work because ...
>
> I want to change my answer because ...

"Listen-for" charts are anchor charts that help students determine what to listen for in someone's argument. They might be single words or indicators such as *clarity*, *vocabulary*, or *makes sense*. Listen-for charts might also be questions that ask the listener, "Is the argument clear?" "Are math words being used?" or "Does the idea make sense?" These listen-for charts also help students think about what *they* might say before they say it.

It is important to keep a few things in mind about scaffolds like anchor references and math tools. First and foremost, students need explicit instruction about the ideas on the charts and how the charts can help. Anchor charts about concepts or discussion techniques should be developed *with* students instead of simply displayed *to* students. Manipulatives, rulers, number charts, and calculators are just tools. The tools do not have answers but rather help students think about and find answers. Using tools is not cheating. But tools can also become distractions when they aren't understood or used appropriately. Students must understand how the mathematics tools work. Students should discuss when it is a good idea to use a tool or refer to a chart.

Set the Stage for Meaningful Discourse

In a routine, the teacher poses prompts, which students engage with. Students share ideas with partners so that all have an opportunity to talk. Then, the teacher leads a group conversation. During that time, every student does not have to share out. You don't have to explore every strategy, and you don't have to discuss every solution. You make choices about what to explore, where to linger, and when to move on during the debrief. You facilitate discussion. You ask questions. From time to time, you will have to insert an idea or strategy. Routines aren't intended to be mini-lessons or mini-lectures; rather, they are opportunities for meaningful discourse.

Because discussion is such a critical component of the routines, Smith and Stein's five practices for orchestrating productive discussions naturally connect with how you can orchestrate discussion during routines. These practices remind us to anticipate, monitor, select, sequence, and connect (Smith & Stein, 2018).

1. *Anticipate What Students Might Do During the Routine*

   Anticipating what students might do helps you consider how you will respond intentionally rather than randomly. Considering student ideas and misunderstandings can also help you think about questions to ask or even content for a routine the next day. You can start anticipating simply by thinking about how you would find the solution to the prompt.

2. *Monitor Student Discussions During the Routine*

   Monitor means that you listen to students as they discuss their thinking with partners. Granted, you probably can't listen to every student conversation. You can be strategic about the discussions you monitor like the discussion of students who you are concerned about. Or, you might plan to monitor different groups on different days to balance whose conversations you listen to and focus on.

3. *Select Strategy and Reasoning to Promote During the Routine*

   Be careful to avoid randomly selecting students for discussion during routines as much as possible. A random selection may compromise the discussion. Anticipating what students might do or think during the routine can help you consider the conversations or ideas that you want to listen for (when monitoring) and select for group discussion.

4. *Sequence Ideas During the Routine*

   Sequencing student ideas in a logical way helps advance student understanding. Sequencing may be quite challenging during a routine. In fact, careful, deliberate sequencing of ideas during a routine may be impossible due to the time constraints or inability to monitor every discussion in the short amount of time. You may be able to offset some of the challenge with your questions. To do this, pose questions that help students make connections between strategies, reflect on efficiency, and make use of structure and patterns within prompts like the following:

- How is ____'s strategy similar to ____'s?
- How is ___'s strategy different from ___'s?
- How does this idea connect to something we have discussed recently?
- Will this approach always work?
- If we think about efficiency, how do these strategies compare?
- What patterns do you notice in the expressions?
- How did you use patterns to help you find your solution?

5. *Connect Strategies and Concepts During the Routine*

   Questions during routines should help students connect solution paths with different ideas and reasoning. Your questions should help students see connections between concepts. Help students make connections between problems, numbers, operations, and representations.

WHAT'S NEXT?

It's time to get started. There are 20 routines waiting for you. Take time to get to know them. Use them to complement who you are as a teacher and what your students need. Modify them to make them your own. Use them as formative insights into your students' understanding. Be committed and creative. Remember that the first few times you use a routine you may find it to be clunky. This is natural. Give it some time before cutting ties. Reflect on how you can make it better or how you might modify it to improve its effectiveness. Be mindful, too, that reasoning and communicating about geometry, measurement, and data in these ways may be new to your students. Be patient with them and give them some time to get comfortable with a routine.

JUMP-START ROUTINES FOR GEOMETRY, MEASUREMENT, AND DATA AT-A-GLANCE

TITLE (FOCUS CONTENT)	BRIEF	INCLUDED CONTENT	PAGE
#1 See It, Build It (Geometry)	Students practice recreating arrangements and shapes.	• Shape attributes • Area • Perimeter • 3D figures • Time • Money • Elapsed time	26
#2 Sorts (Geometry)	Students practice sorting shapes based on their attributes.	• Shape attributes • Polygons • Quadrilaterals • Time	33
#3 Venns (Geometry)	Students use Venn diagrams to compare and contrast shapes, figures, and other concepts.	• Shape attributes • Polygons • Quadrilaterals • Angles • Time	40
#4 Find It (Geometry)	Students look for shapes within composite figures.	• Shape attributes • Quadrilaterals	48
#5 Dots (Geometry)	Figures connect dots to make shapes and solve puzzles.	• Shape attributes • Polygons • Quadrilaterals • Angles • Perimeter • Area	54
#6 The Truth (Geometry)	Students consider three statements about geometric figures determining which are true and which are false.	• Shape attributes • Polygons • Quadrilaterals • 3D figures • Perimeter • Measurement conversions • Symmetry	61
#7 On the Move (Geometry)	Students reason about how shapes and figures move through space.	• Shape attributes • Transformations (translations, rotations, reflections) • Counting and skip counting	68

TITLE (FOCUS CONTENT)	BRIEF	INCLUDED CONTENT	PAGE
#16 I Would Say (Data)	Students practice summarizing data displays.	• Data infographics • Bar graphs • Picture graphs • Circle graphs • Line plots • Line graphs • Tally charts	139
#17 Asked and Answered (Data)	Students determine whether questions about data can be asked and answered.	• Bar graphs • Picture graphs • Line plots • Data tables • Mass	149
#18 Same and Different (Data)	Students compare and contrast data displays.	• Bar graphs • Picture graphs • Line plots • Data tables • Area • Perimeter	158
#19 Mystery Data (Data)	Students use clues and data displays to solve puzzles.	• Line plots • Bar graphs • Time	166
#20 Not Quite Right (Data)	Students determine what isn't accurate within statements about data.	• Bar graphs • Line plots • Picture graphs • Data in infographics • Elapsed time • Area • Perimeter	171

NOTES

PART 2

THE JUMP-START ROUTINES FOR GEOMETRY, MEASUREMENT, AND DATA

ROUTINE 1

SEE IT, BUILD IT

ABOUT THE ROUTINE

In a "quick image" activity, you display or flash an image for a few seconds and then students talk about what they see. This routine borrows from that idea, but students first build an example of the image you flash before talking about how their "build" compares to your flash. This routine is perfect for developing skill with memory, shape recognition, spatial awareness, and vocabulary. It is a good precursor for the routine Find It (Routine #4) or Views (Routine #8). This routine is perfect for any grade as you can easily change the number of shapes and the complexity of the image to increase the challenge. But don't expect that simple images will be easy for all students regardless of their age. At every grade level, you'll find students with refined spatial awareness and memory as well as students who need more time and practice to develop both.

This routine is also a great way to practice vocabulary. Vocabulary in math can be avoided because adults misjudge how capable young students are with language. Terms are replaced with "kid-friendly" language. For example, in first grade, the commutative property might be called the "flip flop" property. This also happens with geometry when shapes are misnamed, or their definitions are completely misrepresented. Take for example the rhombus shown in the image at the start of the routine. It should be called a rhombus. It isn't a diamond or stretched square. Standards require students to learn and use vocabulary with accuracy and precision when talking or writing about math. So then, it is essential that students are introduced to the correct vocabulary from the start and use it during routines like this and others. Plus, if a kindergartener can recognize and name dinosaurs, like brontosaurus, they can surely handle rhombus.

It's critically important that teachers use vocabulary with precision and accuracy as well. But it's OK to make a mistake or speak informally. If you ask, "What's the answer?" just pause and correct yourself by saying, "Sorry, I meant to ask, what is the sum?" In this routine, you might say, "the blue one." If you do, stop and say, "Sorry, I mean the blue rhombus." Doing this shows students that people misspeak occasionally. It also shows them how to correct a statement. Most importantly, it sets the expectation for precise vocabulary use while also providing a brief dose of practice.

As you use this routine with your students, model the use of language and vocabulary. Provide

online resources All routines can be downloaded for your use at **https://companion.corwin.com/courses/jumpstartroutines-geometry**

an anchor chart or vocabulary cards nearby so that students can access them when they don't remember a word. Remind students from time to time why precise language matters. Invite them to politely correct incorrect use of language or vocabulary. This invitation may even increase how well they listen to what you and their classmates say about the content.

HOW THIS ROUTINE HELPS

This routine deepens understanding of geometry by providing opportunities for students to

- identify shapes regardless of orientation;
- decompose and compose shapes;
- use precise vocabulary as they discuss designs (MP6);
- define shapes by their attributes;
- look for patterns in designs and builds (MP7);
- identify shapes regardless of orientation; and
- develop perseverance (MP1).

WHAT TO DO

1. Provide a collection of pattern blocks to small groups of students and a white board or something similar to each individual student. They will use this for their workspace.
2. Prepare an arrangement of shapes on a slide or to display with a document camera.
3. Present the arrangement to students for a few seconds. To do this with slides, put a blank slide before the image. Display the blank slide. Advance to the image for a few seconds and then go back to the blank slide. With a document camera, put something over the image like a binder or cardstock. Move it to show the image and then cover it back up.
4. Have students independently build or re-create the image they saw with pattern blocks.
5. Have partners compare their images with each other then have the class come together to share some of the builds they thought they saw.
6. Have students describe their images. For example, they might say, "I think I saw two blue rhombuses and three green triangles." Another might say, "I think I saw two blue rhombuses and four green triangles."
7. Show your image again and have students describe how their builds are different if they don't match your image.
8. You can repeat the activity once or twice in a short routine.

SOMETHING TO THINK ABOUT: SPATIAL AWARENESS

Spatial awareness describes one's ability to understand, analyze, and interpret the relationships between objects and spaces. This could be reasoning about how objects are positioned relative to one another or how an object or objects move. Humans rely on spatial awareness every day as they move through hallways, stairwells, or any other space. It also includes understanding diagrams, maps, or puzzles. Spatial awareness includes mental manipulation of objects. It also connects with pattern seeking and recognition. This routine practices pattern recognition, shape relationships through space, and visualizing. Other routines, like Views (Routine #8), practice visualization and perspective. Playing games like Memory or Blokus, working with puzzles, building figures with blocks or LEGO bricks, and performing body movements are just some of the many ways you can help elementary students develop their spatial awareness. And the work may benefit more than just geometry. For example, number lines are spatial representations of number and quantity. They are used in the real world and mentally. Using number lines, or thinking about number relationships in general, is an extension of one's spatial awareness (Krasa, 2010). So, in a way, you might think of this routine and some of the other spatial experiences as number or number sense experiences too.

SEE IT, BUILD IT (VARIATIONS): USING TEMPLATES

This book is stuffed with examples of routines. For many, if not all of them, you don't need slides or any technology whatsoever to engage your students. Yet, having an electronic copy that you can share with colleagues or save for future use certainly has value. The many different routines come with templates for you to create your own examples. In this routine, we have provided a master slide with basic pattern block shapes for you to copy and manipulate. There are also templates baked in for pentominoes (Variation E) and cubes (Variation F). If you come up with your own variations, create a template of shapes or objects so that you can easily build new prompts and tasks for your students.

Variation A: Clues to Build It

Even the most engaging routines can lose luster over time. Simple variations can keep them fresh. One way to do that with this routine is to stop flashing images and start giving clues for students to interpret and build. For the example, you might say, "the build has four shapes." Students would build something and compare. Then, you might offer a new clue like, "one of the four shapes is a hexagon." At that point, students would rebuild their image to include a hexagon if their original idea didn't include one. A third clue is given. It could be something like, "the other three shapes are all the same." Again, students would have to rebuild, swapping out the other three shapes for something that's the same. You can continue to give clues or show the "answer" build at any point. In this case, assume you ended after the third build and displayed this image. Then, have students compare and contrast their builds with the image. Someone may have even built it or at least had the same shapes. It's unlikely that the exact image would be built without a fourth clue like, "the same three shapes are in a row above the hexagon." Don't feel pressure to get this experience right the first time. It will take some practice giving clues. Remember to build your own image first to use as source material for the clues, and keep the early builds somewhat simple with just a few shapes.

Variation B: Simple Puzzles

Building composite figures or completing puzzles is a natural variation of this routine. In this version, you don't flash an image for students to re-create. Instead, you tell them which blocks you want them to use (the Use box) and tell them a figure you want them to make (the Make box). This example uses just two pattern blocks. The Make is a triangle on top of a hexagon. It seems simple but you may be surprised to find how challenging it is for some students. And though this is a primary example, it might be the perfect challenge (i.e., place to start) for a fourth or fifth grader. In fact, this variation might be a nice precursor to the Find It (Routine #4). To build these in slides, create a composite figure and then turn all the shapes to black with black borders. Alternatively, you can use a line segment to outline the shape, change the thickness (if you like), and then delete the shapes inside. That's how the Make was created in this example. For real pattern blocks, you could do something similar to this alternative. Make a figure, trace it with a marker, and present that to students. Oh, and you might want to take a picture of the solution before you pose it to students.

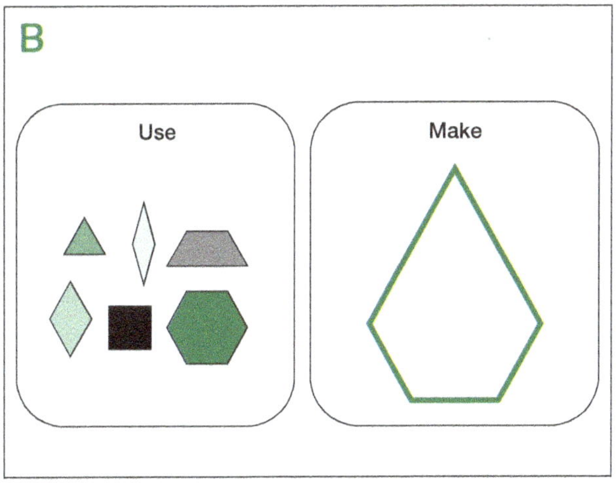

Variation C: More Complex Builds

As mentioned in Variation B, taking a picture of the solution for puzzles is a good idea. This is especially true as you introduce more complex builds. This variation shows what they might look like. How would you make the figure on the right? Is it two blue rhombi flanking a red trapezoid in the middle with a triangle on top? Or is it a red trapezoid in the middle flanked by four triangles and one additional triangle on top center? A picture will help you remember how you built a figure, but be prepared for other possibilities. You can increase the challenge by narrowing their options. This variation tells students to use pattern blocks in general. However, you could set Use conditions. With this example, you could tell them to build the figure with one trapezoid, two rhombi, and a triangle. There's simply no wrong way to do it. Play with it. Have fun. Encourage ideas from your students about how you can modify the experience.

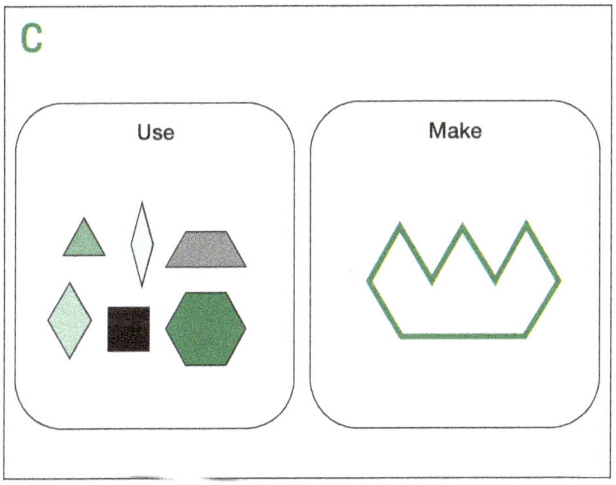

Variation D: Area and Perimeter

This variation morphs from a see it, build it activity to an open challenge to build figures with a given area or perimeter. Obviously, this variation should be done well after students have learned about area and perimeter. In fact, the experience itself stems from a lesson that you have taught, or your students have experienced in another grade. Regardless, it's a good practice experience to maintain their knowledge of area and perimeter. It might even be a good routine to use leading up to an important test. To do it, each student will need some color tiles. Then, you pose a Make like the one shown. We suggest keeping the area somewhat small, about six to 10 squares. If you want students to create something larger, we suggest using graph paper instead of actual tiles. As shown in D2, there will often be more than one solution, which is great for making sure that students don't develop a misconception that area and perimeter are constant.

D1

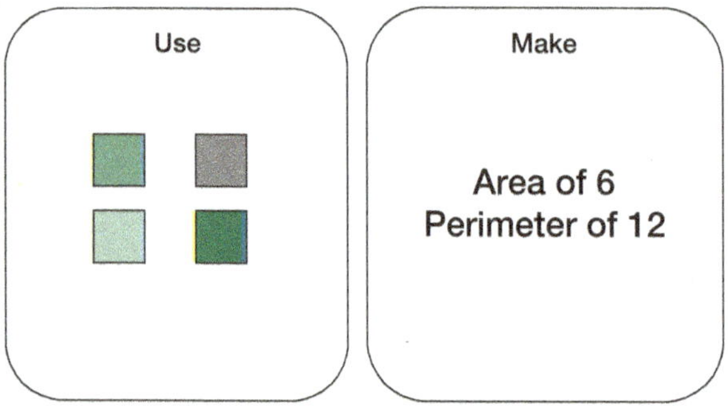

D2

Variation E: Pentomino Puzzles

Pentominoes are figures made of five squares that share at least one full side. You can see five of the 12 pentominoes in the image above. Some manipulative companies sell pentomino sets. You can also download and print pentomino cards from the online resources or use slide templates if you prefer. This variation of the routine builds (pun intended) on the idea of solving puzzles. You can go about it in a few different ways. First, you tell students which pentominoes to use like shown in the example. They then use some or all of them to make the figure. The solution in this case would be the "U" and "L" shaped pentominoes (E2).

E1

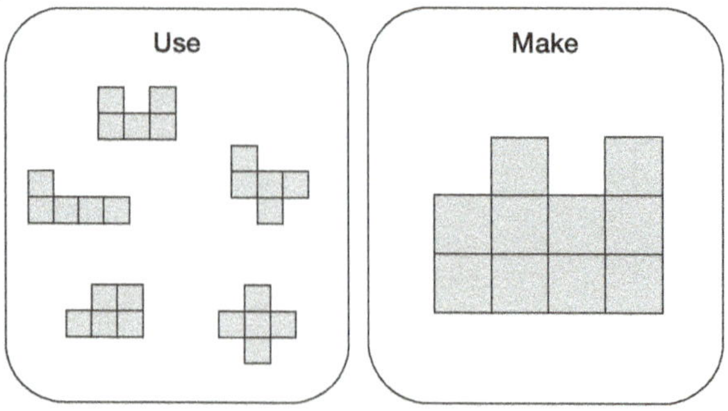

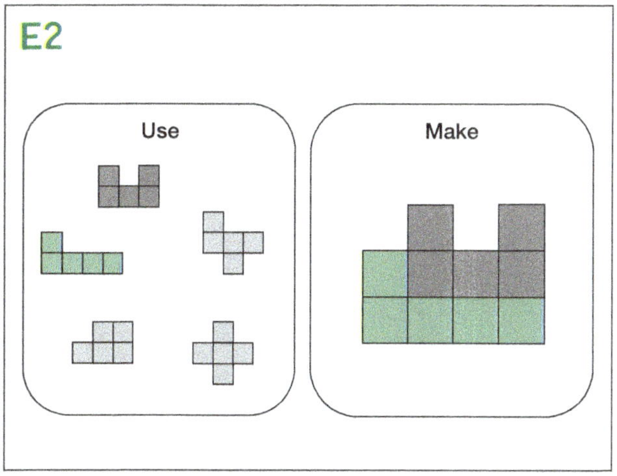

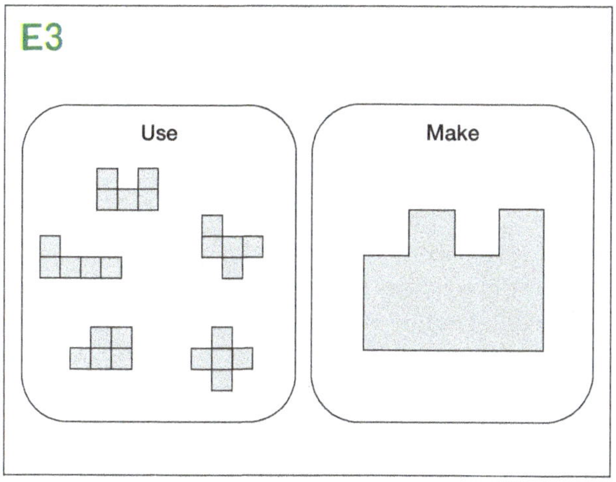

Another option is to not tell students which pentominoes to use. Instead, they can pull from any of the 12. Another way to modify, and possibly increase the challenge, is to provide a silhouette of the puzzle (E3). We suggest starting with puzzles that use only two pentominoes and slowly move toward three or four pentominoes. Remember, create your puzzle and take a picture of the solution to help you "find" it again during the routine. And, as mentioned in Volume Quick Images (Routine #11), routines and their variations are good options for centers and independent activities. So, if you prefer to use slides, consider printing the pentomino cards, making some silhouettes, and putting them in a bag or folder for early finishers or center rotations.

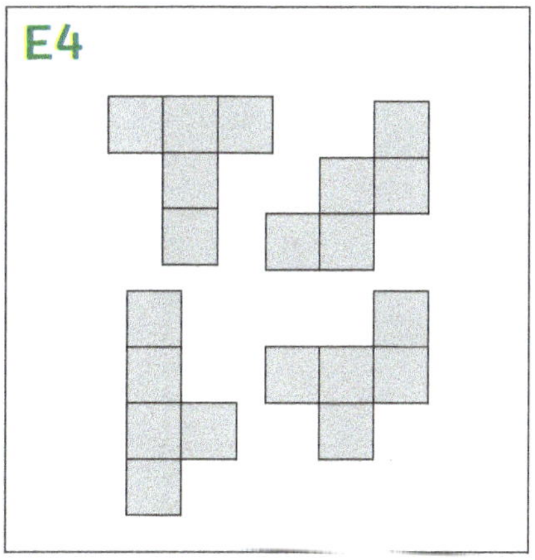

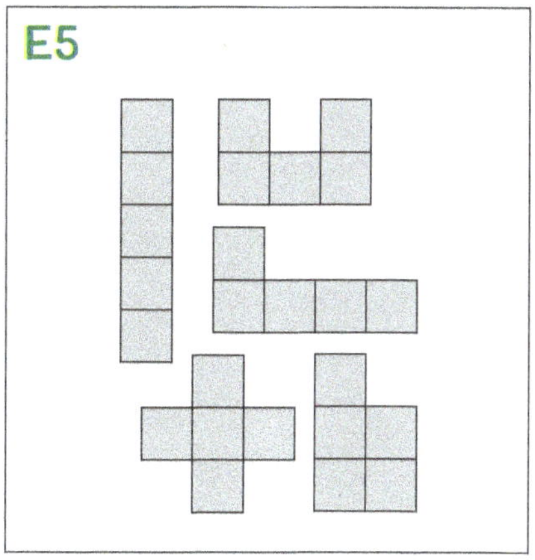

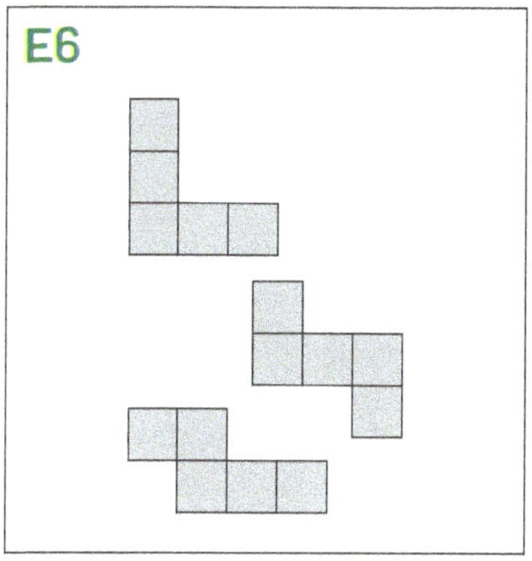

Variation F: 3D Figures

This last variation is an opportunity for students to work with three-dimensional figures. It goes well with Views (Routine #8). It is like Volume Quick Images (Routine #11) but is included here in case you read "volume" and looked past the routine. Yes, it goes well with volume, which is fourth or fifth grade content, but younger students can work with this variation too! Here, each student will need some inch cubes or connecting cubes. You display an image for them to build like the one shown. Then, students try to build the figure independently or with a partner. After a few minutes, you pause the engagement and have students compare their builds to the image. Note that the image in this example may be too complex for students' first few experiences. Start with simple prisms to gauge how well they can remember and build figures. Practice with simple figures and begin to increase the challenge as you gauge their readiness.

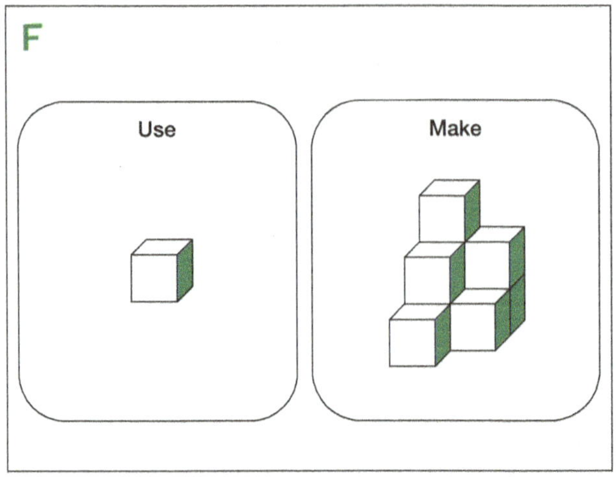

Variation G: Time and Money

This variation is the first of many examples in this book of how you can modify a routine for one content area (e.g., geometry) to practice another content area (e.g., measurement). If your students need practice counting coins, you could pose something like 74¢ as shown in G1. They would have a collection of coins and would build the amount or have a white board and draw images of coins (e.g., a circle with 5 inside it for nickel). A neat thing with this is that students will make the amount in different ways. That gives you an opening to discuss those differences, including which used the fewest coins. You could also do a simple flash and build with coins. To do this, simply swap out the shapes as described in the first few examples with coins. Have students re-create the image and then they can find the total value of the image. You can also tinker with the routine to practice something like time as shown in G2. To do this, pose a time expressed digitally, then students would re-create the time on their physical model or draw the hands on a clock template. You could also practice elapsed time with this version by giving a time and a duration like the examples shown here.

G1

Make	Make
74¢	4:35

G2

Make 3 hours earlier than	Make 15 minutes later than
1:25	6:15

ROUTINE 2

SORTS

ABOUT THE ROUTINE

Students first learn about shapes as early as kindergarten, and some—if not many—have experiences with shapes before they even come to school. They learn about basic arrangements of squares, circles, and triangles. They tell about the differences between them and practice spotting them inside and outside of their class. Some rely on a shape's general appearance, recognizing certain configurations of shapes, like equilateral triangles, and so they'll overlook right triangles among others. Some get tripped up when the orientation of a shape changes and others may look at an attribute that doesn't distinguish one shape from another, like the color of the shape. And even when primary students learn about defining characteristics, like number of sides, they may still reference their rudimentary ideas.

As students move through elementary school, they encounter new shapes, in new arrangements, with new names, and sometimes shared attributes. Obviously, lessons about the names and attributes of new shapes are a must. But there are only so many lessons one can do about what makes a quadrilateral. The skill and understanding you want for your students comes about from a lesson or two and ample practice. That's where this routine, Sorts, comes into play in your instruction.

In this anchor example, students are asked to sort themselves into quadrilaterals and nonquadrilaterals (Figure 1), which is a foundational experience before learning about the hierarchy of quadrilaterals (Figure 2). In this routine, students select a shape card from their personal collection printed and copied from the downloadable content of this book. After selecting a shape, students compare their shape with a partner. Then, once a sort is presented, in this case quadrilateral or not quadrilateral, students get up and move to either side of the room based on the sort. Once there, students confirm with others that they are on the right side of the sort. Afterward, the class shares examples that you highlight and chart like the image shown.

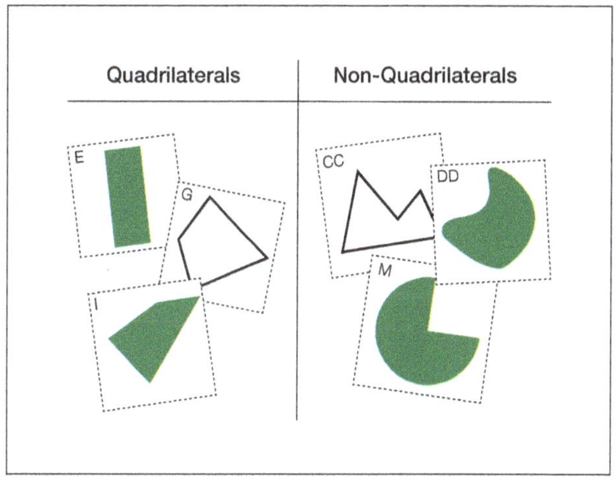

Figure 1

In the images and the downloadable, you'll notice that there are letter labels in the corner of each shape card. This is intentional. The sheer number of cards along with the variety of shapes can make it challenging for students to find an exact card in their collection. For example, it's easier to tell students to find card L than to find the irregular hexagon with three sets of parallel sides.

online resources All routines can be downloaded for your use at **https://companion.corwin.com/courses/jumpstartroutines-geometry**

Moreover, many of the figures have names! But most importantly, as students focus on attributes and comparisons, they can have difficulty remembering the vocabulary. To help them learn the vocabulary, when a card is identified by letter (and it is a shape they need to know), restate the vocabulary after the card is named by letter. For example, if a student says, "card K" you would acknowledge and then say, "card K is a pentagon" and keep the discussion moving.

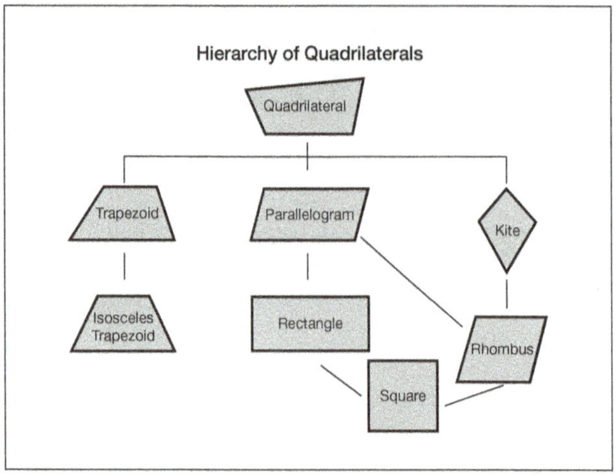

Figure 2

HOW THIS ROUTINE HELPS

This routine deepens understanding of geometry by providing opportunities for students to

- analyze shapes based on their attributes;
- classify shapes by their attributes;
- compare and contrast shapes with similar attributes;
- practice geometry vocabulary;
- describe shapes by their characteristics;
- recognize that different shapes can share some attributes;
- realize countless configurations of polygons and other shapes; and
- collaborate and discuss with their peers.

WHAT TO DO

1. Have each student select a card from their set without looking.
2. Give them a few moments to examine it and talk with a partner about how their shapes are similar.
3. Then, pose two categories. The anchor example uses quadrilaterals and nonquadrilaterals.
4. Have students consider which category their shape falls in and why.
5. Tell students that one side of the room is for one category (quadrilaterals) and that the other side of the classroom is for the other (nonquadrilaterals).
6. Have students get up and move to the corresponding side of the room. Once there, ask students to determine whether others in their group match the category.
7. As students mingle, listen to their conversations. Listen for their reasoning and use of vocabulary.
8. After some time, bring the class back together and ask for shapes (cards) that matched categories. Note that it can be helpful to use a document camera to show the cards so that the entire class can talk about the same card. You can also create an anchor chart or create a table or t-chart on the board and hang cards within the categories as shown in the image at the beginning of the routine.

SOMETHING TO THINK ABOUT: PREPARING SHAPE CARDS

There are two collections of shape cards that you can download, print, and cut out for use with the routine. One set is a mixed set of polygons and nonpolygons (shown here). Another is a basic set of shapes used in most primary classrooms. We suggest you print on heavier paper, like cardstock, and then put them in small plastic baggies or something similar. It is a lot to cutout. So, instead of doing it yourself have your students do it themselves during arrival or dismissal. Solicit a few student volunteers to come in during lunch and cut out cards for you. If you teach primary grades, look for fifth-grade volunteers who want to help. And obviously, this is a great task for parent volunteers if you have them. You should be able to reuse these cards for lessons and centers. It might be nice if they were laminated but it certainly isn't necessary.

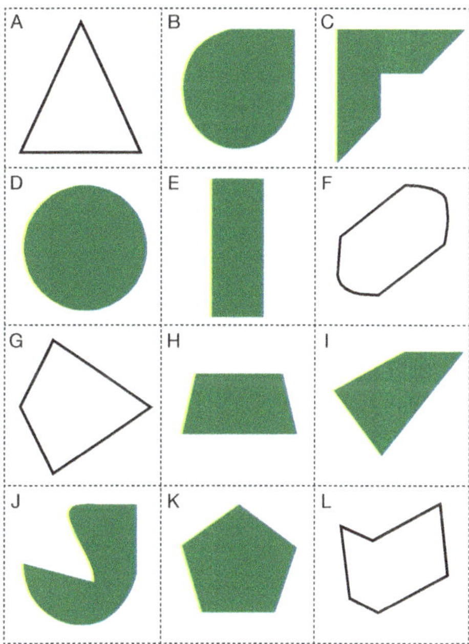

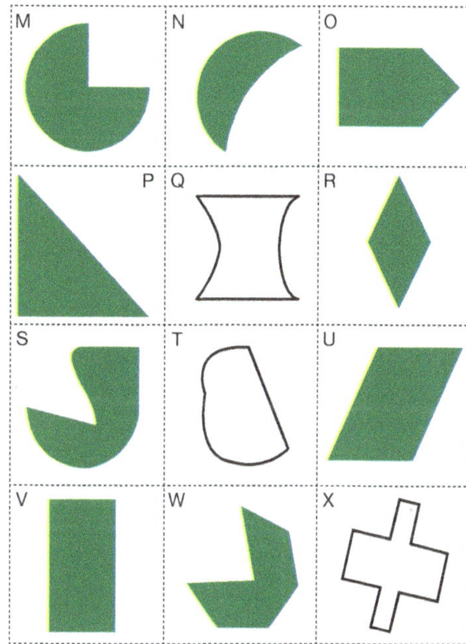

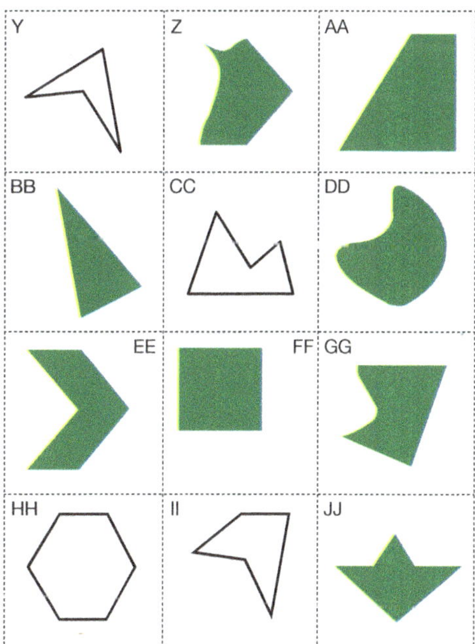

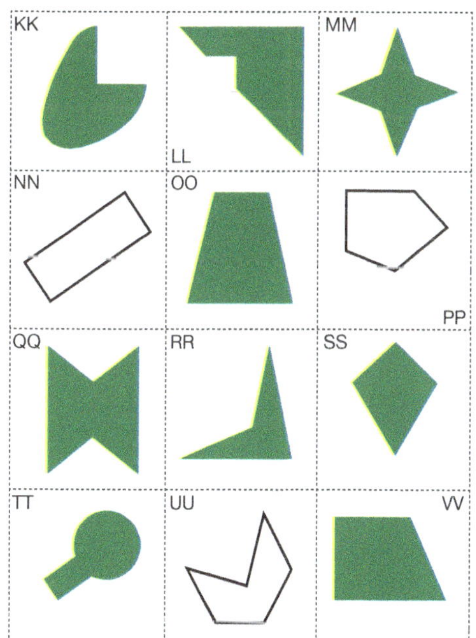

THE SORTS (VARIATIONS): CONCEPT ATTAINMENT

Sorting is a good instructional strategy for concept attainment. Sorting is an opportunity for active participation, critical thinking, and clarification. Often, sorts are done with two categories like an example and nonexample. But you can vary the complexity by asking students to sort things into three or more groups. You can change your recording from a simple chart or table as shown in the examples to using Venn diagrams or something else. And you can certainly change your sorting from geometry concepts to number concepts (e.g., even and odd numbers) to measurement concepts as shown in the variations.

Variation A: Special Quadrilaterals

This variation shows how you can use the sorts to practice special quadrilaterals. It also shows how you can add complexity by offering a third category. The third category—neither—is really important because if you tell students to pull a card at random, it's unlikely that you'll have many, if any, rectangles or trapezoids. That's OK! You can still carry out the routine as described and then once the preliminary sort is complete, have students return to their set of cards and find one example of a rectangle or trapezoid and then sort again. Another way to go about this is to have students look through their set to find an example of one of the three categories before you have them get up and move.

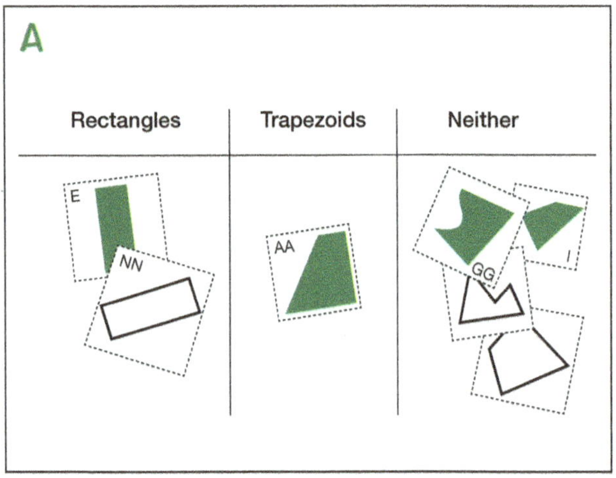

Variation B: Build More Than Two

This variation builds off the three-category example in Variation A. The difference here is that students are using geoboards instead of the sorting cards. This allows for student creativity. It calls for a higher order of cognitive processing (Anderson & Krathwohl, 2001). It may also give you a better angle into their understanding. Routines are perfect opportunities for formative assessment (see "Something To Think About," Venns, Routine #3). When they create examples, you can see if they understand the basic point of the attribute (e.g., number of sides) as well as whether there are patterns in their thinking. For example, do their hexagons typically take the same general shape? Do they ever make shapes with concave sides? You might find that their understanding of shapes may not yet be as deep as you would like.

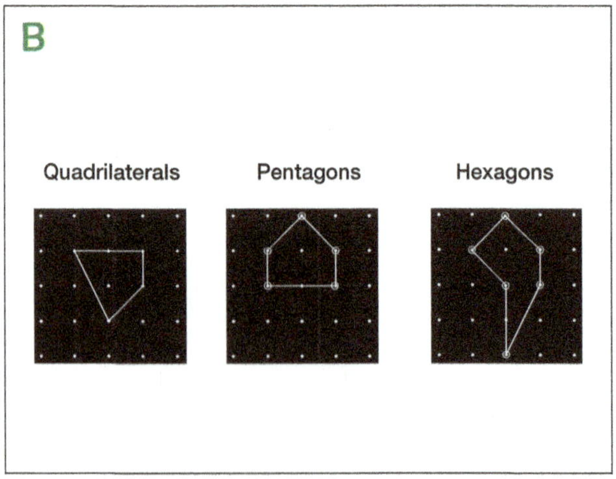

Variation C: Find Your Match

In this variation, students pick a card at random. Then, you have them find someone who matches them through a given category. You might say, "Find someone who has the same number of sides as you do." You might say, "Find someone who has the same number of parallel sides as you do" or "Find someone who has the same number of right vertices." Another way to go about finding matches is to not give students a category at all but rather have them determine similarities. To do this, have students pick a card and move about the room to find a partner. Once they find someone, the two students must identify what attribute their shapes have in common. You can add a direction that pairs should sit down once they find a commonality. This will help you monitor the progress of the routine. Also notice in the image on the left that three students "found each other." Shifting from pairs to triads can create quite a challenge for finding a common attribute.

C1

Not Polygons

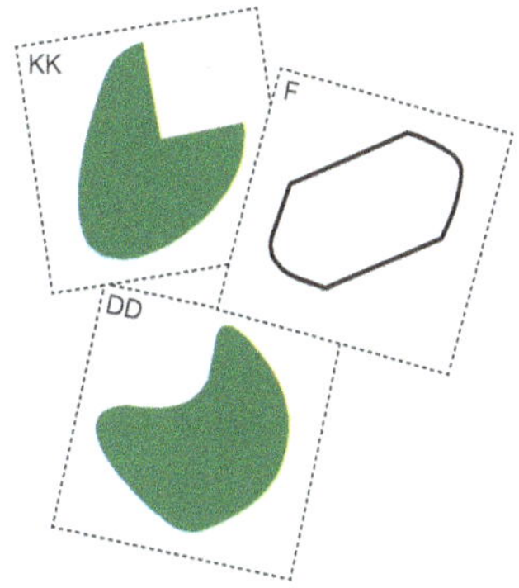

C2

Hexagons

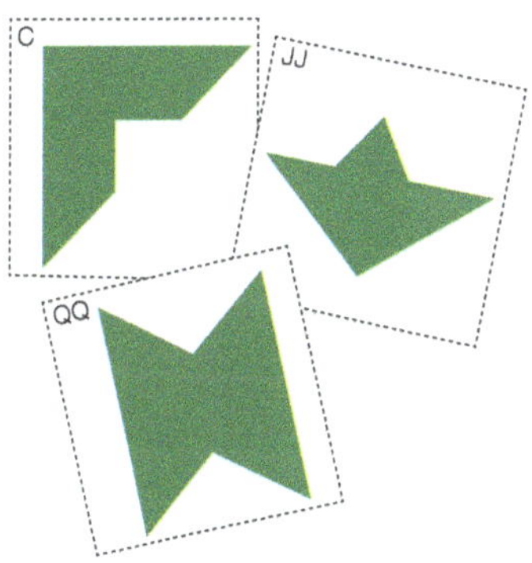

C3

"We're both pentagons."

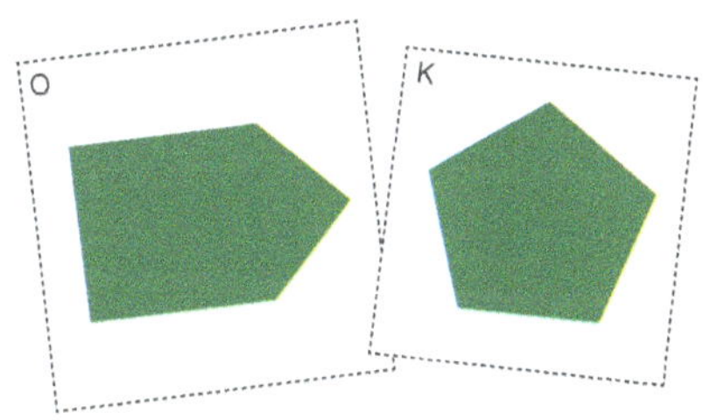

Variation D: Pop Up (That's Me)

Pop Up is a different way for students to consider shape attributes, but it still gets students moving a bit. In this variation, you have students sitting. They pick a shape card. Then, you call an attribute or name. If their example matches what you call, they "pop up" or stand. This notion of popping up is based on the traditional icebreaker, "That's Me." In that experience, people are expected to jump up and shout "that's me" when they satisfy a question, like "Do you have a dog?" In the example, the teacher said, "Pop up if you have six sides." The person holding any of those cards would pop up. Be sure to keep them standing so that the entire class can determine agreement. Once this is in place, have students sit back down, pull a new card, and give a new pop up statement.

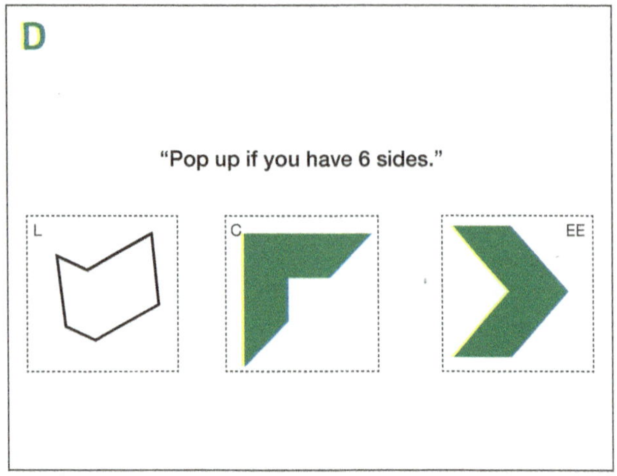

Variation E: Just One Thing

Just One Thing isn't so much about sorting as it is critical thinking and discussion. Here, a student picks a card. They find a partner and share one thing about their shape. Then, their partner tells them one thing about their shape. This causes both partners to listen carefully to what someone else says. There will be times when partners give wrong information, and a classmate will have to give them corrective feedback. This is good! It allows them to practice geometry and communicating. After students talk with a partner, have them move to another partner. You might provide as many as four or five opportunities to share and listen in just a few quick minutes. After a few rotations, bring the class together and highlight one or two conversations. Also note the example in E2. You'll see that it comes from the second set of shape cards. In that set, shapes are white, black, and striped. This is intentional to ensure that students focus on meaningful attributes (e.g., number of sides) instead of color or design.

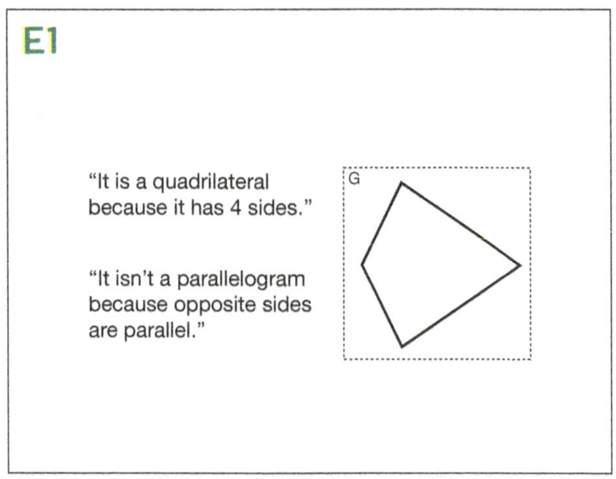

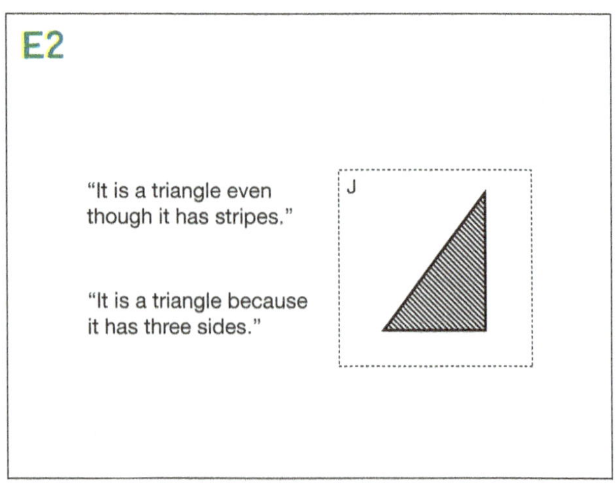

Variation F: Match More Than Two

This simple variation calls for each student to get out a card. You then put them in groups of four or five. At that point, they have to determine what their cards have in common (if anything). It's likely that all four or five shapes won't have something in common. At that point, this small group must look for similarities and differences among the collection. The group in the example didn't find that they all had something in common even though all five have at least one straight side. However, they were able to determine that three were quadrilaterals and that two were not polygons. After students find at least one way to sort, have them sit down to monitor progress as mentioned earlier. Then, once everyone is ready, bring the group together and spotlight one or two groups.

F

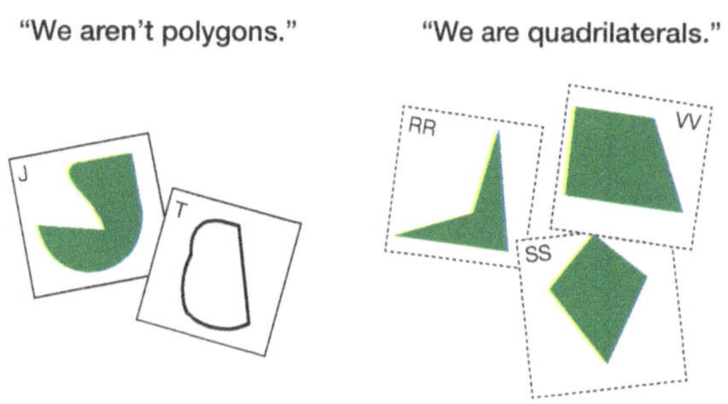

Variation G: Time Sorts

The Sorts routine could be a great opportunity for students to practice telling time on analog clocks. You'll find a template in the downloads of clock faces like you see in the image. All you need to do is add hands to the clocks to create different times that align with the precision of time your students are working with (e.g., time to the minute, 5-minute, 15-minute, half-hour, or hour). Use your master set to create student sets. Then, use the clock cards for any of the versions of this routine that you like. Some of the categories you might use are shown in the table.

G

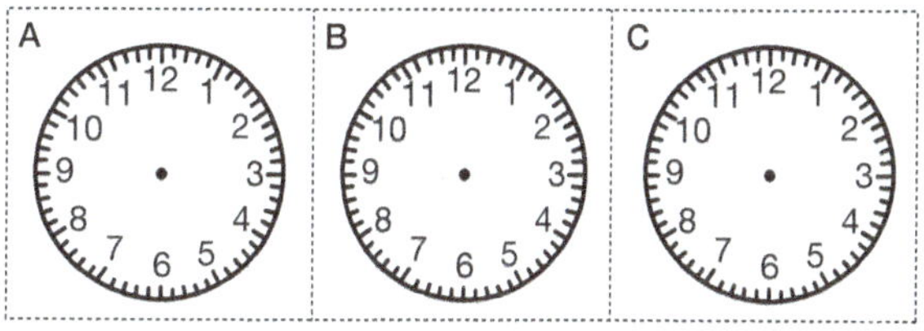

Category	Example	Category	Example
Before 6:00	3:25	After 6:00	8:40
45 minutes past the hour	7:45	30 minutes past the hour	9:30
15 minutes past the hour	4:15	15 minutes until the hour	11:45
An hour when you're probably at school	12:20	An hour when you're probably at home	5:35

ROUTINE 3

VENNS

ABOUT THE ROUTINE

John Venn was a 19th-century, English logician who is remembered for inventing Venn diagrams (Klaxoon, n.d.). In the 150 or so years since their creation, Venn diagrams have become a staple of teaching and learning. They are exceptional tools for concept attainment in math as well as most any other content. These diagrams frame how topics or data points are related, helping individuals develop strength with comparing and contrasting, which contributes to improved reasoning and analyzing. In this routine, Venn diagrams are leveraged for brief bursts of practice with geometry though they can be applied to most any topic in math from place value concepts (e.g., numbers with a 2 in them and numbers with a 5 in them) to multiples (e.g., multiples of 4 and multiples of 6) (SanGiovanni et al., 2024). In this example, the shapes are sorted by their size and number of sides. Shape A would go in section 3 because it is a small quadrilateral. Shape F would go in section 2 because it is large and it is a quadrilateral. Shape C is a large circle placing it in section 1. Section 4 is reserved for shapes that don't match either category.

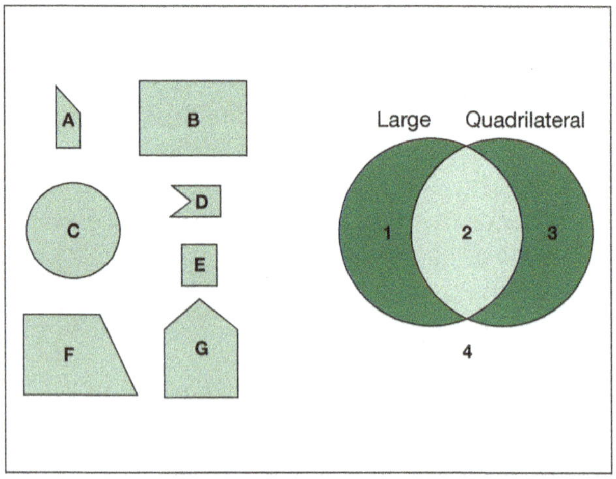

Before doing this routine, or any routine for that matter, you need to first teach the concept. In this example, that would be defining attributes. The shapes categories and shapes most likely align with third-grade content (or later). In younger grades, the categories might be large and square or small and triangle. In either case, students would learn about what those attributes are. They would understand features of shapes and should distinguish between defining attributes (e.g., number of sides) and nondefining attributes (e.g., size). Your lessons might even mirror the routine or vice versa. To do this, you might provide physical models of the shapes or have students build them with AngLegs, toothpicks and marshmallows, or something else. Sorting circles are large, folding plastic circles that come in red, yellow, and blue. They are perfect for creating physical representations of Venn diagrams and could be a nice way to establish a given topic while also informally teaching this routine.

As you can see, the routine doesn't use physical models. Instead, there are images of shapes. You can get these from the downloadable content in this book, make them on index cards, or sketch them on the board. And remember that there are even more shape cards from the Sorts routine (Routine #2). You might also be wondering about the number of shapes to provide. There isn't an exact answer. You want to provide enough to stir

online resources All routines can be downloaded for your use at **https://companion.corwin.com/courses/jumpstartroutines-geometry**

thinking and discussion but not so many that your students are overwhelmed. Five to eight seems like a good number but you may find that you need to start with fewer. You may want to provide 10 or so and that's fine too. If you do increase the number, it is probably a good idea for students to do as many as they can in the shorter amount of time that a routine offers rather than all of the shapes.

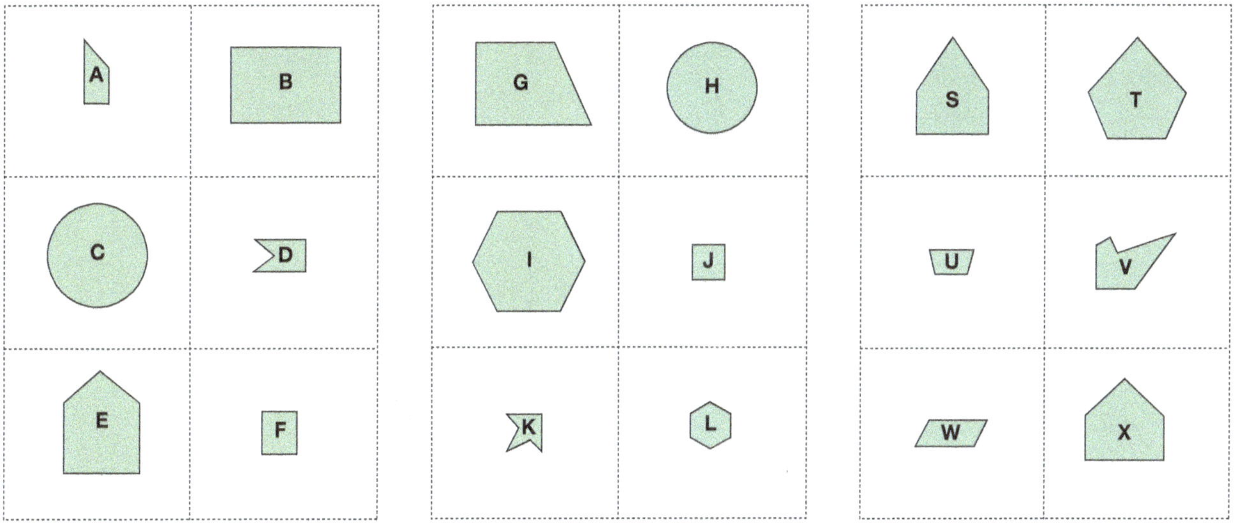

Regardless of how you create the shapes or the number of shapes you use it is important that the shapes are labeled. As mentioned in other routines, labeling or lettering the shapes that students sort is really helpful. In this case, lettering supports discussion as new vocabulary develops. For example, every student can recognize shape D whereas the notion of a pentagon may still be forming. Also, if you or they are comparing two pentagons, it's much better to talk about shape D and shape S or pentagon D and pentagon G instead of "this one" and "that one." Labeling the sections of the Venn are equally important. The numbered sections are easy to identify whereas the left, right, or center may be problematic especially when more categories (see Variation E) are introduced.

HOW THIS ROUTINE HELPS

This routine deepens understanding of geometry by providing opportunities for students to

- analyze shapes based on their attributes;
- distinguish between defining and nondefining attributes;
- classify shapes by their attributes;
- identify relationships between shapes with similar attributes;
- reinforce geometry vocabulary (MP6);
- strengthen reasoning skills for application and problem-solving (MP1);
- collaborate, discuss, and debate with classmates; and
- create shapes that match attributes of other shapes.

WHAT TO DO

1. Pose a Venn diagram to your students.
2. Have them think about a shape that would go in any of the sections (numbered locations) of the diagram. Optional: Have them create an example that would go in a certain section of the diagram.
3. Pose a collection of shapes.
4. Have students independently determine where to place the shapes in the Venn diagram. Optional: Let them record their ideas in their journal, sticky note, or personal dry erase board.
5. Have partners discuss and justify their solutions.
6. Bring the class together to discuss solutions as a whole class. Record solutions as students share their ideas. Be ready to ask questions like the following:
   - » How did you know ___ went in that section of the diagram?
   - » How is shape ____ similar to shape ____? Does that mean they both should be in the same section?
   - » How can two shapes have something in common but go in different sections of the diagram?
   - » How did you know that shape ___ didn't belong in that section?
7. Optional: Introduce one last new shape and ask the whole group to determine where it would be placed in the diagram.

SOMETHING TO THINK ABOUT: FORMATIVE ASSESSMENT

There are different techniques for formative assessment (Fennell et al., 2017) that pay big dividends during your daily instruction. While not a technique per se, routines *are* a great opportunity for formatively assessing your students' understanding of skills and concepts. By listening to their ideas, you see into their thinking. You're able to ask follow-up questions that enable you to probe more deeply into reasoning and insights. You can pose questions that help you see if they understand a concept in a narrow, singular way or if they have generalized a concept and can both transfer and apply it to new examples or situations. Routines aren't a time for grades. They're a time for engagement and discussion. Don't feel like you must hear every student's partner conversation to do this well. Position yourself to listen to certain students that you want to know more about. Ask questions of the whole group during the debrief and be sure that certain students have a chance to talk. Use what you hear to help you decide if something needs to be retaught or simply practiced more.

VENNS (VARIATIONS): WRITING IT DOWN

For the most part, routines are intended to be mental exercises. But some routines benefit from scaffolds like graphic organizers (I Would Say, Routine #16). Some routines are more effective if manipulatives are provided. And some, like this one, need to be supplemented with a piece of paper, math journal, sticky note, or an individual dry erase board. The reason for this is that students need to remember where they placed a shape in the diagram. As they move from one shape to another, they might forget where they placed a previous shape. Ultimately, this slows the routine and increases the likelihood for frustration and disengagement. You can even have students create their own rendering of the diagrams if you like. This will work with any of the following variations as well.

Variation A: Single Category

You can have a single circle Venn diagram as shown in this opening variation. Shapes that match the category, like C, E, F, G, and H, go inside the circle while the others do not. It's a good place to begin for students first working with either the concept of sorting or Venn diagrams for that matter. It's also good for introducing the numbering of sections used in this routine. Remember, as described in Part 1, you must take time to teach the process of a routine before it becomes an efficient, brief practice experience. In the case of this routine, you have to teach them how to use the numbered sections in the diagram. For most students, that will take just a few moments. But for some, it will take a little time to understand how the letters and numbers work. Using this variation can simplify the process, making it clear. To do this, sort with a single circle like you see here. After the sort is complete, put a number on the inside (1) and a number on the outside (2). Talk about how the shapes are either "ones" or "twos." Then, simply present a new shape and ask students what number or numbered space it goes with. Their answers will tell you how well they understand and what you might need to do next.

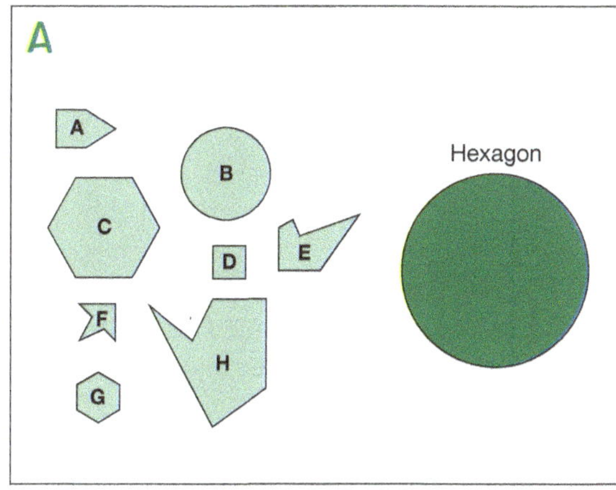

Variation B: Named Polygons and Impossible Situations

Learning the names of special polygons is one thing. Recognizing them in a regular configuration is another. Recognizing them in *any* configuration is a whole other thing. The latter typically presents the greatest challenge to students as they rely on a certain image of a polygon rather than the number of sides. Take this variation for example. Shape G is a regular pentagon that most students will recognize quickly. Shapes H and J have some visual similarities and are likely to be identified by many students. Shape B, however, is unlikely to be the shape you imagine when you think of a pentagon. It's also the shape that your students are most likely to look past when identifying pentagons in this example. There is also one other noteworthy feature in this example and that is sometimes a section of a Venn diagram cannot contain any examples. Here, section 1 could never have a shape because every pentagon is a polygon. This was designed with intention. You may create a similar situation that you don't intend. That's OK! If it happens, simply ask students why or why not a certain case is true. Have them explain and justify their thinking like we just did with pentagons and polygons. And if you notice that you made categories that create a situation like this don't point it out right away. Wait! Give them a chance to discover and question it. If they don't, then ask them if a certain space could ever be filled. But don't feel obligated to turn it into a mini lesson. Give it a moment for discussion and move on.

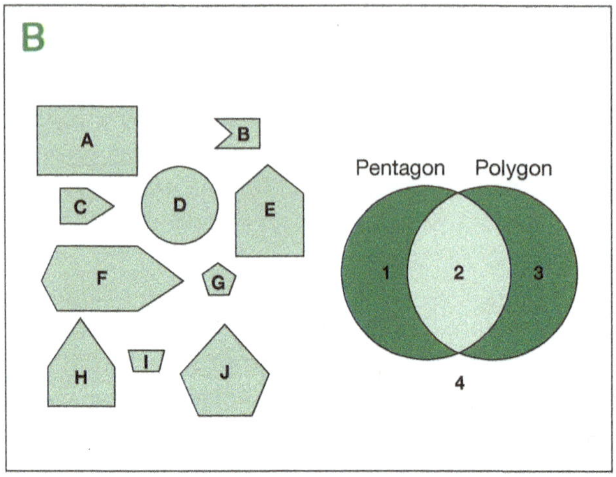

Variation C: Quadrilateral Attributes

Learning and remembering the hierarchy of quadrilaterals or the different types of triangles can be quite a challenge. An obvious first step is to teach the attributes of different quadrilaterals. To do that, you want students to build examples, talk about them, compare them with other quadrilaterals, and so on. You don't want them to memorize the names and definitions of the different quadrilaterals, but you will need to explicitly teach them. Yet for your students to retain this information well, they will need to practice it again and again. This variation of the routine gives you an idea how you might do that. The categories here are foundational. They are a good place to start. From there, you can begin to prompt defining attributes of quadrilaterals like the one in C2. As you do this, add the special name with it. After a bit, you can begin to remove the "definition" and leave only the name. For example, you might have a category of two sets of parallel sides with "parallelogram" written in parenthesis below or beside it. After time, only the word *parallelogram* would be offered.

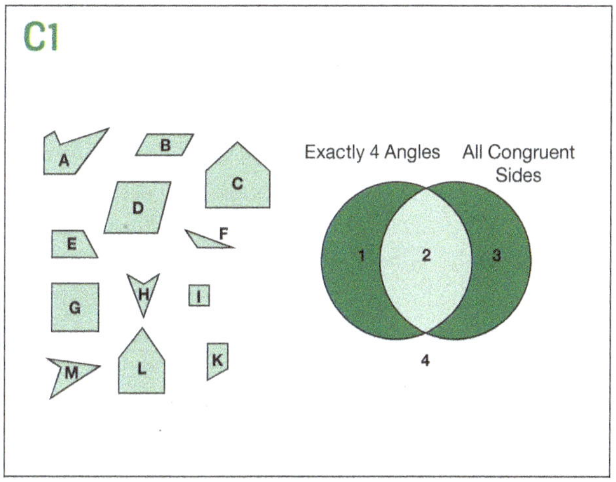

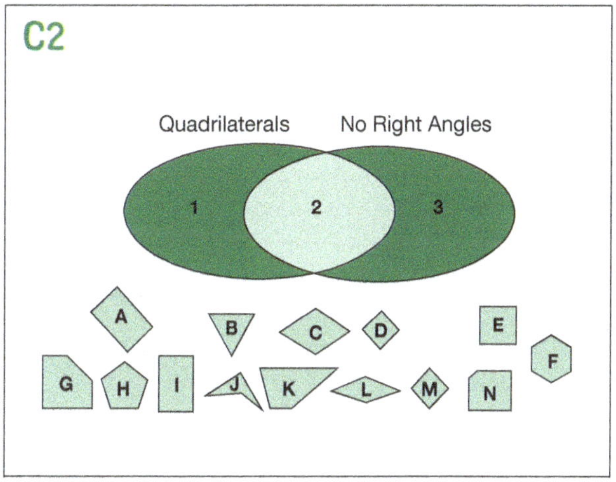

Variation D: Angles

You have read throughout this work how you can create variations of routines to practice all sorts of content within geometry, measurement, and data. This variation of Venns is a good example of how you can do this. Here, the topic is angles, which likely appears in your fourth- or fifth-grade curriculum. You can draw a few angles on your board, create them on index cards, or print some from the downloadable content. Whatever you do, remember that you want angles to open from both left to right and from right to left. You want to make sure that you orient or rotate them in a variety of ways. Be sure that the rays vary in length from angle to angle. In short, make sure that your students aren't fooled or don't rely on a certain configuration of angles to name them. And know that your categories can be more than straight, right, acute, or obtuse. You might include a category like "angles found in squares" instead of "right" or something similar.

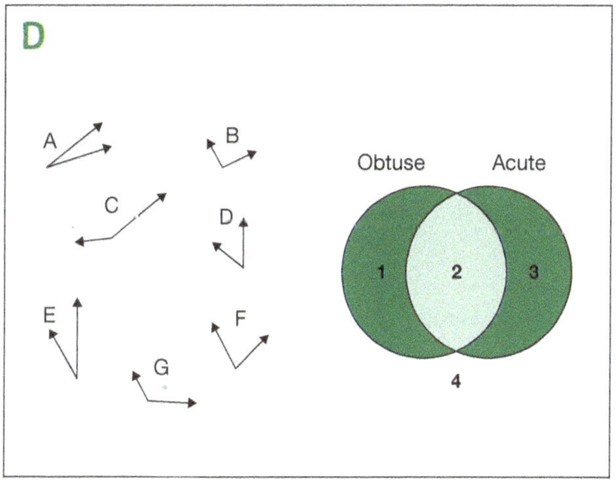

Variation E: Three Categories

"There's a glitch in the matrix." That might have been your reaction the first time you were exposed to a triple Venn diagram as a student, preservice teacher, or just right now! At first, it may seem overwhelming. There is a lot going on with the seven spaces within the diagram. So, when you introduce a triple Venn, give students time to examine it without sorting anything. Have them simply observe, discuss, and ask questions. Ensure that they understand it, and to do this you might need to include categories so that they can more easily describe what's happening. You might also begin with very basic categories, even nondefining attributes like color or size. Working with a triple Venn may seem like a tall task but it really isn't. And working with it gives your students opportunity to deepen their understanding of the content you present while also enhancing their critical thinking and reasoning skills. Here are two answers, in case this is your first time with a triple Venn diagram. Shape G is a pentagon and it has one line of symmetry and at least one set of perpendicular sides so it would go into section 4. Figure F is a rhombus that fits into section 1 with at least one line of symmetry.

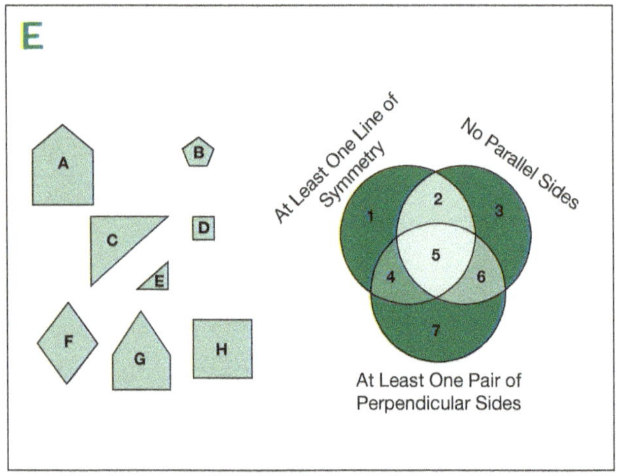

Variation F: Time to Sort

This routine, among many others, can be modified to practice other important topics in geometry, measurement, data, and more. This example shows how Venns could be used to practice time. Here you see four clocks. Students must determine what time the clock is showing and then compare that to categories of "Before 5:00" and "After 9:00." As you know, A (12:15) and B (˜3:38) would fit in section 1. Clock D (˜10:43) would fit in section 3 and Clock C (˜6:09) doesn't fit in either place so it would go with 4 outside of the Venn. You could change the sorting categories for time to other things like the number of minutes shown, such as no minutes past the hour or o'clock (e.g., 6:00), time to the 5 minutes (e.g., 3:35), or 15 minutes past the hour (e.g., 7:15). With time, you could mingle digital and analog clocks. And remember, just because a Venn diagram has an overlap (section 2) it doesn't mean something will fit inside. This is a good conversation to have with students. There is no time that is before 5:00 and after 9:00 unless we're talking about A.M. and P.M., which isn't referenced in this example.

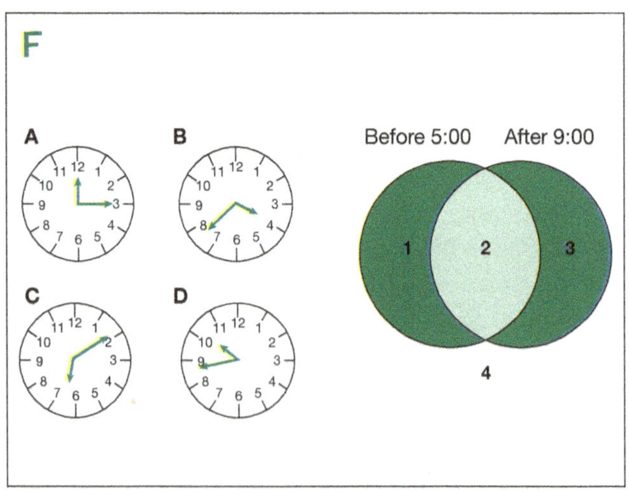

Variation G: Surprise Sorts

This variation of the routine thrives on student creativity and an element of the unknown. First, have students create a shape on sticky notes, white boards, or something similar. You can limit their creations to polygons, a certain set of shapes (e.g., triangles and quadrilaterals) or you can tell them to make anything they like. A nice alternate is to provide each student with a set of shape cards from this routine or Sorts (Routine #2) in which they would pull a single shape at random. Regardless of your approach, once students have a shape, ask them to compare their shape with some nearby classmates. Have them identify similarities and differences. Share out as a class if you like. Then, reveal categories for the Venn and give students time to think about which section their shape would fall into. Have them confirm their placement with a partner and then share solutions. You can have them put their shape on the Venn or if you have a large enough diagram displayed you can have them get up and stand by the section of the Venn where their shape belongs.

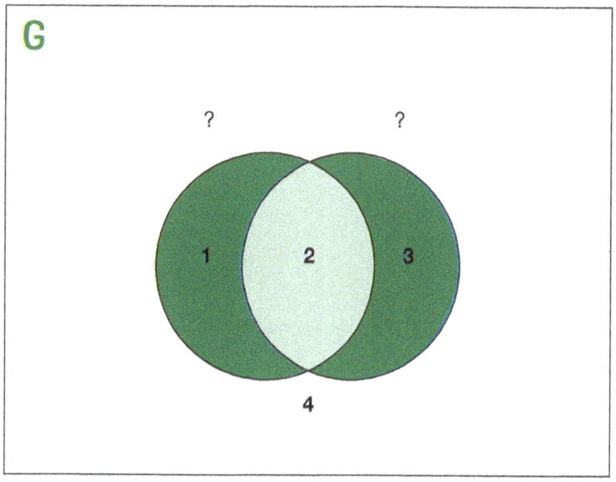

ROUTINE 4

FIND IT

ABOUT THE ROUTINE

Find It is a routine modeled after classic geometry activities of shape hunts or shape searches. In this routine, you pose a figure with some prompts. A subtle, yet important, difference is that you want to offer prompts that don't have one correct answer. For many students, the pursuit of a single solution dampens the joy of doing puzzles. In this routine, you want them to hunt for shapes, find lots of possibilities, engage in discussions, and acknowledge that sometimes there is more to a puzzle (and shapes) than meets the eye.

Find 3 triangles.

Find 2 parallelograms.

Find 2 pentagons.

Find a trapezoid.

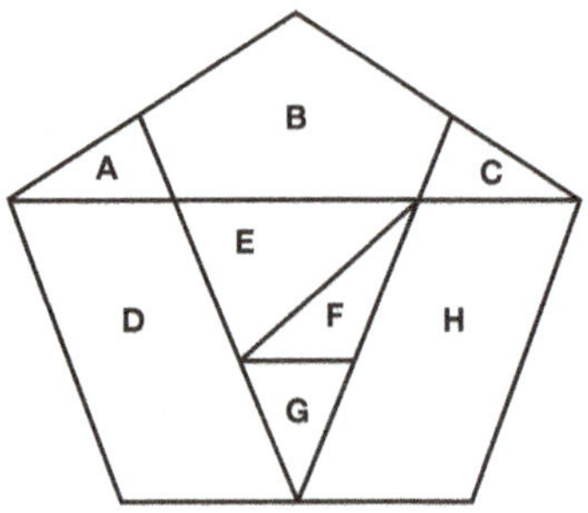

Many possibilities pop in this featured example. Consider the first prompt to find 3 triangles. It's easy to see figures A, G, C, F, and even E. But figures E, F, and G together make a triangle. F and G also combine to form a triangle. Some students might only see independent triangles, like figure A. Exposure to others' observations and explanations encourages them to think more deeply about shapes and shape composition. As students become keener finding composite examples, you can change your prompt to something like find 3 triangles other than A, F, and G. Figure C remains an easy find but thinking will be needed to find others.

This routine helps students move past van Hiele's lowest level of visualization (Grouws & Cebulla, 2000). It helps them begin to analyze the properties of shapes and understand the relationships between these properties, even if they haven't fully acquired a formal definition. You should see students be able to describe properties of the shapes they identify, pointing out sides and angles. They should recognize that different shapes can share some properties. Work with this routine and activities like it will help shift focus from recognizing shapes to thinking critically about their characteristics.

Routines are typically mental exercises. Yet Find It is a routine that comes with a strong recommendation to provide a printed copy for students to work with. A good way to do this is to draw or print an image and put it in a plastic sheet protector. Then, give students dry erase or washable markers so they can trace shapes as they find them. Having more than one color marker can be helpful so that the different shapes "pop" more easily. But there is no one best way. Some teachers find it helpful for students to use their markers to find all of the triangles (first prompt in the example), discuss the findings, and then go on to the next. In situations where students will compose shapes, teachers recommend that they trace it with their marker, find the smaller, component shapes, and record them before looking for something new.

online resources All routines can be downloaded for your use at **https://companion.corwin.com/courses/jumpstartroutines-geometry**

HOW THIS ROUTINE HELPS

This routine deepens understanding of geometry by providing opportunities for students to

- identify shapes regardless of orientation;
- decompose and compose shapes;
- define shapes by their attributes;
- find regular and irregular examples of certain shapes (e.g., quadrilaterals);
- analyze composite shapes;
- better understand how regular and irregular figures are related;
- recognize that prompts and puzzles can have more than one solution; and
- develop perseverance.

WHAT TO DO

1. Pose a figure with a number of line segments intersecting it.
2. Label the smaller partitioned shapes within the larger shape.
3. Create prompts for students to find a number of specific shapes within the composite figure.
4. Give students some time to find and make a list of their examples.
5. Give partners a few moments to share their findings.
6. Bring the class together to share their collective findings. As examples are shared, ask students to justify their thinking with questions like the following:
    - How did you know the shape was a ____?
    - How is this shape similar to the other ____ we found?
    - How did you know that ___ wasn't a ____?
    - Did anyone put two smaller figures together to make a ____?
    - How did you know this larger figure was actually a _____?
7. After discussing the first prompt, move to the next prompt like, "find two parallelograms" as shown in the example.

Note that you might not have enough time to go over all four prompts in a single setting. When you decide to suspend the discussion or simply run out of time, pick up the next day with the same figure and prompt. Consider giving students a few moments to find examples again (if needed).

SOMETHING TO THINK ABOUT: CREATING EXAMPLES

Having your students create figures and prompts for this routine is a great way to engage their creativity while giving them a different way to practice. This also helps lessen your burden. You can do this in all sorts of ways. You can print large open shapes like squares, rectangles, parallelograms, hexagons, and so on. Then, have students use a ruler to create line segments within the figure. You can also choose to have them add labels as shown in the opening example. Having them create an example is a good use of independent time or even homework. Speaking of which, making this a homework assignment is a great way to connect with caregivers and enlist their support. You might even find some families will be quite creative or enthusiastic providing more than a few examples. Keep in mind that you want your students to experience the routine with your examples first, so they are comfortable with the task. Also keep in mind that some will be really good, and others might not be as ready to use in your class. It's important to honor each student's contribution regardless of whether you will use it as an example or not.

FIND IT (VARIATIONS): PUZZLES ARE PROBLEMS

Problem-solving comes in all shapes and sizes. Problem-solving encompasses much more than word problems. Problems can be routine and nonroutine (Kablan & Uğur, 2020). Nonroutine problems are somewhat unusual. They call for individuals to create a strategy. They elicit sense-making, creative thinking, and mathematical reasoning power. Puzzles are great problems! They help students do all of this and more. But any puzzle, done repeatedly, can lose its novelty. You can keep this routine fresh by changing it up. Ideas for doing so are highlighted in these variations.

Variation A: Put 'Em Together

The first example of this routine is a great place to start with students. There are clear examples of parallelograms, triangles, and trapezoids. For the most part, students simply had to look for examples within the larger shape. This variation calls for students to find examples of a given shape by composing smaller shapes. Look for students at first to compose only two shapes. That works fine for this example because A and B make a square, E and F make a rectangle, and so do C and D. But you can challenge them by asking for more examples. To find two more quadrilaterals, they will at least have to combine B, C, and E or even A, B, C, and D. Another easy way to tap into the greater potential of this variation is to not put a limit on the number you want them to find. Instead, ask them to find as many quadrilaterals as they can!

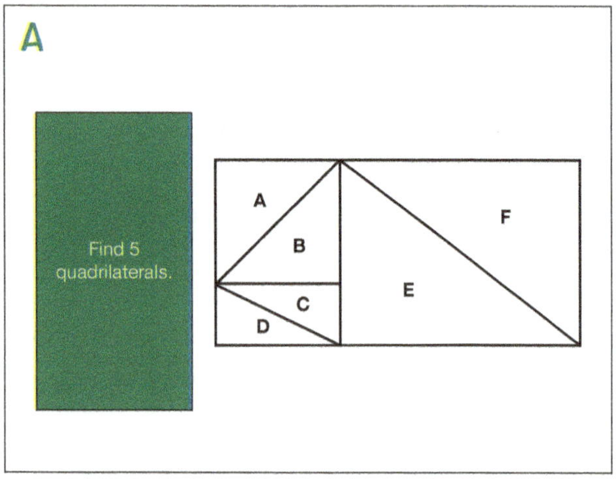

Variation B: An Open Challenge

This variation presents some nice options. It is somewhat open in that it doesn't ask for a certain number of hexagons for students to find and it doesn't give direction about how many smaller shapes to combine. This openness has advantages. Asking students to find just one hexagon allows for different entry points as well as more than one right answer. In this example, G alone is a hexagon. F, G, and C combine to make a hexagon as do F, E, B, A, and D. With different solutions offered, you can focus the discussion on what makes a hexagon and how their solutions satisfy that characteristic. An important aspect of this example is that many students only see hexagons or other shapes, like pentagons, in regular configurations. Because of this, they rely on visualization for recognition. But, as you know, a hexagon is any figure with six sides and so the examples given earlier are all correct responses.

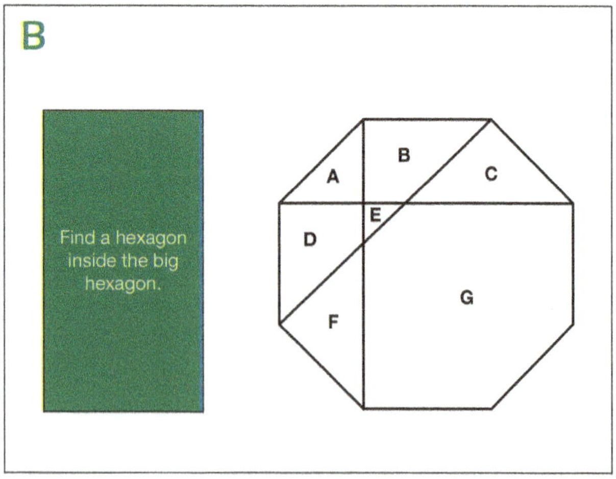

Variation C: Reuse It

This is another example of how you can prompt students to find examples of irregular polygons. The slight difference here is that they are asked to find more than one example, and it's offered to you as a reminder that there is no one way to go about this or any other routine. In this example, A and B form possibly the most obvious example of a quadrilateral. B, C, D, and E also form a quadrilateral, as do A, B, and E. The outer shape is less conventional. You might find that these shapes along with increasing the number of diagonals or partitions creates more challenge for your students. We offer this example for one other important reason. You can (and should) reuse your creations. This image could be reused with prompts like find five triangles, find a triangle made of two figures, or find two triangles made from two or more figures. And, if you're wondering, you can use this same figure with different prompts on consecutive days or you can spread them out over time.

The example in C2 also shows how you can reuse a figure with different things for students to find. In the black box, you see questions about triangles, parallelograms, and trapezoids. Again, you can pose each of these over different days. However, some teachers have found an advantage of posing all three on the first day but only talking about the first shape (triangles in the example). Providing all prompts at once can expedite the conversations on following days because students begin to look for them while they wait for a whole group discussion.

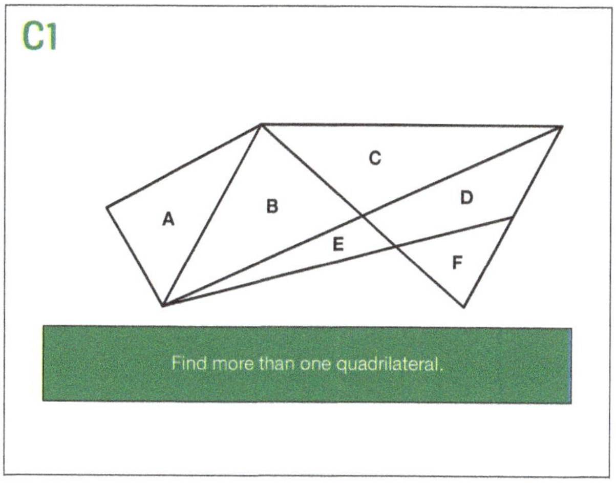

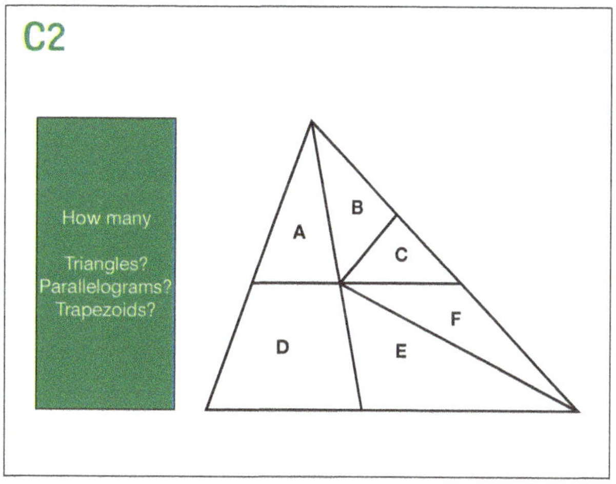

Variation D: What Do You Notice?

This variation is rather basic and might be a nice place to start. Instead of prompting students to find anything, you simply ask them what they see. Ask them what different shapes they see and how many of them they see. Use their observations to question others. For example, a student might say, "I see four triangles." You would then use that to ask the whole group what four triangles they think their classmate saw. In open situations, be ready for students to look for shapes they are most familiar with. In other words, expect them to notice shapes like triangles and quadrilaterals rather than octagons or trapezoids. To offset this, allow students to notice whatever they like. Ask follow-up questions as described. Then, pose something you notice that stretches their thinking beyond those comfortable shapes. Also note that this version is a nice angle to bring to any variation of the routine. To do this, simply ask students what they observe for any configuration before you pose your challenge.

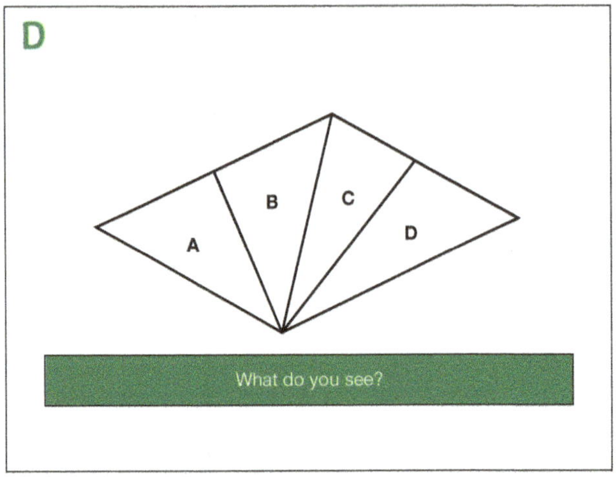

Variation E: Simple Puzzles

Simple puzzles like this are a great problem for students. Though it isn't nearly as complicated as the other examples, it will still provide plenty of challenge. Here, the outer figure counts as one of the squares (3 x 3). Inside, there are nine small squares and four medium (2 x 2) squares. You can create these with more squares, with triangles, with rectangles, or any other shape. Variations like this are also perfect puzzles for primary students. Again, this is a routine, but you can easily use a routine as a center or an independent task (see "Something to Think About" in Volume Quick Images, Routine #11).

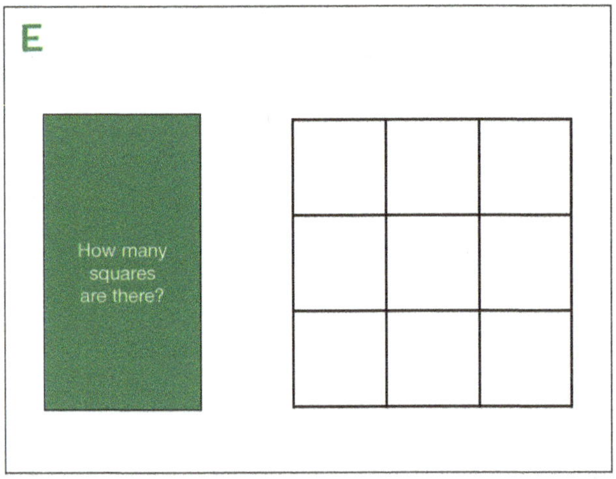

Variation F: Decomposing Figures

This last variation is a lead-in toward decomposing figures to find area. This example asks students to find three rectangles however they like. A student might draw a vertical line on the right side creating a "vertical" rectangle on the left and two smaller rectangles as shown in the left example. Another student might draw two horizontal lines that create three rectangles like shown in the right example. This might be an easy task at first, but you can change the prompts, asking students to find a different number of rectangles (e.g., four or five). Again, this is perfect for decomposing an "open" figure to find area, but you can also use it to create a challenge with any of the shapes shown in the other variations. For example, you could give a hexagon and ask them to draw lines that create at least three triangles.

F1

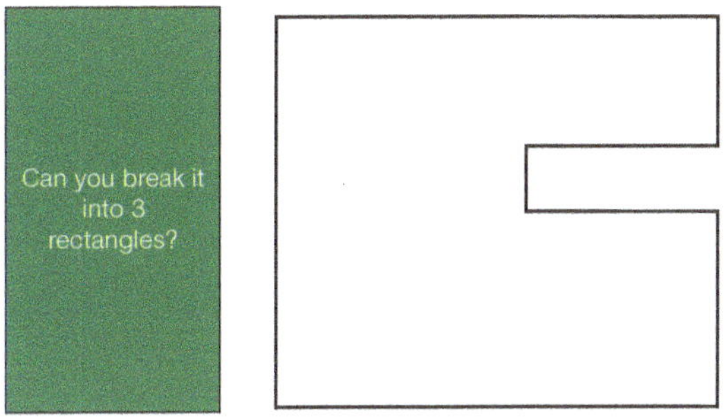

F2

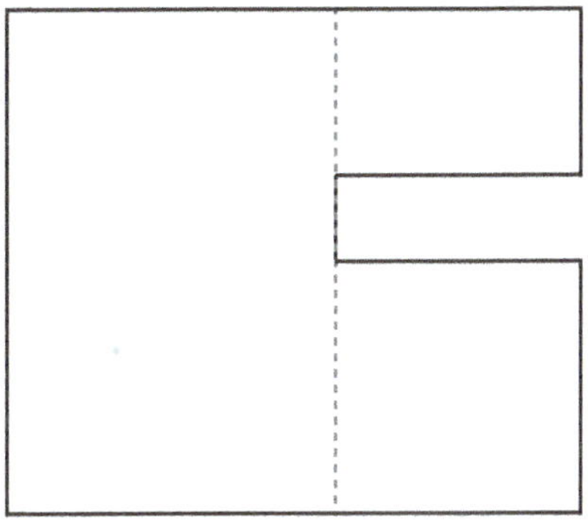

F3

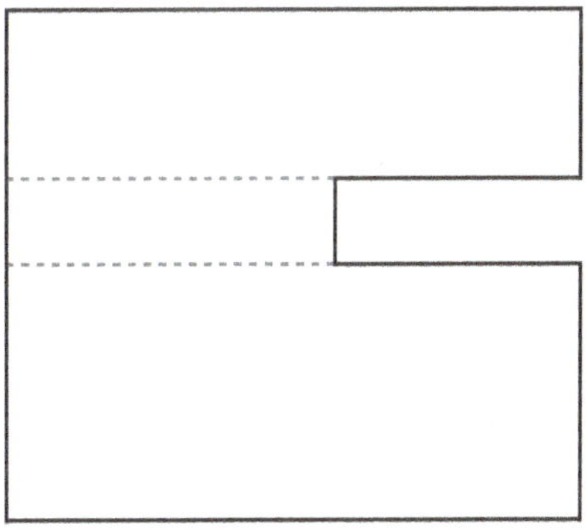

ROUTINE 5

DOTS

ABOUT THE ROUTINE

At some point in your life, you have likely done a dot-to-dot puzzle. They have been a prominent feature of children's activity books along with coloring-by-numbers and number-coded messages. If you haven't done a dot-to-dot puzzle, the simple premise is that a person connects dots to create an image. Sometimes the dots are numbered to direct how to complete the puzzle. Sometimes the dots make up the whole image and other times they are part of a drawing or image that becomes complete once the dots are connected. And, if you're wondering, these puzzles *are* the source of sayings like, "let me connect the dots for you," or "if you connect the dots."

This routine is a take on the timeless classic but with a subtle twist. There is not a grand image to complete. There is no sequence for connecting the dots nor any direction how to do so. Instead, students must complete a challenge by connecting dots however they wish. It reinforces shape recognition and creation, which are both fixtures in most, if not every, set of curriculum standards. It's perfect for any grade and can be easily adjusted for simple bursts of practice with shapes, geometric figures, measurement topics, and more. It plays out best for engagement, reasoning, and discussion when it's a rather open experience with more than one right way to complete it.

This opening example provides just six dots. The challenge is for students to connect them in some way to generate two triangles. Though seemingly basic, there's a good chance that it will lead to a rich discussion in a primary grade while giving the teacher great information into student perspective and understanding. Consider the two solutions that students might offer in the images on the following page. On the top left (A), there are two equilateral triangles. On the top right (B), there are two scalene triangles. Primary students aren't expected to know these terms, but they must know that all triangles have three sides and three corners. Yet, many students only "see" triangles in a certain configuration or orientation. This routine can help you determine whether your students think more globally about the shape. Be ready for only one type to appear, most likely the equilateral triangles on the left. If it does, challenge students to create something different the next day or create an example of your own that doesn't show equilateral triangles and have them compare.

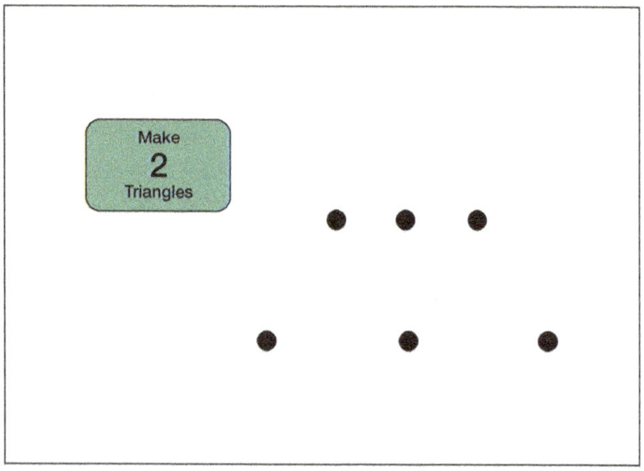

These examples also feature congruent triangles. Again, a term that primary students aren't required to know, but a notion you should be on the lookout for. In a prompt like this, look to see if students create congruent or similar figures. It's not a problem if they do but it might signal a narrow view of shape. The examples that follow show how students connected the dots to create

online resources All routines can be downloaded for your use at **https://companion.corwin.com/courses/jumpstartroutines-geometry**

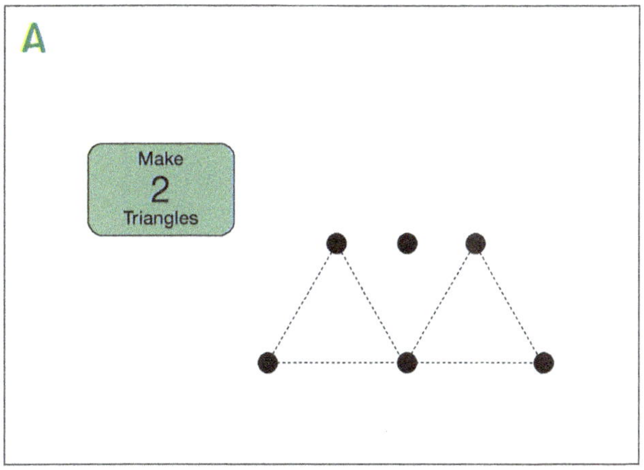

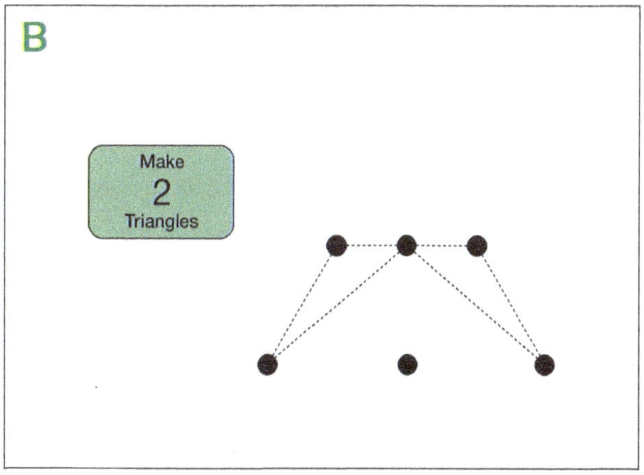

two different triangles. On the left below (C), the student created an isosceles and equilateral triangle. On the right below (D), the student created a right triangle and equilateral triangle. These triangles also have somewhat different orientations. These students are no more correct than the previous but it might do better to help you know that they fully understand the attributes of a triangle.

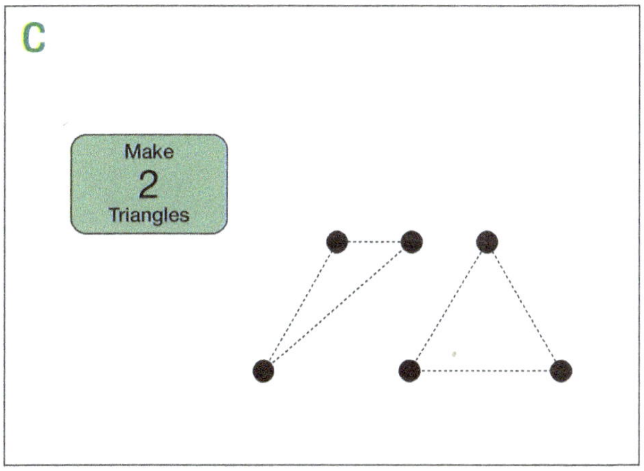

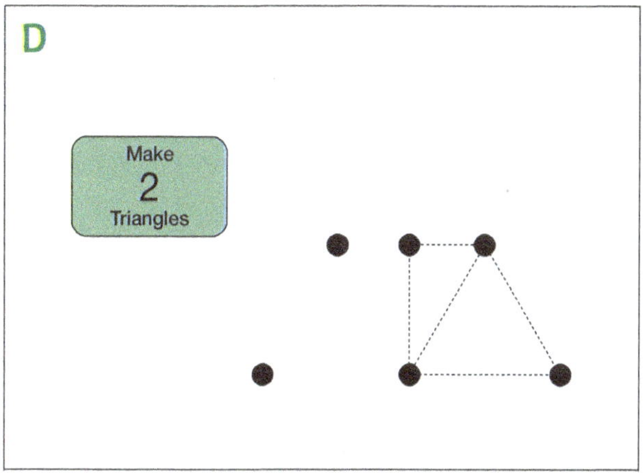

HOW THIS ROUTINE HELPS

This routine deepens understanding of geometry by providing opportunities for students to

- identify and distinguish between shapes by their attributes;
- create shapes by considering their attributes and properties;
- think strategically and critically to solve problems (MP1);
- strengthen perseverance (MP1);
- defend their reasoning (MP3); and
- consider different possibilities and alternative solutions.

WHAT TO DO

1. Create a dot configuration.
2. Optional: Provide students with a replica of your dots on a laminated sheet or paper in a sheet protector.
3. Pose a prompt or challenge such as, find two triangles.
4. Give students time to find their solutions.

5. Have partners compare their solutions. Some prompts you want them to discuss include the following:
   - How does your example show _____?
   - How are your ____ the same as mine?
   - How are your ____ different than mine?
6. After students have discussed their thinking, bring the group together to talk about their examples. Ask about any examples that students disagree with and why.
7. Optional: Provide your own solution to the puzzle. Ask students to determine whether your solution satisfies the challenge. Compare student examples with your examples. Remember, it is important that students clearly understand that your examples are not the *correct* answers.

SOMETHING TO THINK ABOUT: DOING IT FIRST

Anticipating what students will do with a task is a critical action for meaningful discourse in math (Smith & Stein, 2018). Anticipating what students will do with routines, especially routines like this one, help you think about how you might respond to their ideas, examples, and potential missteps. Anticipating helps you think about what you want to look for in their work, like anticipating if all students will do two equilateral triangles or if they will create two of the same triangles no matter what kind they make. Knowing your students and the content helps you anticipate what they might do. But it's also helpful if you take a few moments to complete the task or the routine yourself before doing it with students. Doing the task first helps you anticipate what they might do, and it helps you think for a moment about the solutions that you might be most expecting (SanGiovanni et al., 2023).

DOTS (VARIATIONS): CONNECT WITH CREATIVITY

A simple way to implement this routine is to provide dot paper or isometric paper. There is also a downloadable that has fewer dots than both of these. Any of these are good for any variation of the routine and are even required for some of the variations. But a good challenge for your students is a puzzle that only gives a few dots like the featured example. The thought of creating these might feel overwhelming but there is an easy solution. First, create some shapes. Then, create points on their vertices and consider adding more dots. With all the dots in place, erase or delete the shapes you started with.

Variation A: Starter Puzzles

Simple "starter" puzzles are perfect for kindergarten and first-grade students. But these puzzles are nice places to begin with older students too. The few dots and the singular challenge create a "low floor," increasing access to the task for students. But a high ceiling comes about through the many solutions students can consider. The debriefing conversation presents an opportunity for all to deepen their understanding about a particular shape and its attributes. In this example, there are only six dots and a challenge to find one quadrilateral. Students can't just connect the five "outer" dots as doing so creates a pentagon. And students cannot intersect line segments for obvious reasons. They must consider which dots to connect and how they might do it. There will be different solutions, as shown in the examples, ranging from parallelograms of different sizes to irregular quadrilaterals.

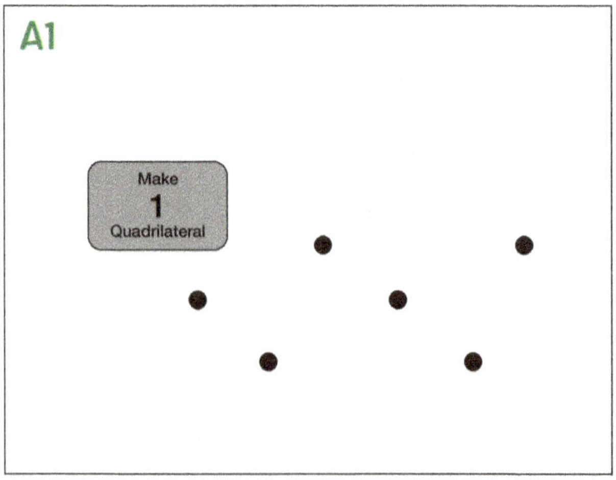

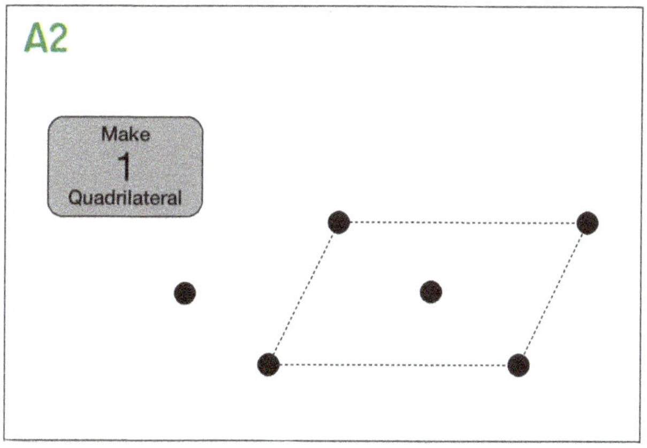

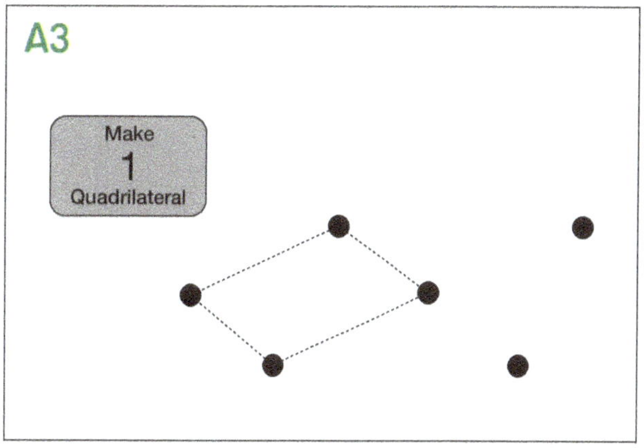

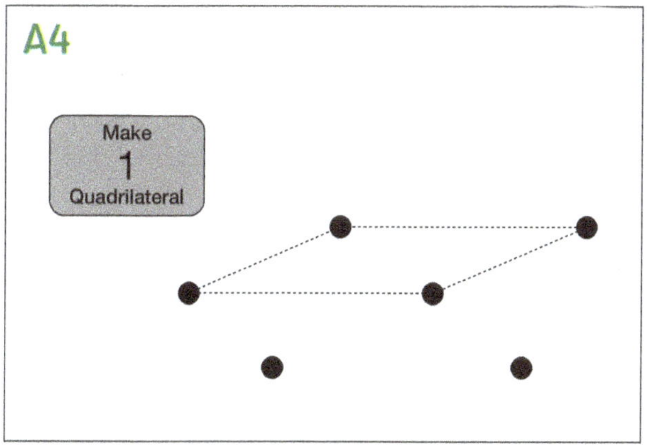

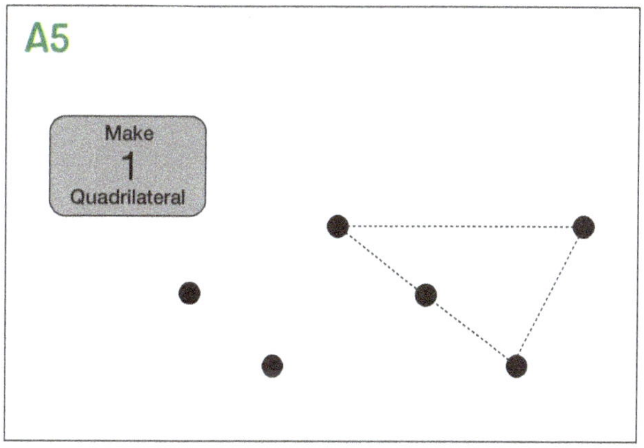

Variation B: Create and Explain

Puzzles are great for engagement and problem-solving. Yet, by making a small adjustment to the routine you can use it to promote student individuality, agency, and creativity. In this variation, students are tasked with making a certain number of connections between dots. Any dots can be connected, and segments can intersect. After making connections, students then look for all the shapes their connections created. In the example on the right, the student's six connections created three right triangles, a trapezoid, and even a pentagon (can you find it?). A nice outcome of this variation is that your students will create a large collection that you can reuse as part of a routine or independent work. Simply take their creations and ask what shapes can be found. Oh, it's a nice touch to have the creator of the work autograph or write their name to honor and give them credit.

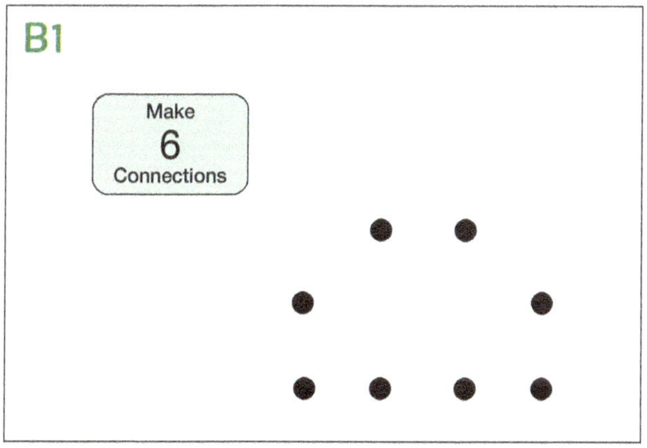

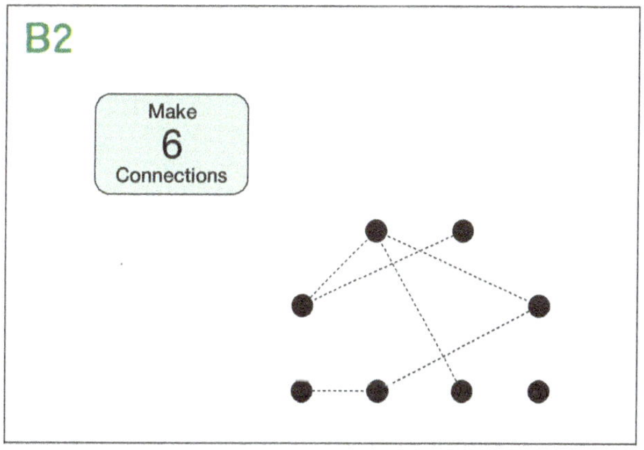

Variation C: Bigger Challenges

Variation C is a much bigger challenge to both create and solve. First, remember the tip about how to create these. The dots in this challenge were created with the two rectangles you see in the example on the right. Then, some other dots were added. The example on the right isn't the only correct answer but it does satisfy the prompt. There are two quadrilaterals, and one is a rectangle. There are actually three rectangles in the prompt. This is likely to spark a lively debate about whether the prompt was satisfied or not because three is not two. We suggest including "no less than," "at least," and "or more" in the challenges. While you can require exact answers, know that they can increase the difficulty quite a lot.

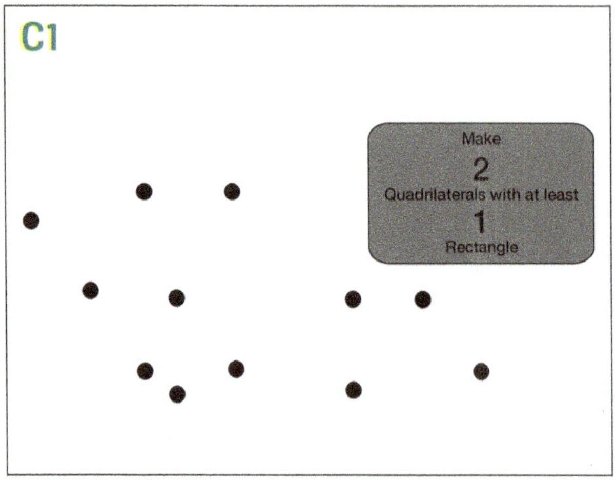

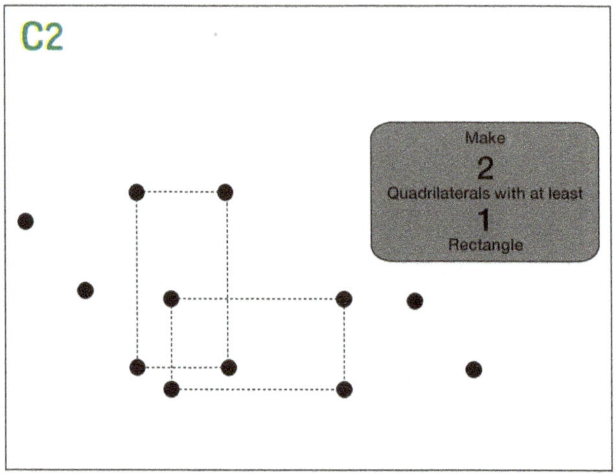

Variation D: Basic Dot Configurations

Variation D is provided for two reasons. First, it is a reminder that this routine is the perfect challenge at any grade. Finding three squares doesn't seem complicated for adults but it could take a few moments for a young student to find them. And when they do, they'll see that there are many squares, which might lead to the question of how many squares are there in all. This variation is also shared as an example of how dot paper or basic dot configurations can be used in this routine. Here, it's a 4 x 4 grid. That's typically a good size for younger students though 5 x 5 is also reasonable. In later grades, you will likely need larger arrays as students look for more complex shapes and even perimeter and area.

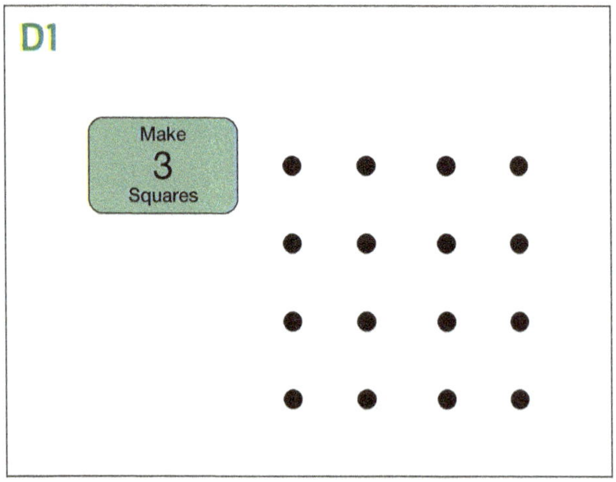

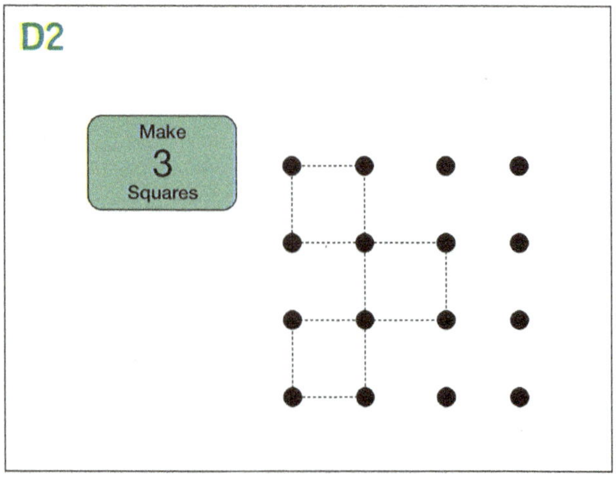

Variation E: Other Geometric Figures

Using the same four-by-four dot grid, this variation lifts up a simple, yet effective, way for students to practice other geometry figures. Here, you see the prompt, "make 2 acute angles." The student has made two with important differences that can be challenging for elementary students. The top angle has a "level" side, which is indicative of early work with angles. However, it opens to the right, which is opposite of that same early work with angles. That angle alone signals that the student is developing a good understanding of angles. The angle on the left is another indication. Neither side of the angle is "level," and the opening of the angle is both opposite of the other angle and rotated toward 10 o'clock. Other figures you can ask students to create include obtuse and right angles along with intersecting, parallel, and perpendicular line segments.

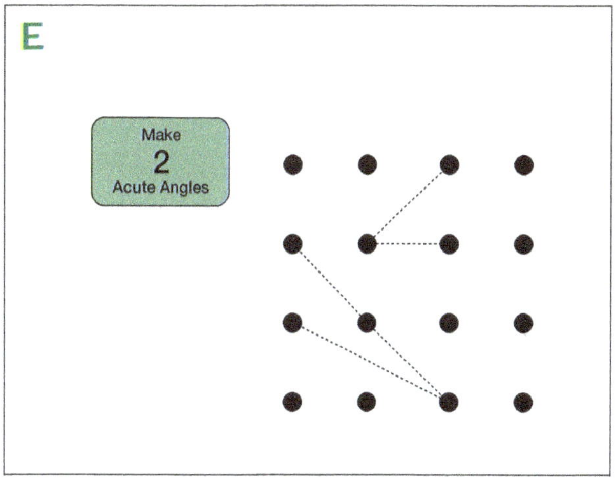

Variation F: Perimeter

This variation is a perfect follow-up routine for practicing perimeter. In this experience, you provide a dot grid that is relatively large. These are 7 x 5 though you probably want them to be even larger. You pose a challenge like, create a figure with a perimeter of 16. Students do just that and then share their creations with a partner. Partners confirm perimeters and then the class examines a few, comparing the overall shape, size, dimensions, and even orientation of the different examples. Again, creating a laminated dot grid for them to draw their examples on will be helpful and it would make sense for you to have a presentation dot grid, too, for obvious reasons. Remember to have students show how they counted or found the perimeter of their examples. At first, this can be simple counting methods and over time you may charge them with incorporating equations. It's reasonable to expect students to stick with rectangle creations at first. After some practice, you might challenge them to create a figure with a given perimeter (e.g., 16) that isn't a rectangle. An example of what such a figure might look like is on the bottom. Another, possibly better, way to approach irregular figures is to not tell students to do it but instead wait for it to come up naturally in discussion or in someone's example.

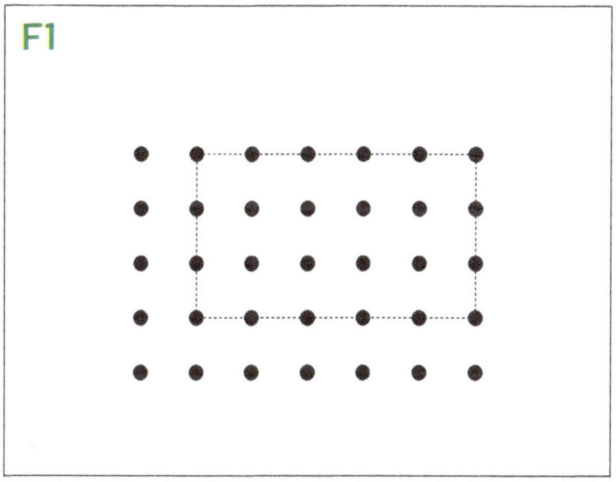

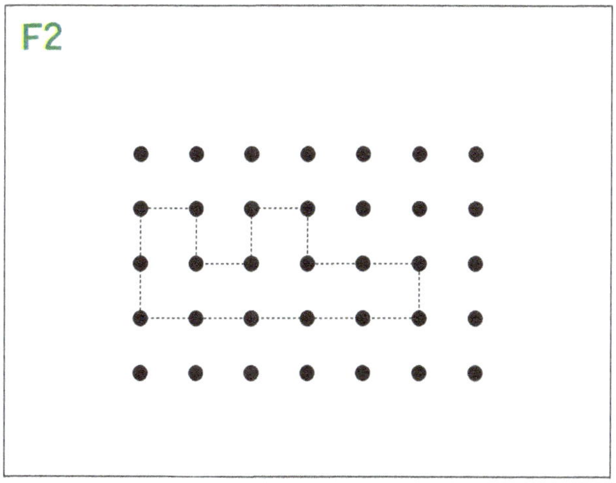

Variation G: Area

After reading about a perimeter variation, you probably figured that an area variation would be next—and it is. Here, you ask students to create a rectangle with a specific area, such as 12 as shown in the example. Students create and share. Again, you want students to prove how they found the area of their example and at some point, you want them to record the equations. However, students don't need to know how to calculate area before working with this routine. Afterall, first exposures to area focus on tiling and counting. That method of "proof" is fine until multiplication is connected to area or the formula is introduced. Just like with the perimeter variation, you can shift from rectangles to irregular figures as shown in G2. In later grades, teachers can even include basic parallelograms and other figures. G3 shows one more clever way to work with area and multiplicative comparison. In this experience, present a rectangle and then ask students to create a rectangle that is a few times larger. G4 is 5 times larger than the original rectangle presented to the students.

G1

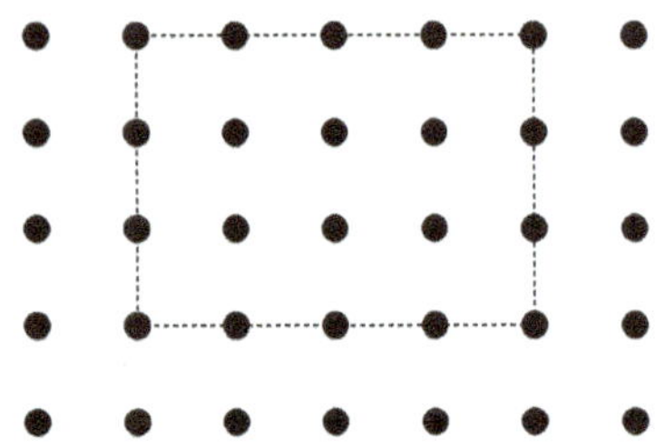

G2

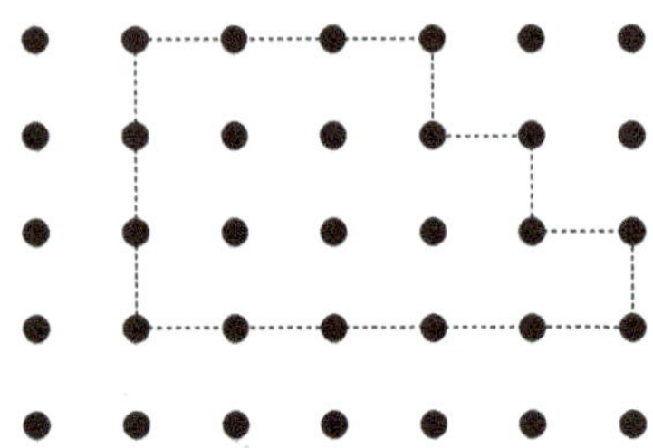

G3

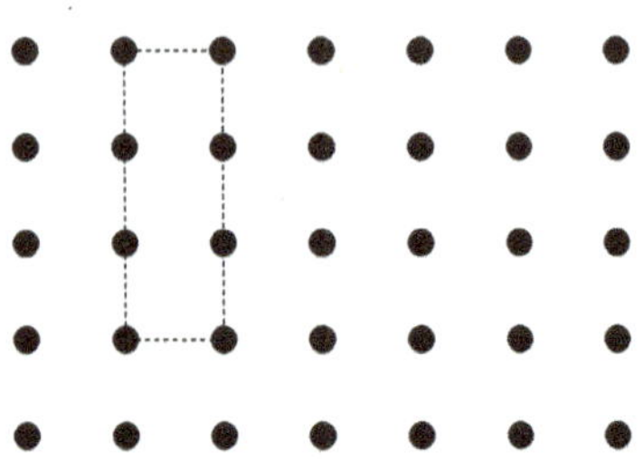

G4

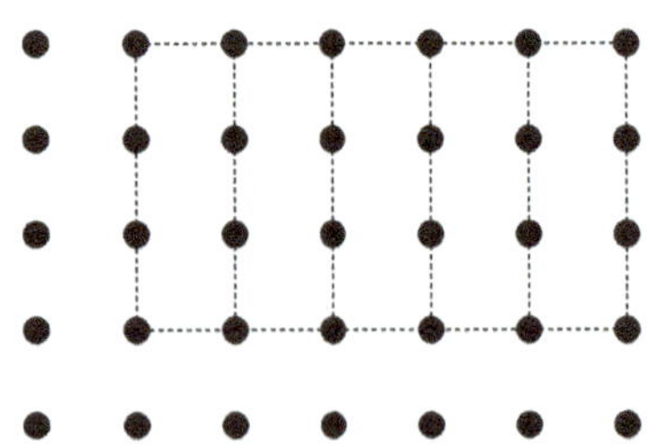

ROUTINE 6

THE TRUTH

ABOUT THE ROUTINE

Two truths and a lie is a familiar icebreaker or get-to-know-you activity. In those settings, participants create and share two truths about themselves and a lie. Partners consider the statements and decide which of the three offered is the lie. In some cases, the lie is obvious. In other cases, it's nearly impossible to figure out. Well-crafted ideas cause partners to reason and think critically about the statements and the likelihood that they could be true.

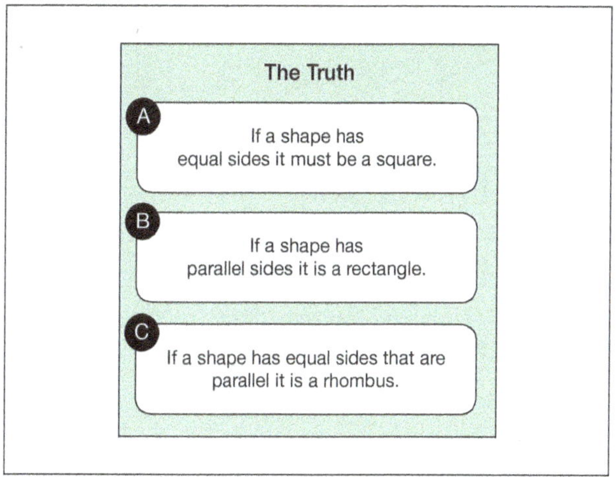

This routine, The Truth, is a take on that classic game framing a fun and engaging experience for your students. In this version, students are presented with an idea and must determine the one truth instead of the one lie. You can make statements about shapes, attributes, or even relationships within classifications and hierarchies. The anchor example is about the characteristics of special quadrilaterals. You can also use images or manipulatives as described later.

Keep in mind that you can modify the routine so that there are two truths and a lie if you prefer. Regardless of the format you choose, the routine provides valuable practice in brief bursts. In all instances, this routine helps students think critically about the concepts and choices presented. It helps them look or consider both examples and nonexamples. Each of these skills, along with content, can then be reinforced through multiple experiences. Ultimately, it helps prepare students for different situations, including standardized tests, in which students must think critically about possibilities and distractors.

Templates are available for download though it's just as easy to write a few statements on your board for students to discuss. Writing so many statements may seem overwhelming at first but be clever and use your resources. First and foremost, make mental notes of the errors or misidentifications students make in class. Those are perfect examples to use in the routine. Share what you create with your colleagues. Ask students to craft statements and select the ones that are good fits for the whole class. Consider using an AI tool asking it to create "elementary geometry statements" for two truths and a lie. And, if you must, trim the statements from three to two. When you do, think about having a true and false statement some days and two true or two false statements on other days.

online resources All routines can be downloaded for your use at **https://companion.corwin.com/courses/jumpstartroutines-geometry**

HOW THIS ROUTINE HELPS

This routine deepens understanding of geometry by providing opportunities for students to

- think critically about concepts, examples, and nonexamples (MP1);
- consider multiple representations of a given shape or figure;
- look for relationships between shapes, figures, or attributes (MP7);
- construct and critique arguments for strategies and solutions (MP3); and
- work with assessment-like, multiple choice items and distractors.

WHAT TO DO

1. Pose statements to students for them to consider as shown in the examples.
2. Ask students, "Which of these statements are true?"
3. Have partners discuss which they think is true and why.
4. After students have had time to discuss, bring the class together to discuss their ideas.
5. Come to agreement as a class about which statement is true.
6. Optional: After it is clear which statement(s) is true, have students review one of the false statements and discuss how it would need to be changed to make it true.
7. Optional: After it is clear which statement(s) are true, have students create a new statement with their partner that is similar to the true statement.
8. Acknowledge and thank students for their engagement, communication, and initiative.

SOMETHING TO THINK ABOUT: LETTERING OPTIONS

You probably noticed that each statement is labeled with a letter. Labeling examples is a good move for clear and effective communication. It's simply easier to talk about statement C rather than the "third sentence." Sure, descriptors like top, bottom, and middle work fine when just three statements are presented. But when a fourth, maybe even a fifth, statement is offered, conversation can grind to a halt because it's hard for everyone to stay focused on the right statement. Lettering options isn't just a good idea for this routine but many others. In fact, you might find other situations in math class that flourish when objects are labeled. For example, labeling tangram pieces has advantages when students don't know the names of the shapes or when two pieces are the same shape and size.

THE TRUTH (VARIATIONS): USE PHOTOS AND REAL OBJECTS

As you'll see, a good way to modify the routine is to use images for students to analyze. You can provide them something to draw with to help them see the statements if you don't provide images. You can draw these images yourself on index cards and display them with a document camera. You can also make them in a slide and present them. One other approach to consider is to take pictures of real-world objects that represent different shapes and figures. For example, you might show a yield sign and a one-way sign for students to work with statements about triangles and rectangles. Another nice option is to display images of the manipulatives you and your students use like pattern blocks or attribute blocks. It can also be a good idea to put these in your students' hands as they work with the routine—especially for those working in the lower levels of the van Hiele hierarchy.

Variation A: Primary Grades

The Truth is perfect at any grade. In younger grades, images work well. The value in this example is that it presents triangles in different configurations and orientations. This is critical for growing primary students' understanding of shapes and their attributes. But to do this, you can't tell them that one of the shapes is the true triangle. Instead, you have to ask for the example that isn't a triangle. You could include a square or circle but this example highlights another misstep that students sometimes make. D is the truth. The figure in D isn't a triangle. In fact, it isn't a polygon at all because it isn't a closed figure. It could be interesting to have a real triangle in the same size, configuration, and orientation as another example to have students compare with. Also note that this variation offers a fourth statement. There is no limit to the number of statements you use. Three statements or considerations is a good starting point. A fourth can be helpful but be careful not to use too many.

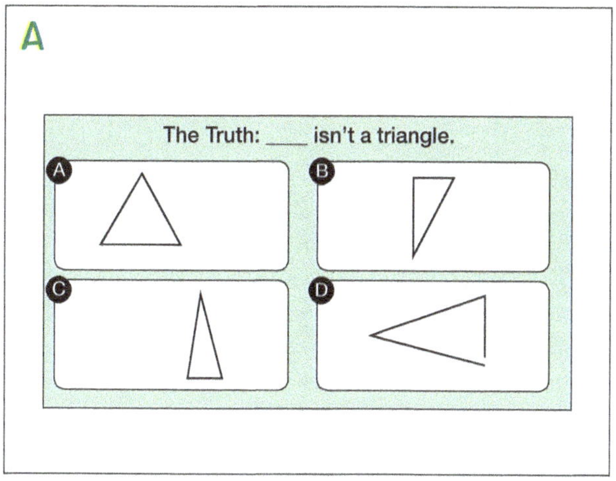

Variation B: Reasoning Without Images

Using images, like in Variation A, is a good place to start with primary students. However, you also want them to reason about shapes by mentally visualizing them and eventually by "just knowing" facts about basic shapes like triangles or squares. This variation presents statements as text only. It is completely appropriate to read the statements to your students. You might also plan to provide white boards or have them use their journals to sketch shapes so that they can analyze the images and compare them to the statements to determine which statements are true.

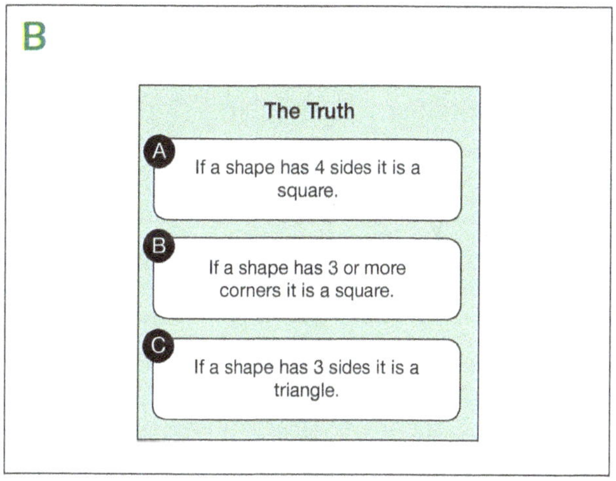

Variation C: Two Truths

As new figures are introduced in later years, students will need time to experience the images before moving to written statements. This variation shows what that looks like.

Here, students are presented with shapes and have to recognize and name the shape. Doing so represents Level 0 (Visualization) in the van Hiele hierarchy. To defend their thinking, they might match a shape in the routine to an example in the classroom. They might also identify attributes and characteristics, which is evidence of their advancement to Level 1 (Analysis). This variation also shows how you can provide a fourth statement and potentially more than one truth.

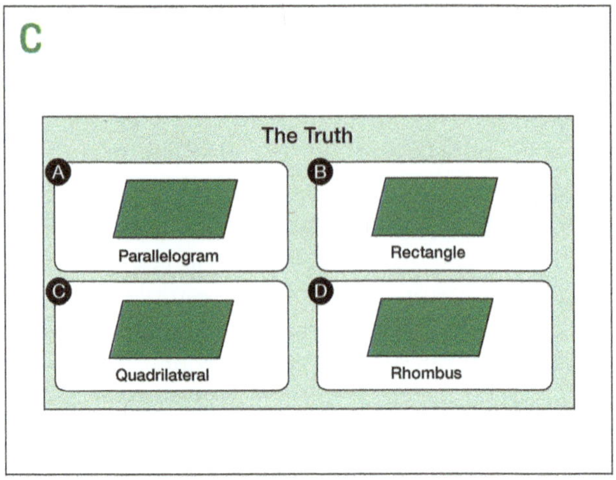

Variation D: Different Definitions

Math has been traditionally presented as true or false, yes or no, and obviously right or wrong. This creates problems when mathematicians don't agree on interpretations or definitions. It creates even bigger problems when math teachers are unaware of differences and insist that a certain strategy, procedure, or example is or isn't correct. That is the sole reason to share this example. It is not a variation but rather a talking point. At first glance, it may seem that statement A is the one and only truth. All rectangles are parallelograms therefore if something is a rectangle it is also a parallelogram. But the second statement could be true, too, depending on the interpretation of a trapezoid because—as noted—mathematicians don't always agree. There is an inclusive definition of trapezoids stating trapezoids have at least one set of parallel sides. So then, a parallelogram must be a trapezoid, too, because it has at least one set of parallel sides. The exclusive definition says that trapezoids have exactly one set of parallel sides therefore excluding parallelograms. While you may teach students both definitions and explain that mathematicians don't always agree, it is probably best to check with your district's math office for guidance.

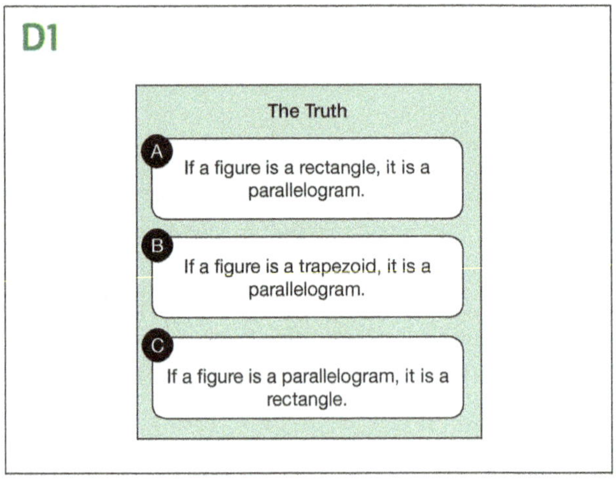

Variation E: 3D Figures

Though no routine has featured three-dimensional figures, like cubes, cones, and spheres, the concepts will work well with any routine that goes after attributes or characteristics. This variation of The Truth is a good example of how that might work. Here, you see three statements about different figures. The clues mention attributes about them including the shape of their faces along with the number of faces and edges. In this example, B is the truth as cubes have more than six edges and pyramids can have a base, or face, that is a triangle, quadrilateral, or other polygon. You see that there are images included for each of the figures. You might find this isn't necessary. Or you might find that students can only determine attributes with a drawing or object to consult. This is fine until mental images and deep understanding of the figures takes hold. You can also leverage the routine to focus on just one figure. For example, you could make the topic statements about cubes. Then, you could pose statements like, "Cubes have two square faces," "Cubes have four square faces," and "Cubes have six square faces" with the latter being the truth.

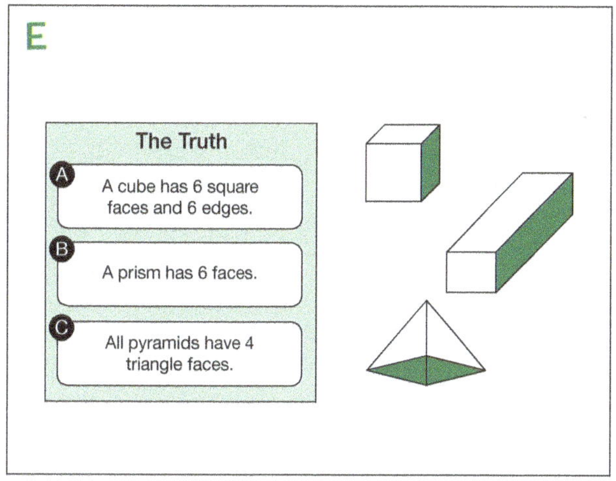

Variation F: Perimeter

If the perimeter is 28 units, then both A and C are the truth. This isn't the first example of more than one truth, but it does speak to a possible advantage of more than one truth within the routine. For example, when learning about perimeter, some students have difficulty understanding that two figures can have the same perimeter though they have different dimensions. In this example, that challenge is confronted as both A and C have the same perimeter. In addition to this challenge, occasionally students "eyeball" their conclusions. They rely on what they see and what they assume. For example, they might think that a perimeter of 28 is somewhat large and assume that D is the truth because it seems to be largest. Or someone might assume that B will be 28 because it has the only two-digit dimension. Again, this routine offers a nice opportunity to expose and assess. Ultimately, if you prefer to have only one truth, you could easily change this prompt to a perimeter that is 28 and an area of 48, which then elicits only C as the truth. Other questions like C is the largest area (true) or B is the smallest perimeter (true) will work well too.

F

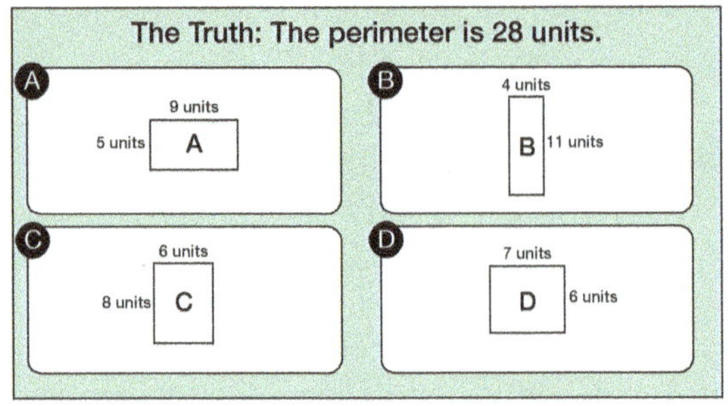

Variation G: Conversions

Conversions within and between units of measure have been highlighted in different routines in this book. The Truth is yet another way to practice conversions. This example is seemingly basic though you can expect that statement D will trip up a few students who see 1 and 12 along with inches and feet. Inverse statements like those are good to include in this version of the routine. In general, the intent here is to practice the basic conversions (e.g., there are 12 inches in a foot). Because of this, we don't suggest using an anchor chart to support students as they work with this routine as mentioned in other experiences. Instead, use this and experiences like it to introduce and practice those basic conversions. In time, you can begin to shift to more "complicated" conversions (e.g., 72 inches equal 6 feet) and supplement them with anchor charts if needed.

G

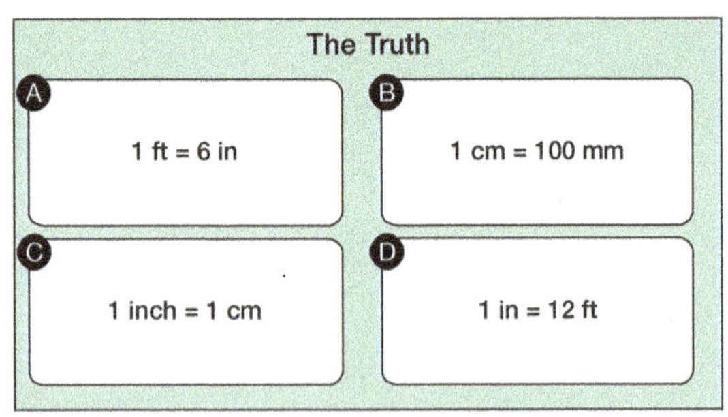

Variation H: Symmetry

In many curriculum standards, symmetry seems to be jammed in as an afterthought that distracts from the "real work" to be done in a given grade level. As with other elementary geometry concepts, there isn't much more to teaching symmetry than a lesson or two. Students gain proficiency with it through practice and experience. Overall, the concept isn't too difficult for students to acquire except when shapes have more than one line of symmetry. This variation addresses both the needs for more practice and work with multiple lines of symmetry. It functions like all the examples. Simply pose three or four images with lines of symmetry and challenge students to find the one that is true. Then, have them explain their thinking. Note that in this example, students might be drawn to C not because it is correct but because it only has one line of symmetry.

H

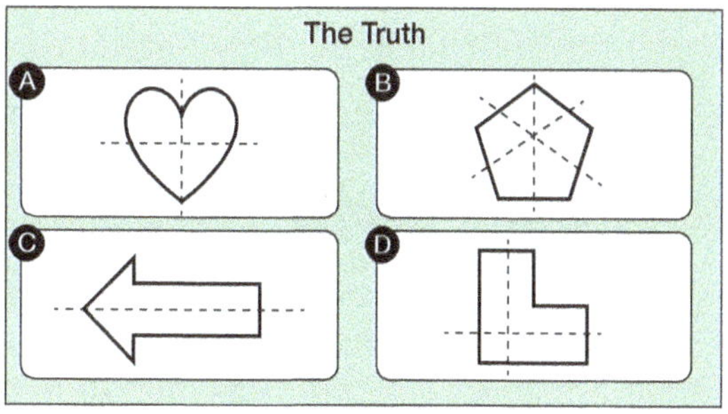

ROUTINE 7

ON THE MOVE

ABOUT THE ROUTINE

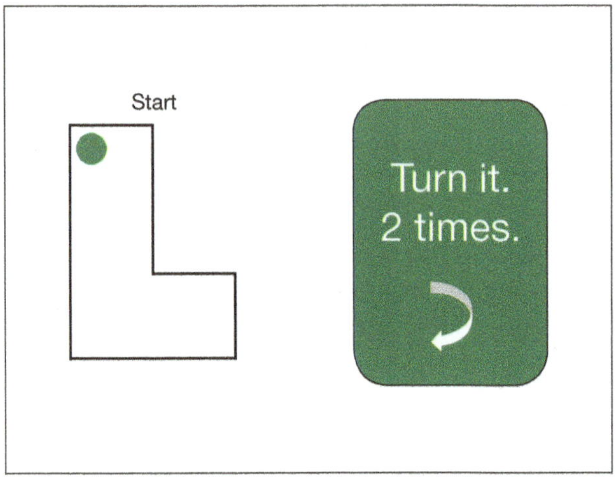

Transformations were once in most elementary mathematics curriculum standards. Today, those transformations like reflections (flips), translations (slides), and rotations (turns) typically appear in middle school mathematics. And though you aren't necessarily required to teach these ideas, developing your students' understanding of them will further refine and enrich their spatial awareness. Along the way, you have an opportunity to reinforce understanding of shapes and their attributes regardless of orientation.

Spatial awareness and reasoning refer to the ability to understand and interpret shapes or objects as they are moved. These skills are essential for many tasks in daily life, such as navigating through spaces, solving puzzles, and understanding diagrams. Spatial awareness and reasoning are closely tied to cognitive abilities that involve mental manipulation of objects, patterns, and environments (Cohen, 1999; Miller & O'Connell, 2004). Reasoning about how shapes look different as they are manipulated or moved is one of many ways to develop your students' spatial awareness and reasoning.

One aspect of spatial awareness is imagining how a shape or object will look after it has been moved in some way. Mathematically, the terms for basic manipulations are *rotations*, *reflections*, *translations*, and *dilations*. In the past, dilations haven't been included in elementary transformations and so they aren't included in this routine. These transformations are commonly, and informally, referred to as turns (rotations), flips (reflections), and slides (translations). We always advocate for accurate, grade-level terminology. That being said, it's reasonable to use informal language with students unless called on specifically in your curriculum standards.

Spatial awareness and reasoning are part of everyday tasks like driving a car or packing a suitcase. It is a natural part of many STEM fields including engineering and architecture. It contributes to problem-solving. This routine is a perfect opportunity for students to develop their spatial awareness and reasoning. It promotes explaining and justification. It does well to help students galvanize their understanding of the shapes identified in your grade-level standards. It can be a good way to enrich and extend that grade-level content. But most importantly, it is supposed to be fun and engaging. If you find that isn't happening for your students, step away from it for some time and come back to it later in the year.

Before you begin to use any routine, you must be sure that students understand the concepts. In this case, you want to establish what turns, flips,

online resources All routines can be downloaded for your use at **https://companion.corwin.com/courses/jumpstartroutines-geometry**

and slides are, as well as some language commonly used when describing these transformations, such as clockwise and horizontal. This is probably just a single lesson that produces an anchor chart for reference during the routine (see "Something to Think About" in More or Less, Routine #14). It is recommended that for the first few experiences, you use a single transformation as shown in the example. It is also recommended that turns are relegated to increments of 90 degrees. So, in this example of the L it would rotate clockwise, two 90-degree turns ending with the long side of the L on the right, the short side on top, and the dot on the lower right side. Speaking of the "dot," that element is added to help students keep track of the movement of the shape. You can hole punch the dot if you find that your students have difficulty keeping track of the dot when the image is flipped over.

HOW THIS ROUTINE HELPS

This routine deepens understanding of geometry by providing opportunities for students to

- identify shapes regardless of their orientation;
- analyze shapes based on their attributes;
- mentally manipulate a shape through different transformations;
- visualize a shape as it is manipulated;
- imagine how a shape moves through space and how it will look different;
- consider how a shape looks different after it has been manipulated;
- physically manipulate shapes (see variations);
- collaborate and discuss with their peers; and
- move student thinking from van Hiele Level 0 (Visualization) to Level 1 (Analysis).

WHAT TO DO

1. Create and project a shape. While any shape will do, be mindful of symmetrical shapes. They may be a bit more challenging for early use. With any shape, be sure to add a dot for reference.
2. Have students imagine what it might look like if the shape was turned, flipped, or slid.
3. Pose a transformation to students. In the example, the "L" was to be turned two times.
4. Give students a few moments to think about how the shape will look after the transformation. Allow students to sketch the new image on a dry erase board or something similar. Be aware that some students might draw the shape as you show it and then transform it (e.g., turn their white board two times). This is fine for early experiences with the routine.
5. Have students share with partners their results.
6. Solicit an idea from a student. Then, ask if any students have different ideas.
7. Talk about the first shared idea, asking students who created that example to agree or disagree with the idea. Explore other student ideas in the same way.
8. After discussion, show students the correct result along with each phase (after each turn in the example).
9. Celebrate students for their effort and discussion.

SOMETHING TO THINK ABOUT: ACTIVITIES FOR SPATIAL AWARENESS AND REASONING

It is possible to train and improve spatial skills (Krasa, 2010). Logic games are a good way to develop problem-solving and perseverance (SanGiovanni, 2023). Games like Blokus, Pentago, Qwirkle, and Connect Four also develop spatial awareness and reasoning. Jigsaw puzzles, pattern block puzzles, and tangram puzzles are good challenges to support these as well. Puzzles like these are great for independent work or collaborative experiences. One nice feature of any of these puzzles is that they aren't competitive, which can be a turn off to students who are deep thinkers, process differently, or simply don't like competition. Of course, there are many computer-based games that are good for spatial awareness and reasoning like Tetris or Minecraft. Any of these are good to include in your mathematics instruction. Granted you don't want to use these every day, but they can be incorporated once a week or two. And you might be surprised how students who aren't strong "number crunchers" get excited about working with these spatial activities.

ON THE MOVE (VARIATIONS): REVERSING A SITUATION

Giving students an answer and asking them to craft the problem is an example of how you can reverse a situation in mathematics. It is a good way to improve the quality of a task, which increases rigor, novelty, and the number of entry points (SanGiovanni et al., 2020). Reversing is a great tactic for use with your routines. This is a good way to stretch your students' thinking and how you can keep the routine fresh. Reversing is highlighted in Variation C along with these other options.

Variation A: Transformations in Different Directions

The opening example prompts students to turn a shape (the L) two times. This variation gives you a few other things to consider. Obviously, it shows a flip instead of a turn. But it also shows how this transformation, a flip, can be executed in different ways, flipping vertically or horizontally. As you see, it asks students to flip the triangle three times. You can also see the arrows that show the directions of the flips. The first two arrows show a vertical flip and the last shows a horizontal flip. The result is shown in A2. As mentioned in the opening, it's a good idea to start with one transformation. It's also a good idea to keep that transformation consistent at first. So, turns move 90 degrees and clockwise. Flips are done vertically or horizontally. After students gain their footing with a transformation, introduce a different direction. For turns, keep it at 90 degrees but offer counterclockwise. Use vertical and horizontal for flips. You can be as regimented with slide directions though you may find it unnecessary.

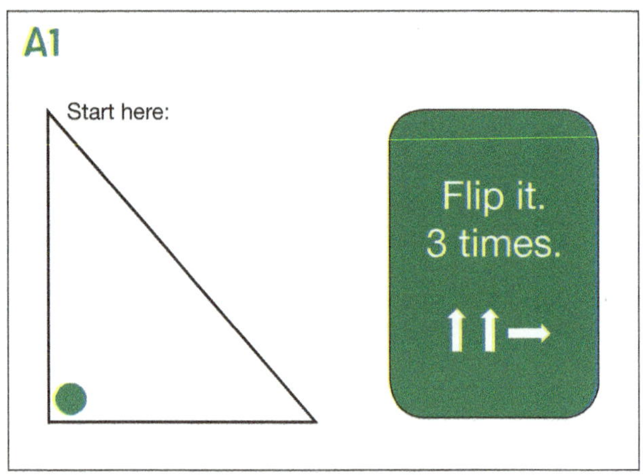

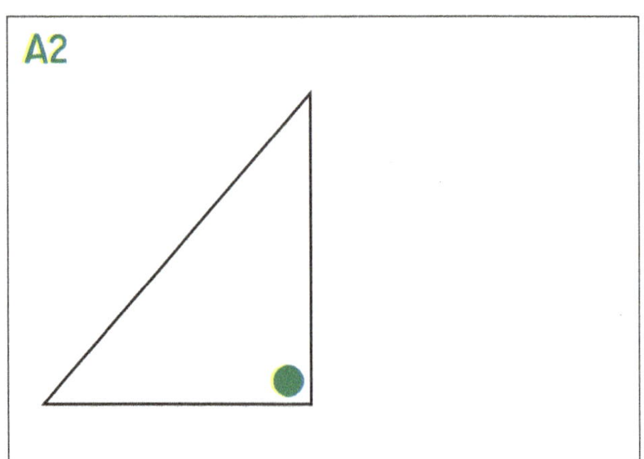

Variation B: Open to Interpretation

This variation is more open and more likely to spark discussion. In the first two examples of the routine, the transformations were accompanied with arrows to insinuate a direction. Those arrows are basic shapes that you can insert in PowerPoint or Google Slides. You can just as easily sketch them on the board. They are good to provide to students as you begin to work with the routine. In time, you can begin to remove them and simply say flip, turn, or slide as shown in this example. Assuming students have been exposed to the different ways these can be carried out (i.e., flipped vertically or horizontally), you will see that they come to different solutions. The following images show two different possibilities for the "H" in this example. The one in B1 was flipped horizontally, turned counterclockwise, and then flipped horizontally again. The one in B2 was flipped horizontally, turned clockwise, and flipped horizontally again. But how would it look if it was flipped vertically twice or once horizontally and once vertically?

Variation C: What Happened?

The first set of examples frame a typical experience with transformations. Students are presented with a shape along with a set of transformations and then have to determine the resulting look or orientation. This variation provides a different way for students to think about transformations. It has them determine the movement of a shape when given its starting point and its ending point. It can have more than one right answer. The picture of the heart could be simply rotated counterclockwise 90 degrees. But it could also have been flipped vertically, then horizontally, and then turned 90 degrees clockwise. You don't need to require multiple answers for each experience. But, letting students try their ideas first, providing a little wait time, and posing a clever question like, "I wonder if there's another way to____?" can go a long way toward helping students consider more than one possibility.

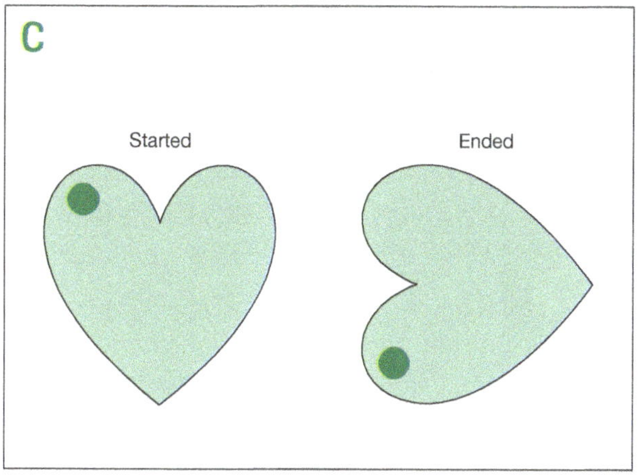

Variation D: Geoboards on the Move

A mini lesson on transformations can be done with a variety of manipulatives like pattern blocks, tangrams, or geoboards. After using them with a lesson, you might find it helpful to have students use them for a short time with this routine before phasing them out of the experience. Even then, you can have them available as a support when students need help visualizing the shape and its transformations. The example shows a right triangle with a single, 90-degree clockwise turn. Some teachers find it helpful to re-create a few geoboards on a piece of chart paper that they laminate and draw on during the routine to explore student thinking. There are several virtual geoboards available online. Your students can work with those as well, but we strongly encourage using the real thing because it can be physically manipulated.

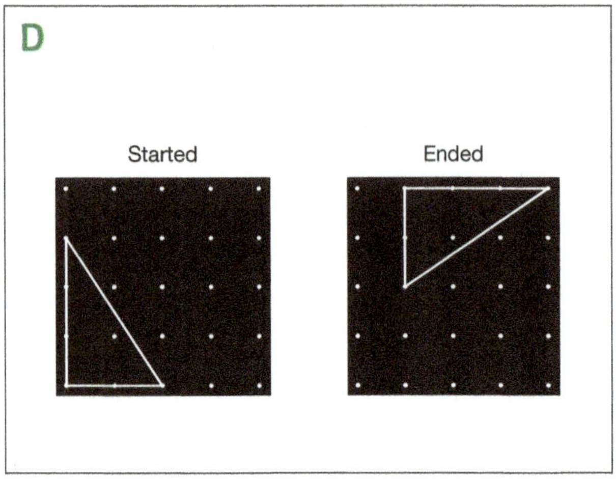

Variation E: On the Move With Shape Cards

Finding or creating shapes for this routine might be the most challenging aspect for you. The shape cards included with Sorts (Routine #2) and Venns (Routine #3) are great places to start. These shape cards offer a bonus as students can hold them and move them. They do not come with a dot or point of reference so you'll need to add that with a marker. However, the letter on the card does serve as a reference point and usually works just as well. Printing these on transparency sheets or film can be helpful for seeing the results of flips. Understandably, many schools no longer have these sheets. So, you can also print on white copier paper and trace with a Sharpie marker, or you can print them and trace them on patty paper.

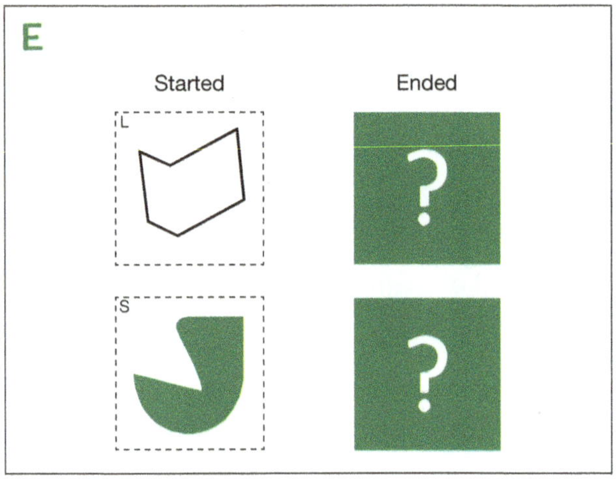

In this variation of the routine, students are shown a card. You tell them about transformations to apply to it, then, what the shape looks like after the transformations have been applied. If each student has their own set of cards, you can simply have them hold up their card to show you the ending result. This provides a quick, easy way to assess the whole group at once. There will be times when students have different results. Those are the best opportunities for discussion!

Variation F: Slides on a Number Chart

This last variation is a great way to practice counting by ones and tens both forward and backward on a hundred chart. First, you give students a starting number like 47. Have students identify it on the chart. Then, provide a series of slides. Students have to determine the final number after moving in those directions on the hundred chart. Students share their answer and reasoning with a partner before ideas are shared with the whole group. In this example, the starting number is 47. Students then move up, up, right, right ending with 29. Keep in mind that this uses a traditional number chart and that bottom-up number charts (Bay-Williams & Fletcher, 2017; Bay-Williams & SanGiovanni, 2021) could be nice options as well. However, if you use that chart the value of the arrows will change (i.e., an up arrow will mean 10 more instead of 10 less). This version of the routine is just the starting place. In time, you want to add +10, −10, +1, and −1 to your arrows as shown in the image in F2. This will help students connect the arrow to the computation. After a few weeks with that experience, begin to phase out the arrows altogether as shown in the example in F3.

F1

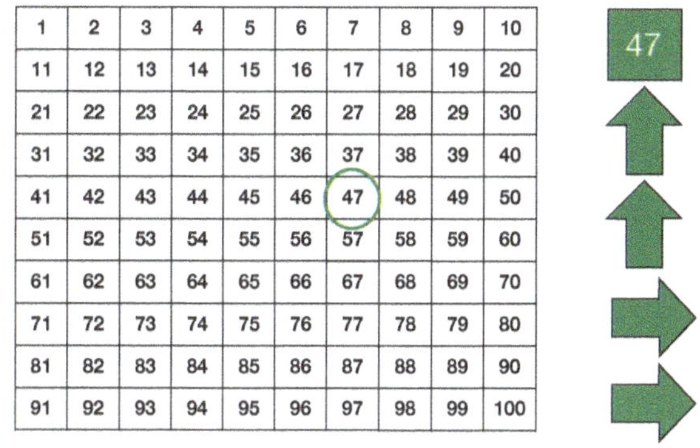

F2

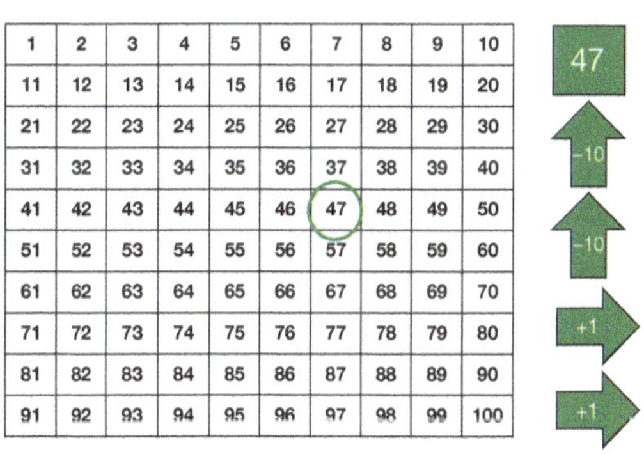

F3

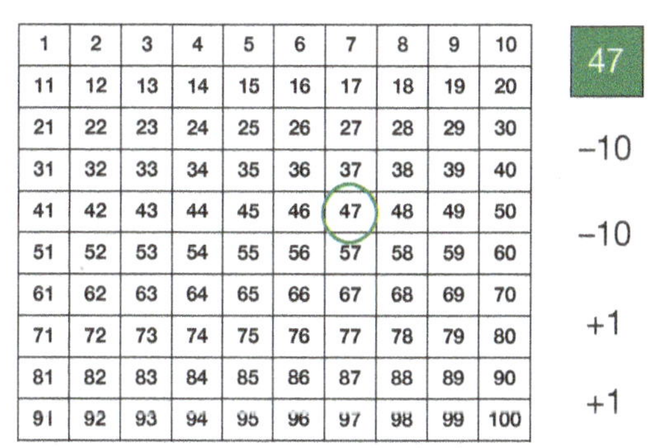

ROUTINE 8

VIEWS

ABOUT THE ROUTINE

Have you ever walked down a street and wondered what a building looks like from the air? Have you imagined what a certain piece of furniture would look like in different spots of your living room? Mental manipulation, imagination, and visualization of shapes and figures in different orientations is a powerful tool that we use often, like in these situations, among many others. It's something that many of your students do when they work with puzzles or build things with their LEGO bricks. Yet not every student does these things. Some lack interest. Many lack access and opportunity. You can counter the latter with this routine.

In this routine, Views, you show a figure and have students envision what the figure looks like from different angles or "views." Students then draw or sketch the view. The views they create should be

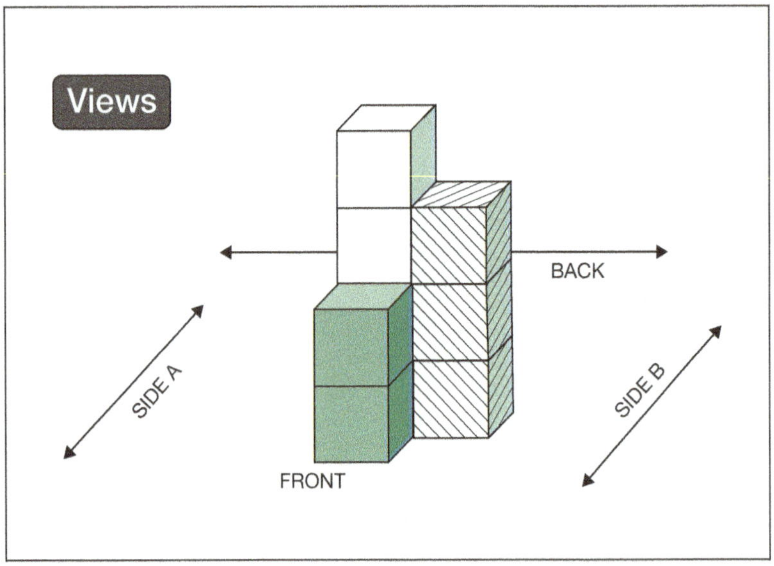

online resources All routines can be downloaded for your use at **https://companion.corwin.com/courses/jumpstartroutines-geometry**

SOMETHING TO THINK ABOUT: A TIME TO SHINE

Some students are naturally strong with numbers. They have refined number sense. They calculate with ease, often doing so mentally. Their strength with numbers allows them to shine in many math experiences. Yet, their strength with numbers doesn't prove to be an advantage with spatial experiences and other activities like this routine, among others. These activities can be quite challenging, even off-putting, to students who "know" they're good at math. It's one reason why you must do them with your students. These geometry experiences create an opportunity for struggle that these "number crunchers" need. Moreover, these experiences are valuable for those who are still developing number sense or still working to recall facts. Those students can shine during these experiences. It can help repair their confidence and signals that they can do math! This alone is a reason to make geometry experiences a somewhat regular undertaking in your math class.

VIEWS (VARIATIONS): ROUTINES AND DIFFERENTIATION

You can tweak the directions of these examples. For instance, you can have students talk to each other before they draw their view of the figure, or you can allow students to choose the view they want to draw, which provides different entry points. You can provide manipulatives or drawing materials so that students can make models or diagram their thinking, find solutions, and discuss their ideas. You can modify the targeted goal or product of a routine by having them create a figure based on a view that you give them. In short, variations of routines allow for differentiation. You'll see examples in the variations that follow along with all the other variations of routines in this book.

Variation A: Basic Prisms

As you might have figured, basic prisms are a good starting place for this routine though simple 3D figures, discussed in Variation H, might be an even better place for your students. Here, students are presented with a 5 x 3 x 3 prism. Each "layer" of the prism appears to be made with a different block (white, stripe, gray). This layering helps student envision the prism from different views. The following images show what the prism looks like from the sides, front, and back. Don't be surprised when your students *are* surprised that only the white blocks can be seen from the front and only the gray blocks can be seen from the back. Or, that all three types of blocks can be seen from the sides, but the order is reversed (gray, striped, white). This might seem obvious to adults but that isn't the case for elementary students. The image of a prism should work fine. But, if you can build it with colored blocks or connecting cubes, or better yet have your students build it, it can be physically moved around for better viewing. This, too, is a very good idea for your students' first experiences with the routine.

A1

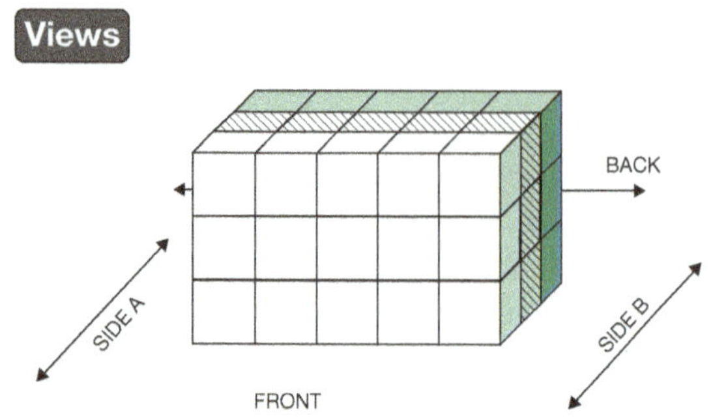

A2

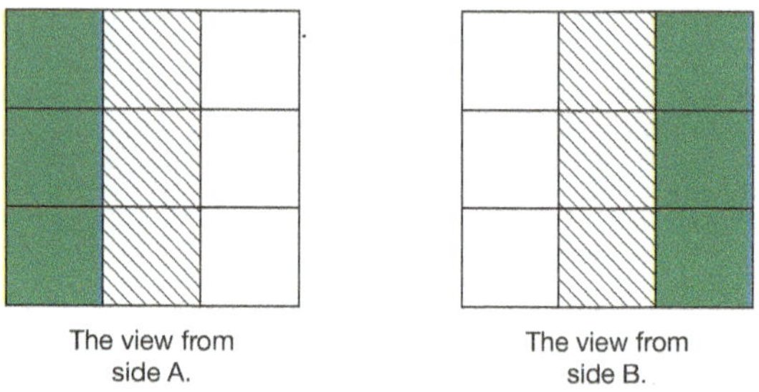

A3

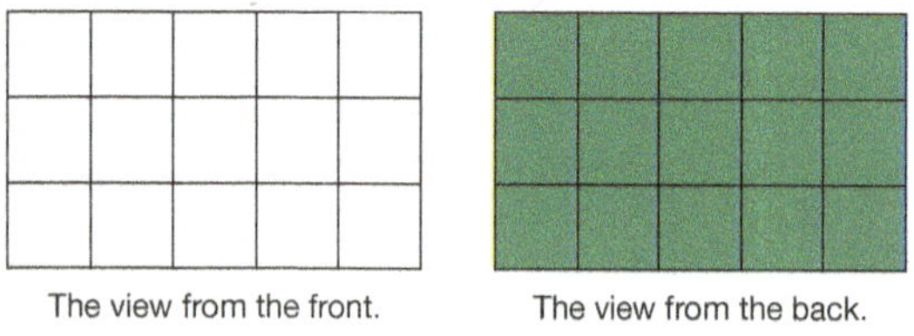

Variation B: What Is the View?

This variation causes students to think about a figure from all the different angles and one more that hasn't been mentioned yet. In this version, present a figure and then an image of that figure from a certain view. Students then determine which angle or view of the figure you have shared. Give them some time to think and then have them write their answer on a personal white board or sticky note. Have them hold up their answer when you signal. Take a quick look at their answers and then facilitate a discussion about their reasoning. The images show what this figure would look like from side A, side B, the front, and the back. Yet, they don't match the mystery image shown. That's because in this example, the view is from the top! Variation F will talk more about a view from the top.

B1

Views

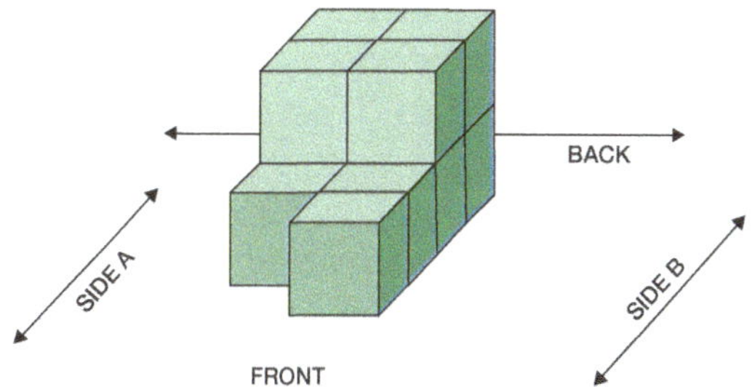

B2

?

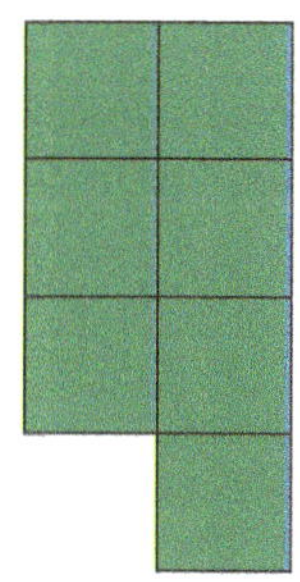

This is the view from ____.

B3

The view from side A.

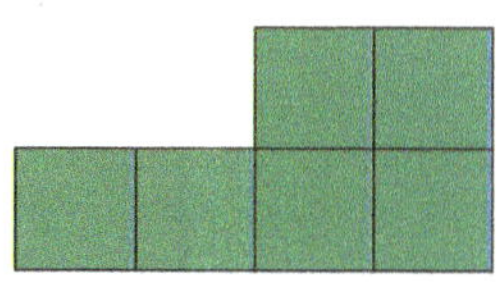

The view from side B.

B4

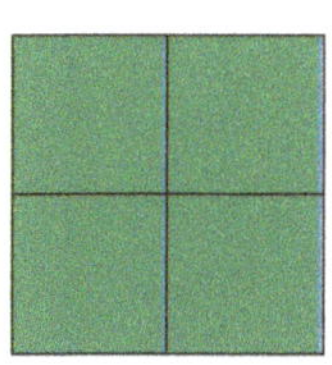

The view from the front.

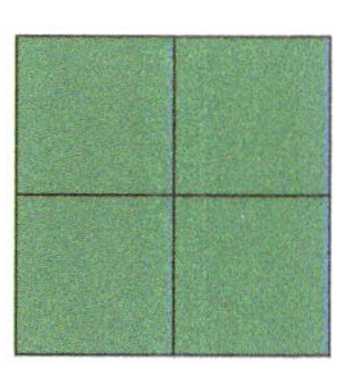

The view from the back.

Variation C: Build and Compare

In this variation of Views, you give directions for the number of blocks you want students to use to build a figure. Remember, blocks with different colors work best. After students create an image, they compare how their figures would look from different angles. Look at what Nate and Rachel built with the directions given. Their figures are different and so the view from side A is also different. This variation is a nice springboard for a center activity or for multiple days with the routine. To do this, have students create a figure and use your phone to take a picture of their creations. Project the image and have students determine the different views during the routine or print the images for a center activity. You can do this with a single student creation where students think about it from different views, or you can show an image of two figures for students to compare as shown here. If you decide to use photos, consider creating a large, white placemat with the front, back, and sides labeled as shown in the different images. You can place the student objects on that placemat for the image.

C1

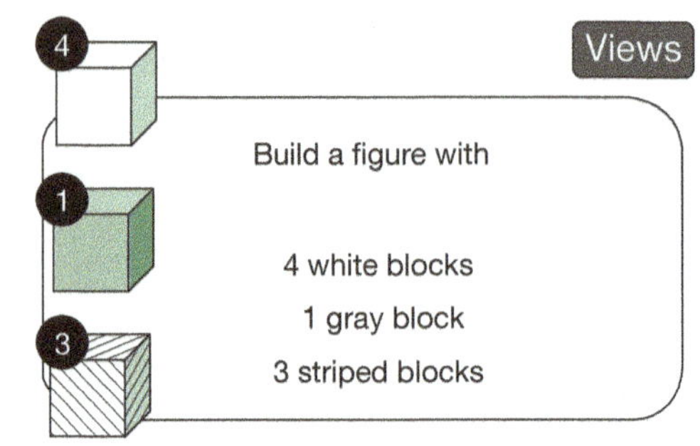

C2

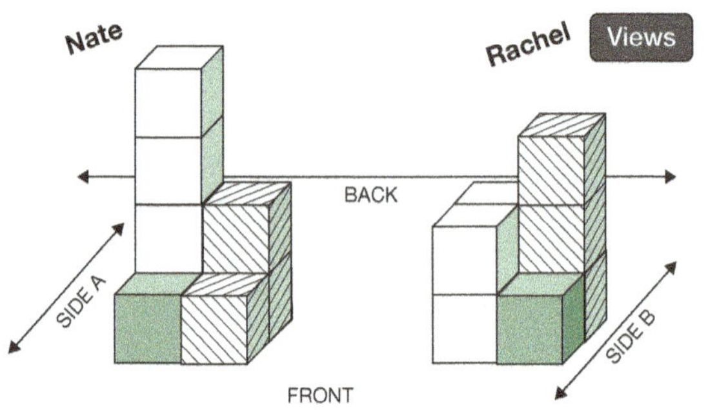

C3

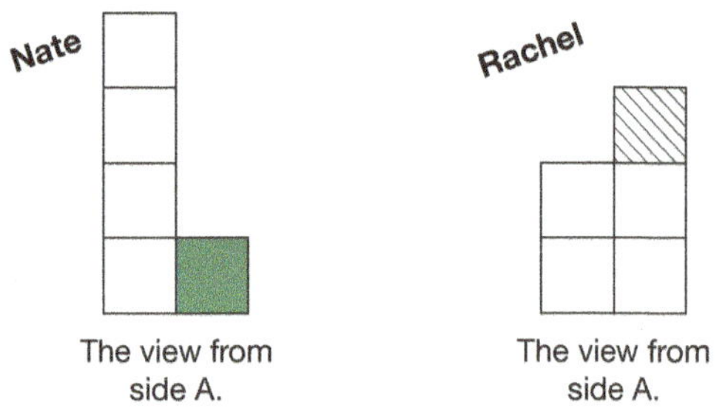

Variation D: Silhouettes

In this variation, students create silhouettes of the figure rather than drawing each square. It presents a different experience that may or may not be more challenging for your students. To complete the silhouette, they will still have to imagine each block of the figure. In fact, that's a nice strategy for figuring out how to draw the silhouette. The images show what this figure looks like from the front and from side A. A student could use those to then draw the silhouettes of the figure from the front and side A as shown. It's also fine for students to not draw the blocks first. Instead, they can draw a "rough" sketch of the figure and talk about that. There is no right or wrong way to go about it. Let them try. Observe what they do and be prepared to offer some suggestions, like drawing each block or drawing a rough sketch, when they get stuck. Better yet, look for students who use these or other viable strategies and spotlight their approaches when others get stuck.

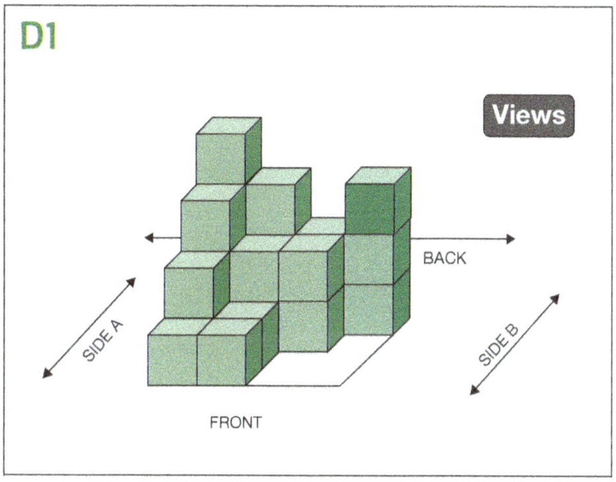

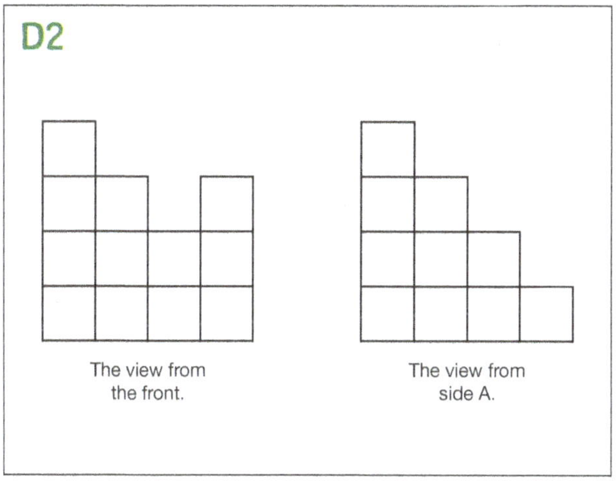

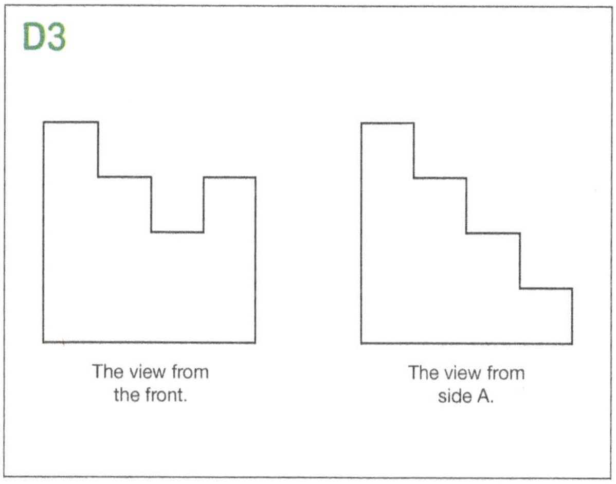

Variation E: A View From Across the Line

Years ago, elementary students learned about transformations of shapes and other figures. These transformations are discussed and featured in On the Move (Routine #7). A classic lesson about reflections, or flips, called for a student to build a figure that their partner, sitting directly across from them, or beside them, would rebuild from their own perspective. This variation of Views revisits those experiences. In this variation, you present a pattern block design like those shown on the left of both images. Draw a dotted line above or beside the design. Then, have students build the figure or draw a picture of it from the view on the other side of the dotted line. This is shown on the right side of both images. It's recommended that you begin with simple shapes of just one or two pattern blocks at first. As your students progress, you can begin to introduce more complicated figures as shown with the triangles and trapezoid. Pattern blocks prove to work best for this experience though you could also use shape cards from other routines (Sorts, Routine #2 or Venns, Routine #3). Pentominoes featured in See It, Build It (Routines #1) could also work.

E1

E2

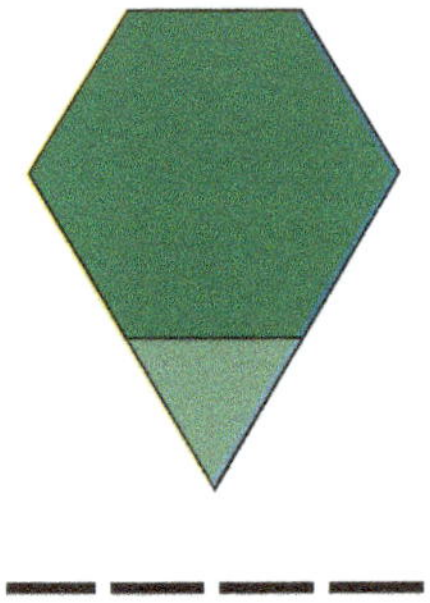

E3

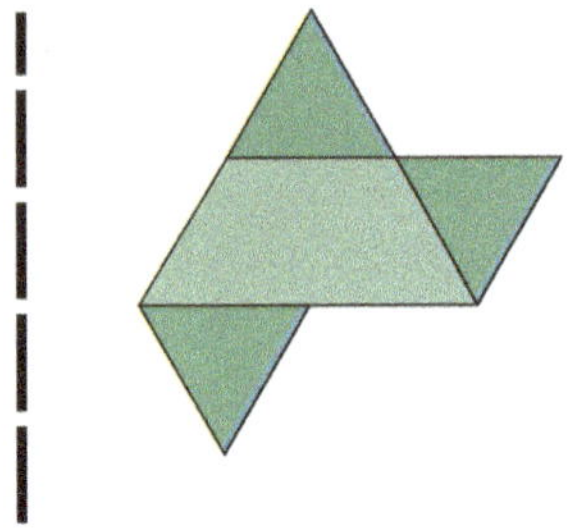

E4

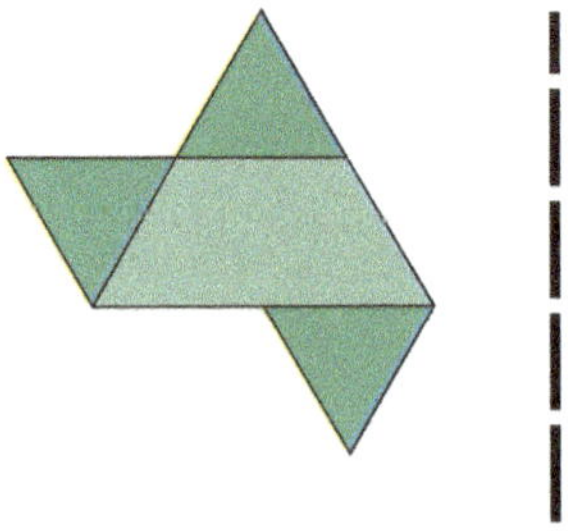

Variation F: From the Top

A view from the top was mentioned in Variation B where students had to figure out which view of a figure was being presented. In this variation, a view from the top is the only perspective they are to focus on. This perspective, in the context of maps, is commonly referred to as an aerial view. It would be fine to share this term with students when they first confront this variation. Here, they have to imagine what the figure looks like "from the top." It's a good variation for somewhat complicated figures like the one shown. This figure will look like a 2 x 4 arrangement from the front, back, or either side. In short, it might not trigger a very rich discussion. However, a view of this figure from the top reveals two "notches" that appear in distinct places as shown in the image. Know that a view from the top works with any figure and doesn't have to be reserved for unique situations or figures like this one.

F1

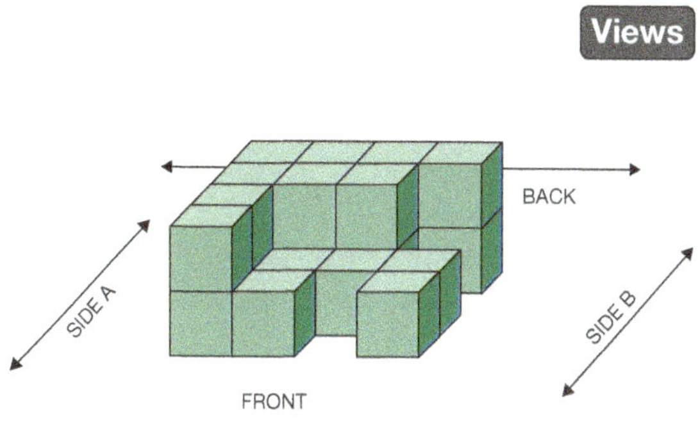

F2

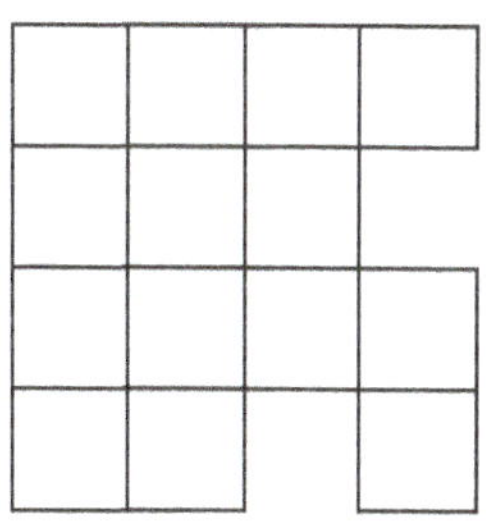

The view from the top.

Variation G: Blueprints

Blueprints is a fun variation of this routine where students aren't presented with a figure to consider from different views. Instead, you show them a map or blueprint of the figure. That is, the number in each square tells you how many blocks are in that stack or column. This information is used to envision a figure to determine what it would look like from different views or one specific view. Go ahead and try it! Look at the blueprint. Then, determine whether the images of the views from the sides, front, and back of the blueprint are correct. You might be thinking this variation is really hard and it might be. Don't be afraid to try hard things with your students. They'll be quick to let you know when something is too difficult. When they do, stick with the activity for a bit longer to see if it really is too difficult. Cut ties if it is but think about how you can differentiate for students before you do. For example, this would be a good variation to provide blocks for students to build a model of the blueprint so that they don't have to rely solely on mental images.

As mentioned in Variation A, basic prisms are a good starting place for this routine. Likewise, they're a good starting place for the blueprint variation of the routine. The image shows a blueprint for a prism that is four blocks wide, three blocks deep, and four blocks tall.

The views of that prism from side A and from the back are shown. As you know, the views from side B and from the front will be the same as those, respectively.

One more example of a blueprint for a figure and views of that figure from side B and the front are also shown in the images.

G1

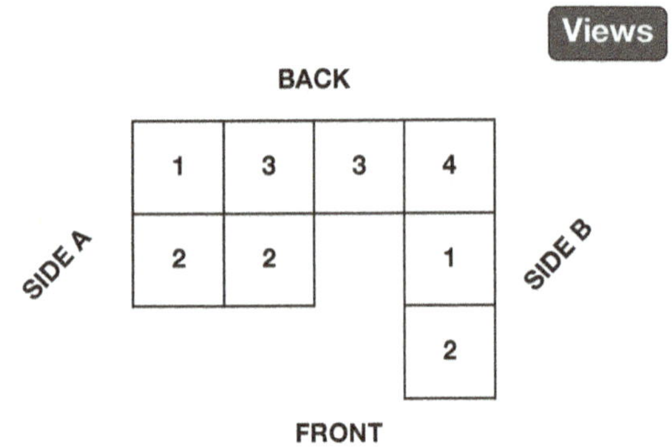

G2

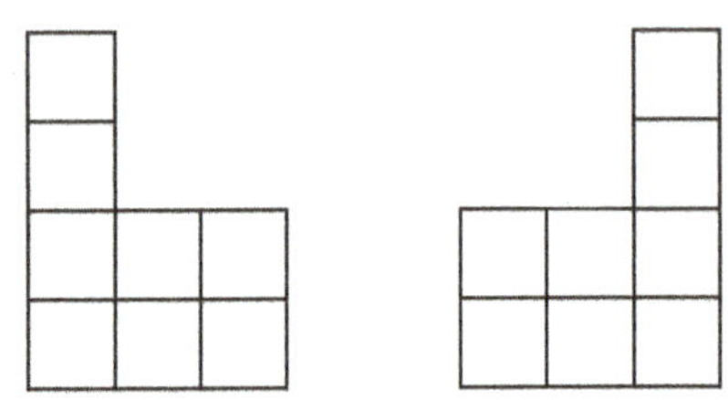

The view from side A.

The view from side B.

G3

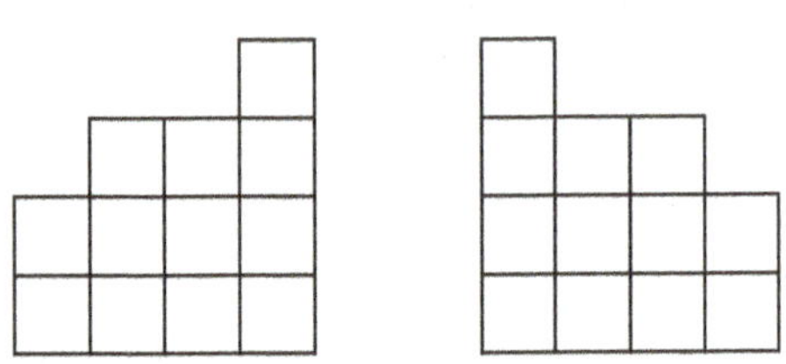

The view from the front.

The view from the back.

G4

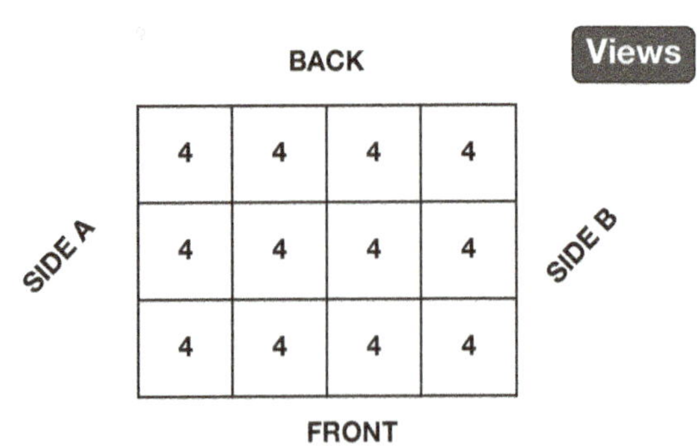

G5

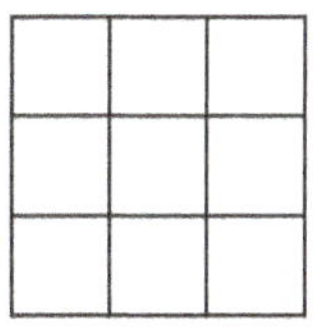

The view from
side A.

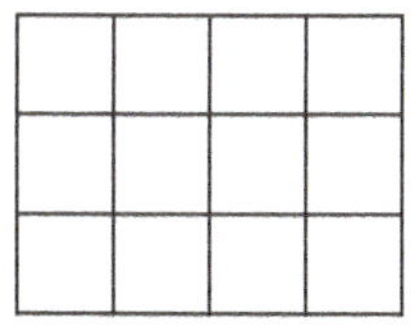

The view from
the back.

G6

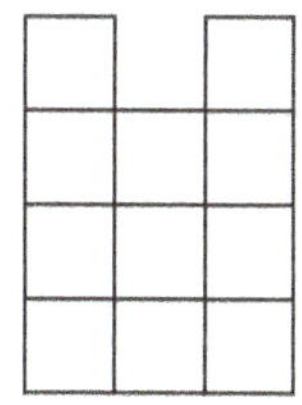

The view from
side B.

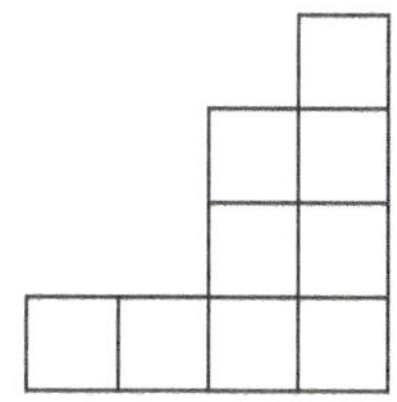

The view from
the front.

G7

Views

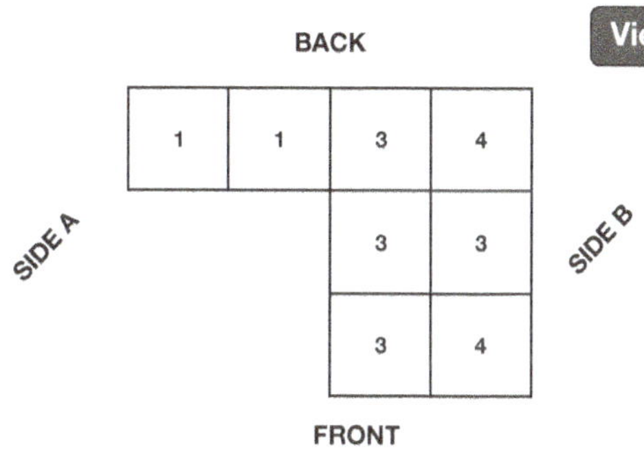

Variation H: Common 3D Figures

All the figures in this routine are 3D figures but this variation uses common 3D figures like spheres, cubes, cones, cylinders, prisms, and pyramids. This example tasks students with envisioning how a cylinder and a cone look from different views. It's perfect for helping students think about the look of these figures from different angles, which can contribute to understanding nets, 2D figures that when folded create a 3D shape, in later grades. The net of a cylinder is shown in H1 and the net of a cone is shown in H2.

Students don't need to know about nets to work with this variation of the routine. They only need to have learned about these common figures, which happens early in their elementary experience. In fact, this last variation might be a nice place to start the routine because of the familiarity with these figures and the views of these figures from the different positions is pretty simple, as shown in the images. A cylinder looks like a rectangle from the front (or back) and like a circle from either side. The cone looks like a triangle from the front and back, or either side for that matter, though it does look like a circle from the top.

H1

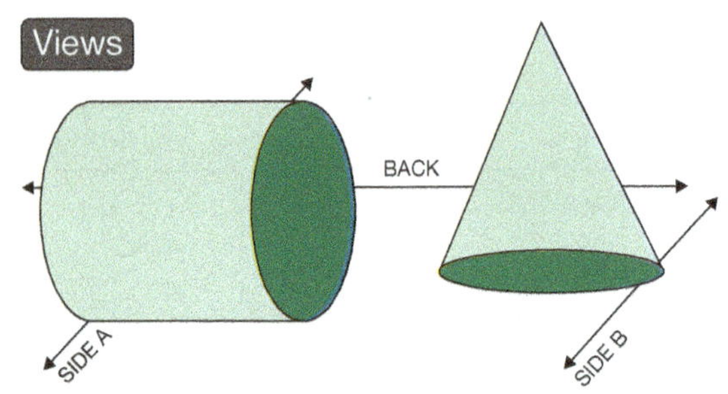

H2

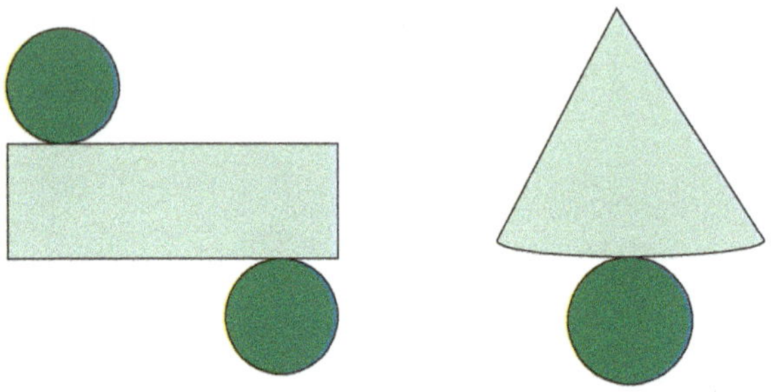

H3

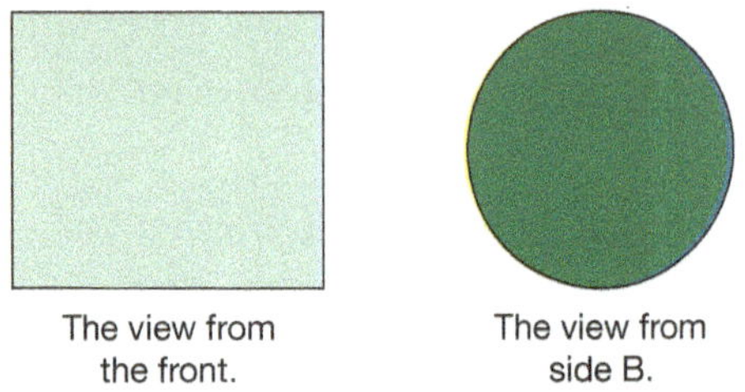

H4

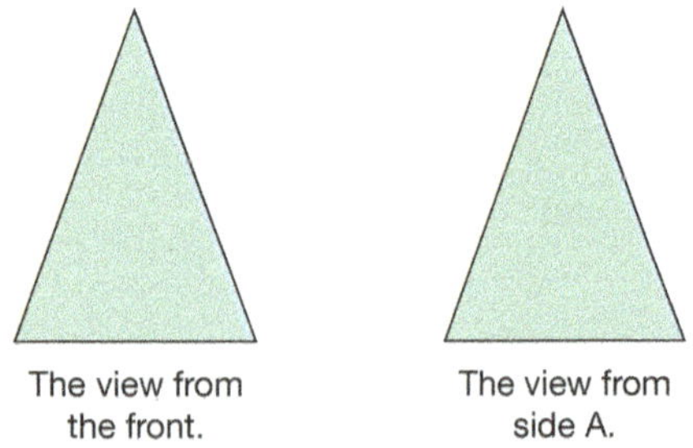

ROUTINE 9

WHAT'S THE ORDER?

ABOUT THE ROUTINE

Measurement is a fundamental skill that adults can take for granted. We interact with measurement, determining the size of things, every day. Measurement is rooted in comparison of objects even without numbers or units to make such comparisons (Beckmann, 2013). Young children will tell that one toy airplane is longer than another even though they don't know that the longer is 24 inches and the shorter is 15 inches. As described in Part 1, instruction begins with measurable attributes, usually length, and comparison before moving to other attributes and then introducing unit or reference amount.

Mastery of measurement skills and concepts comes from instruction and lots of practice measuring. This routine, What's the Order?, is a great opportunity for a burst of high-quality practice. The routine itself is straightforward with no bells and whistles though there is a subtle twist in which each object is placed at different locations on the ruler. This counters the misconception that one must line things up with 0 on a ruler.

Using this activity routinely across the entire school year can pay dividends. To do it, pose a few objects without the measurement tool. Have students predict the order of them from longest to shortest or shortest to longest. Once standard units have been introduced, like inches or centimeters, have them also predict how long each object is. After predictions are made, display the measurement tool, and have students determine the order of objects before discussing solutions as a whole class.

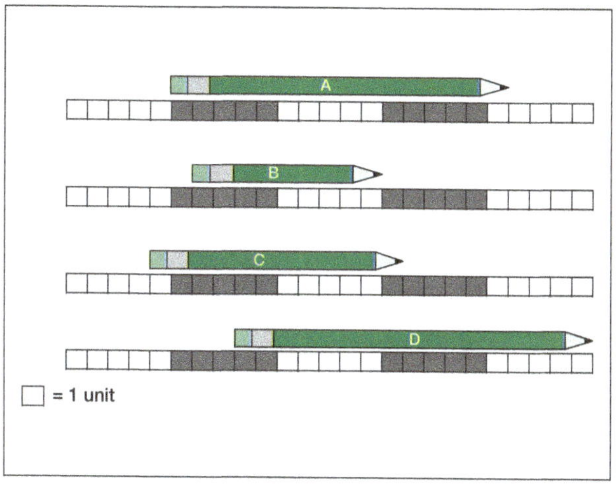

In this example, you'll notice that the measurement tool isn't a ruler. In fact, it's a representation of a bead string with the real thing shown on the following page. Bead strings are good tools for building skill with measurement through nonstandard units. You can use full strings of 100 beads or shorter 20-bead strings. These are good tools because they're flexible and set in intervals of 5 or 10 that can reinforce efficient counting. Other nonstandard units include things like paper clips, strings, or sticks of connecting cubes. In fact, a nice variation of this routine would be to have students order objects with a given tool like a bead counter and then do it again with a different unit like paper clips. The order won't change of course but the number of units will!

The downloadable content for this routine includes this example and the variations. It also includes

online resources All routines can be downloaded for your use at https://companion.corwin.com/courses/jumpstartroutines-geometry

a customizable, editable template. You'll find bead strings and rulers in those templates. The numbers on the rulers are created with textboxes so that you can change them. You can also shift the objects along the ruler or swap them out with your own. Remember, it's a good idea to have one slide with the objects for students to predict their order before having the next slide appear with the measuring tools.

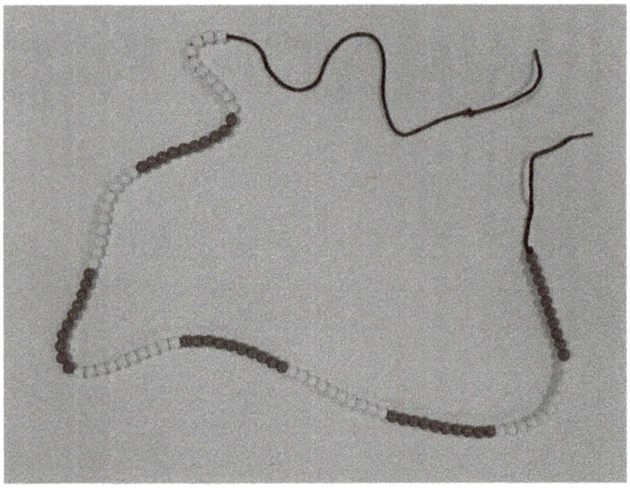

HOW THIS ROUTINE HELPS

This routine deepens understanding of measurement by providing opportunities for students to

- measure objects;
- compare and order objects;
- reason about the length of objects regardless of their position on a ruler;
- select and use tools for measuring (MP5);
- attend to precision (MP6);
- strengthen reasoning skills for application to measurement and problem-solving (MP1); and
- collaborate, discuss, and debate with classmates (MP3).

WHAT TO DO

1. Collect a set of objects.
2. Identify a measuring tool like a bead counter as shown in the opening example.
3. Optional: Show the objects first and ask students to predict the order of objects by their length.
4. Display the set of objects and the measuring tool. Ideally, each object would be adjacent to its own measurement tool. In the example, each pencil is above its own bead string.
5. Have students determine the order of objects with a justification. When using three or more objects, as shown in the example, you may want to provide students with a sticky note or white board to record their solutions. This can help lessen the burden on their memory.
6. Have students compare their solutions with partners.
7. Bring the class together. Record different solutions, if they exist. For example, ask the group for the order in the example. Someone might say D, C, A, and B. Record that on the board and ask for another solution. Another offering might be D, A, C, and B. Others can be recorded if offered. When you have possible solutions recorded, have partners identify which they agree with and why.
8. After a few moments, have students or partners who offered solutions justify their thinking. Record their ideas to illustrate their thinking for others. As you do this, be sure that you record the values students speak to.
9. After recording ideas and values, have the class conclude the correct order. If disagreement continues, show the correct answers and demonstrate how they are established.

SOMETHING TO THINK ABOUT: SLIDES, DOCUMENT CAMERAS, OR DRAWINGS

The pandemic created all sorts of challenges and innovations for teaching and learning. Some of those innovations were great and some were not. The use of slide decks is one that, while not an innovation, has had staying power. Using slides to present a task is a good use of the tool. Using a slide deck as a script poses significant challenges to teaching math. Among other things, it can undercut your responsiveness, differentiation, and opportunities for student exploration. The message isn't to use or not use slides but rather to be mindful of how this or any resource is used. The routines in this collection are provided through slides. You have access to editable templates to make new examples to use with your students. However, don't feel obligated to use them in that format. For this routine, and many others, you can use a document camera or your white board. For example, in this routine, you can use your document camera to show a few objects and a ruler or bead counter below them for reference. You can also put objects and measurement tools on your board with magnetic clips or something similar. The point is that you want routines to be easy to use and efficient practice bursts. The way you create them should also be easy and efficient.

WHAT'S THE ORDER? (VARIATIONS): ANY MEASURABLE ATTRIBUTE

This routine works with any measurable attribute. Length is featured in most examples. Money appears in the last variation. However, you could just as easily have students compare liquid volume with cups, pints, milliliters, or anything else. Images of beakers or measuring cups would be a nice touch but you can just as easily put the values in a circle. To increase the challenge for older students, you can mix up the units (e.g., pints, cups, and quarts). You can get some ideas from other routines like Close, Far, Between, and More (Routine #12). The following variations also give you some ideas about how you change the experience with whatever measurable attribute you use.

Variation A: Linker Cubes

This variation is offered for two different reasons. The first is that it has students compare only three items. This is a natural move after comparing two objects. In time, students can move to four or more objects. Another reason this is a good example is that it uses sticks of connecting cubes. It's natural for students to compare them through the number of cubes within the stick. That reasoning is fine, but you want to lift up how long they are in units. So, when they say, "C is the shortest because it has three cubes" you should acknowledge and then ask, "But how many units long is C?" Doing this reinforces finding length through a unit of measure. The number of cubes is a unit of measure but it won't work with pencils (opening example) or with mixed objects like in later examples.

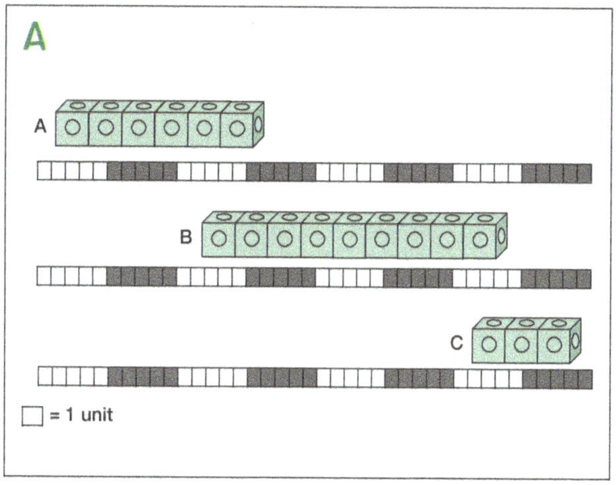

Variation B: Different Objects

This variation continues the use of bead counters but offers different objects for students to compare. Each object or set of objects is labeled though it's completely fine for students to speak to "the paper clips," "the cubes," and "the pencil." It is important, though, for you to require them to make comparisons using the number of units long each object is. In an example like this, students are likely to identify the cubes as the shortest length. They might "eyeball" the paper clips and the pencil but stress that the two are close in length and that they need to be measured. Be mindful of this as you use or create different objects. It's fine to have three that have clear differences. When you do, be ready for those who say they "just know." Connect those statements to the measurements as proof.

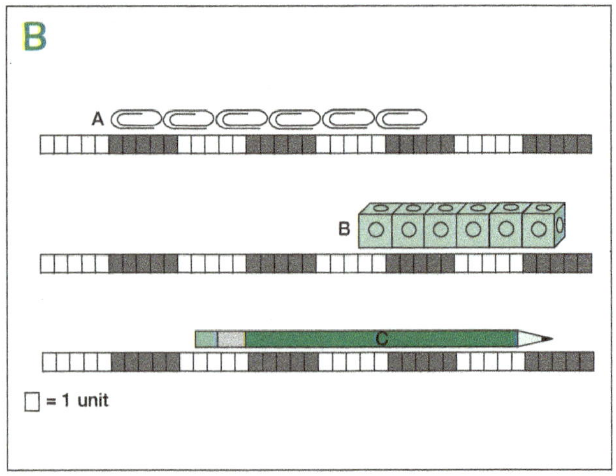

Variation C: Standard Units (Centimeters)

Measuring with standard units like inches or centimeters is a natural adaption of this routine. In this example, each ruler shows centimeters. Students must determine the length of each pencil so that they can put them in order. Be on the lookout for students who rely on the appearance and their visual perception to order the items. Yes, C is clearly the longest and B is the shortest. But the point of the experience is to make use of the exact lengths. That being said, it's reasonable for students to speak to clear examples but when two or more are close to the same length they should use exact measurements to prove their solutions. Students can find them in different ways. Some might count forward and others might count backward. Students might count by ones while others might count by twos or some other interval. Compare their approaches and talk about efficiency but avoid insinuating that one approach is correct over another. We don't suggest that you require that students use equations to justify their solutions. However, you might record the equations for them to model how it might be done.

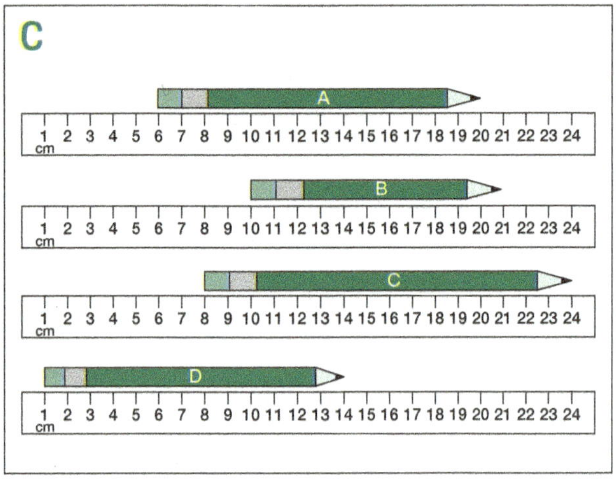

Variation D: Where's the End?

This is a neat variation of the routine that doesn't ask students to put the pencils in order. Instead, they have to figure out the starting or ending point of the pencil on the ruler. It's a great practice for growing their reasoning skills. It also connects with other important mathematics concepts like the compensation strategy for subtraction as shifting the difference or constant difference is used to find the solutions for each. In this example, the pencil is 11 centimeters long. For the second ruler, the pencil begins with 3. Knowing that it is 11 centimeters long you can add that to 3 finding the end point of the pencil (i.e., its tip) to stop at 14 on the ruler. The third pencil begins at 12 centimeters and ends at 23 centimeters. The bottom example ends at 14 meaning it begins at 3. You can do this with cubes, pencils, paper clips, or strips of paper as described in Variation F. You can even see what happens if you flipped the pencil over (i.e., tip on the left and eraser on the right) in one or two of the unknowns. You might be surprised by what you learn!

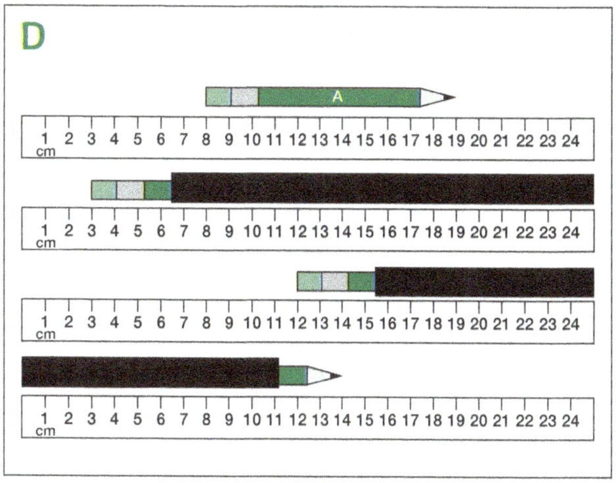

Variation E: Cuisenaire Rod Trains

Cuisenaire rods are often reserved for work with fractions, but they hold potential for so much more. They are a good tool for teaching multiplicative comparison, combinations of 10 or 100, as well as addition and subtraction of two-digit numbers (SanGiovanni et al., 2023). As you might know, there are 10 rods in a set of Cuisenaire rods with each rod being 1 centimeters longer than the next. With this in mind, you can create "trains" consisting of a few rods. During the routines, students determine which train is the longest, which is the shortest, and so on. In this example, trains B and D are both 19 centimeters long. Train C is 18 centimeters and train A is the shortest, measuring 15 centimeters. Listen carefully as your students describe their thinking. Some might say that C is the longest because it has the most rods but that isn't true. Others might think D is the longest because it has the most brown (longer) rods. The justification you're listening for should describe the difference between the beginning and the end of the train. For example, B is 19 centimeters because it measures from 57 to 76 centimeters. Keep in mind there are other ways to think about the measures as well. For example, it is reasonable for students to think of train C as 18 centimeters because it has six green rods that each measure 3 centimeters. Also look for ideas of substitution or comparison. The image in E2 is a good "cheat sheet" to make for yourself so that you know the length of each rod.

E1

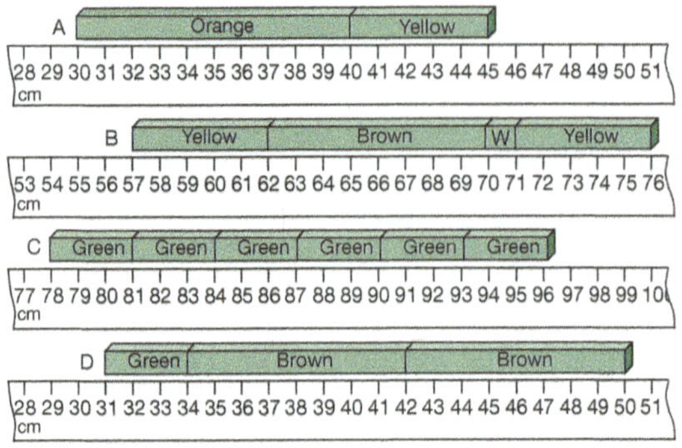

E2

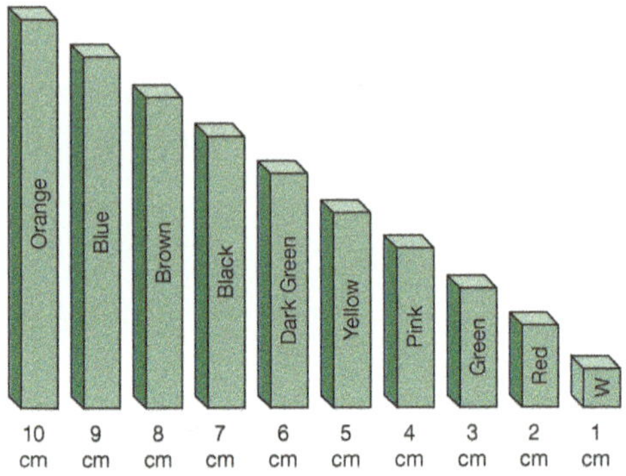

Variation F: Paper Strips and Fractional Lengths

Finding objects that measure to an exact inch can be hard. Finding objects that measure to an exact half-inch or quarter-inch might be even harder. A simple way around that challenge can be to use strips of paper cut to the lengths you want. The models in the image represent this idea. They show a rectangle, which represents a piece of construction paper or something similar cut to certain lengths, like B which is 7¼ inches. You can make a set of these and label them with different letters. During a routine, you can pull out three or four of them to use. And, they don't have to be in order (i.e., A, B, C, and D). As long as the different strips have different letters you'll be fine. The image was made with PowerPoint and each "strip of paper" is actually just a rectangle with a letter in it. In the online resources, you'll find a template with lettered boxes. To make new examples, you can copy the slide and drag the edges of the rectangle to make it larger or smaller.

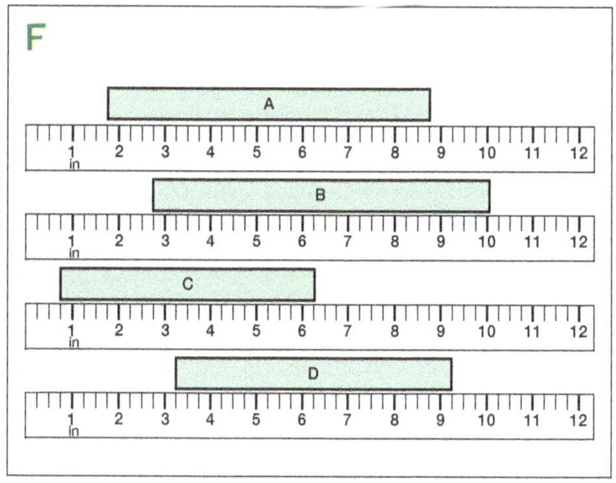

Variation G: Thermometers

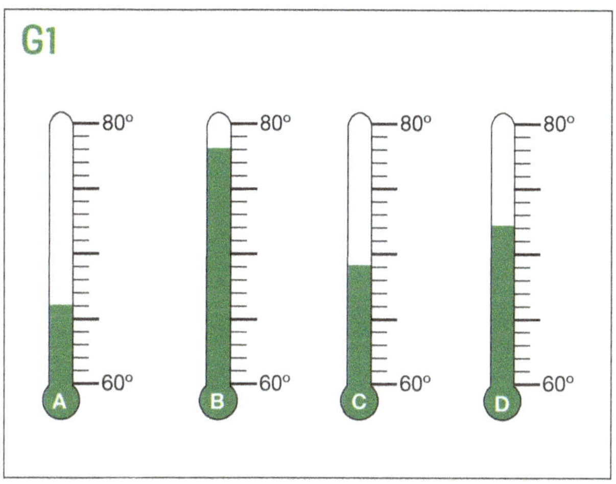

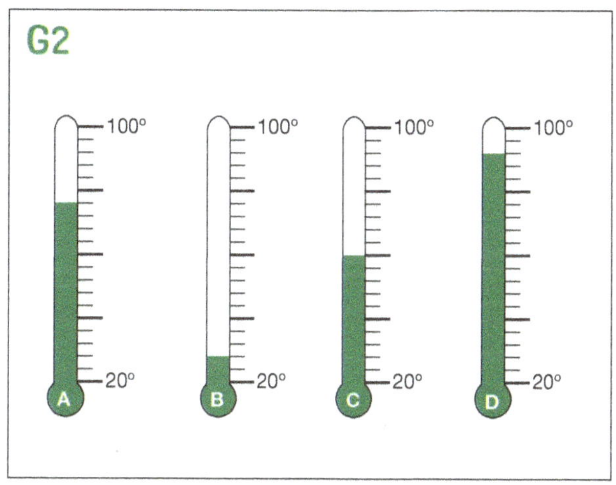

Thermometers are vertical number lines! They may not appear in your curriculum. After all, when is the last time you used a real thermometer instead of an app or a digital thermometer? But that doesn't mean you can't play around with them in this routine. Working with thermometers is a good way to strengthen and extend your students' understanding of number lines while "previewing" the vertical number lines that they will experience in later grades with coordinate grids, among other topics. There's also another potential advantage to using this tool. Notice the thermometers in G1. They have a scale of 1. That is, each tick mark is 1 degree. You should work with those on the left first before transitioning to a scale of 2, 5, or 4 like the thermometers in G2. But why do this? It can be a nice segue into open number lines or an anchor point for teaching bar graphs and picture graphs with different scales.

Variation H: Money

Money is a measurement topic in primary grades, and it appears in problem-solving standards in later grades. Recognizing different coins and recalling their value is one thing. Finding the value of a mixed set of coins is a different challenge altogether. Students need to remember the coins and their value, but they also need to be able to skip count by different intervals and from different starting numbers. It's unreasonable to expect students to find mastery with this skill in a week or two. That's why counting money is an important topic to consider for this routine and others. Take note of an important aspect of this variation. Here, values for coins are used rather than images of the exact coins. This is a good starting point for students with fragile skip counting skills. As that skill matures, and their knowledge of coins in general grows, you can begin to use real coins or images of them. Also note that you might consider using just one image of a coin mixed with the values in circles. For example, you might replace the 25¢ circle with an image of a real quarter for each set of coins and leave the others as they are. This will allow students to focus on recognizing the quarter and its value. Later, you can introduce the next coin, the next, and so on.

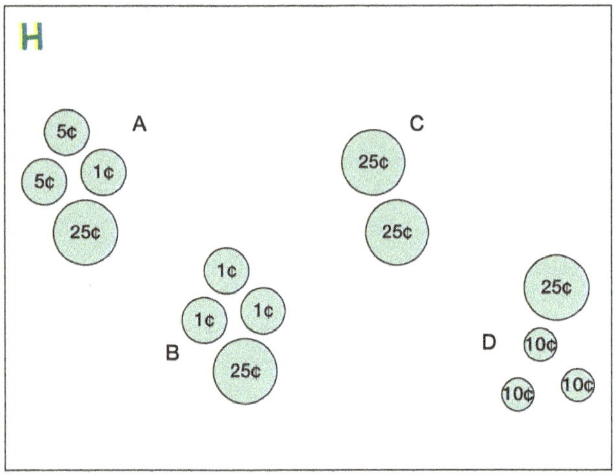

ROUTINE 10

THAT'S A FACT

ABOUT THE ROUTINE

That's a Fact

5 15 50 100 500

The cafeteria table is about _____ hands long.

The cafeteria table is about _____ hands wide.

We estimate measurements every day. We estimate the length of objects in our house, the weight of a package, or the size of a table. We estimate the price of things, how long something will take, or the capacity of various containers. Estimation is essential in our daily lives. Our ability to estimate improves the more that we do it. And with a better sense of estimation, we in turn have a better guide for reasonableness and accuracy.

In this routine, That's a Fact, students select missing numbers to complete measurement statements making them true or establishing them as a fact. Students will have to call on experience and judgment. They will sometimes be close and sometimes way off. That's OK! Estimation for adults, especially with the examples here, is easier because we have so many more years of doing it. This routine alone provides your students with just that, experience estimating, sharing ideas, and comparing to actual numbers all of which improve their sense of measurement and estimation.

In some experiences, you can have them estimate the length of an object in terms of a familiar benchmark like the length of their hands. This is highlighted in this opening example. Something for you to keep in mind is that cafeteria tables vary in length. For this discussion, let's assume they're 6 feet long or 72 inches long. If a student's hand is roughly 4 inches, then it's reasonable to estimate that the table is about 15 hands long. But you can't expect these sorts of calculations from your students. Instead you want them to think about how long 1 hand is and even 5 hands. They can do this with partners right there at their table groups or on the floor. It should help them realize that 5 is too small while 100 and 500 are way too big. It's understandable for them to argue 50 and depending on the length of your school's table or even the age of your students (i.e., size of their hands) that number might be about right. Keep in mind that the numbers we present can (and should) be changed to suit your situation. You can change them, and you can reduce the number of possibilities.

Estimation can be really hard at first and may be best nurtured when done collaboratively. In other words, this routine is likely to be most successful when students have opportunities to consider multiple possibilities through different perspectives, insights, and experiences. With this in mind, the routine may be better implemented

online resources All routines can be downloaded for your use at **https://companion.corwin.com/courses/jumpstartroutines-geometry**

in a math council format rather than a think-pair-share format. To do this, pose the prompts and groups of three or four can come to common agreements and justifications before sharing ideas with the whole class. In this approach, there is no time during the routine where students would work with the situations independently. You may shift to a think-pair-share format as students gain experience with the routine and estimation.

Estimation is special because everyone can do it, and there isn't truly a wrong answer but rather better answers. There may (will) be a wide range of estimates but essentially each student can participate. There is no procedure for estimating and thus no one way to carry it out. This routine is unique in that students need minimal proficiency with measuring. They should understand an attribute of an object, such as length, and have some sense of number and magnitude. Yet, even students who are still developing understanding of any of these can engage in the routine. In fact, working with this routine is likely to help them better understand measurement attributes and concepts of number, magnitude, and estimation. As with other routines, That's a Fact is best when students share ideas and listen to the ideas of others. With this in mind, certain behaviors or dispositions are prerequisites. Students should have understanding and experiences with group discussions, sharing perspectives, listening to others, and respecting the opinions of others.

HOW THIS ROUTINE HELPS

This routine deepens understanding of measurement by providing opportunities for students to

- determine how ideas about numbers and measurement are relevant and evident in their lives (MP2);
- develop their understanding of the magnitude of numbers (MP2);
- reason about nonstandard, familiar benchmarks (such as hands);
- develop a sense of reasonableness for better accuracy when measuring (MP2);
- make better sense of their world as it is described with numbers and measurements;
- compare and contrast situations (MP1);
- justify and communicate their reasoning (MP3); and
- consider the reasoning and strategies of others (MP3).

WHAT TO DO

1. Create a few statements about the relative length, mass, capacity, etc. of objects. A look around your room will give you an idea of things to ask about. Trivia books, books of records, or internet searches can also be quite helpful for finding and creating these statements.
2. Remove the values from the statements.
3. Present the statements separate from the values and include additional incorrect values.
4. Ask small groups of students to discuss and agree on the likely values for each statement with a justification for their selection.
5. Once students arrive at solutions, discuss group ideas about the solutions. Highlight student reasoning during discussion. Honor and explore both accurate and flawed reasoning. Questions to ask might include the following:
    - How did you decide on how many hands long the cafeteria table is?

- How does your desk compare to the length of a cafeteria table? How could that help you make an estimate?
- Did anyone see how long 5 of your hands were? How did that help you?
- Were there any numbers that were easy to ignore? Why?
- Which number was the hardest to figure out? Why?
- What might be some other estimates for the number of hands long the cafeteria table might be?

6. Reveal solutions to the statements and discuss possible surprises.

SOMETHING TO THINK ABOUT: THE IMPORTANCE OF ESTIMATION

Estimation plays a critical role in learning and doing mathematics. It infiltrates most every aspect from computational fluency to problem-solving, number sense, and of course measurement as we've discussed so far. Your students cannot estimate enough! You can do it every day by having students estimate their sums or differences before doing a problem. You can incorporate estimation jars or estimation stations. You can use routines like this and others. When you work with estimation, it is critical that exacts are found so that students can compare and calibrate their reasoning. But when you give exacts, be mindful that students might misinterpret that one, close estimate as *the* answer. So, when exacts are given, have students look back at their estimates and others. Have them determine which estimates were better and why. Point out that estimates aren't to be exact and that there can be multiple good estimates and some better estimates.

THAT'S A FACT (VARIATIONS): MIX IT UP

It's a good idea to vary when and how students estimate. Estimating with different activities that ask them to reason differently helps them craft new strategies. Different experiences provide opportunity for students to transfer approaches from one setting to another. Changing the how isn't complicated. You can have them estimate quantities, determine "close to" numbers, estimate calculations using different methods, and you can vary the type of units (i.e., standard and nonstandard), the unit of measurement, or the attribute being measured. The following variations offer some ideas about how you can vary this routine.

Variation A: Standard Units and Different Numbers

The obvious change in this variation of That's a Fact is that it uses standard units. This is a natural progression from nonstandard units but it doesn't mean that the two should be isolated. Helping students identify a nonstandard unit that is close to a given standard unit can be helpful. For example, the width of two fingers (pointer and middle) are about an inch. These nonstandard references can help students make their estimates and justify their thinking. But you have to help them establish these references. Another thing you'll notice about this variation is that each statement has its own set of numbers to complete the statement. This can be helpful when two different statements are going to be about the same. You don't want to get into a fruitless debate about how 5 or 6 could be used to complete two different statements. Instead, just give two sets of numbers. Also note that the second statement has a blank for the container. We did that to speak to using an actual container (in this statement) or object so students can see and potentially hold the item in order to make their estimate.

A

That's a Fact

1 3 5 10 30

The book is about _____ inches long.

1 6 10 30 100

The _____ holds about _____ ounces of water.

Variation B: Typical Benchmarks and Ranges

Having a personal benchmark for an inch, as mentioned in Variation A, can set the stage for using other familiar objects, like the average height of a human. Granted, some people are much more than 6 feet tall and others are much less, but 6 is a reasonable number to use. Using nonstandard references like this works so well it's a common technique used in photography to help the viewer understand the scale of something. The example asks for a certain number of feet. So, the height of the door might be about 8 feet because it is a little more than a person. In fact, simple comparisons of people's height to that of a door, without exact measures, is something that begins in kindergarten. We also want to point out the last statement about the tree. It is there to show you how to use common items and landmarks that students see repeatedly during the day. Doing this helps them add to their collection of mental references.

B

That's a Fact

Adults are about 5 ½ feet to 6 ½ feet tall.

So, the door to our classroom is about _____ feet.

So, the height of a car is about _____ feet.

So, the tree in the front of our school is about _____ feet.

Variation C: Estimate and Confirm

This variation shows how you can estimate with familiar objects and nonstandard units. It also speaks to the value in having students estimate and confirm with an exact. As mentioned earlier, it's critical to provide the exact number to grow your students' skill with estimation. In this example, numbers are provided but your students might prefer a different number. For example, 12 is the best estimate of the choices but they may argue for 8 or 9 instead. When this happens, you are encouraged to change the 12 but they must agree to what new number will be used instead. You should also remind them that an estimate isn't the exact number necessarily and that both 8 and 9 are pretty much the same. This will also help when students want to change 12 to 11 or 13.

C

That's a Fact

12 50 500

A pencil box can hold about _____ markers.

4 14 41

I can hold about _____ markers in my hand.

Variation D: Relevant Facts

This example isn't so much about variation. It's about relevance. Making math relevant to students is a must-have for meaningful instruction. Relevance allows students to see math in their world and themselves in math. With that in mind, imagine it's October and your school had a Fall Fest just last week. The fact about the pumpkin would be a great way to make math relevant in this imagined context. The bottom fact speaks to the relevance of a family pet. It also shows seven different number choices. Typically, this wouldn't be a great idea but the fact calls for a range instead of an "about" number. If you think seven numbers would be too distracting for your students, you can give them no numbers and have the class come to consensus about the values for the range. Oh, and you might be wondering about how you confirm the exact figures when these real-world examples aren't accessible in the classroom. In these situations, we suggest that you and your students use a reliable online tool to confirm. In other words, just "Google it."

D

That's a Fact

8 80 800

A typical pumpkin weighs about _____ pounds.

1 5 12 20 50 65 100

A house cat usually weighs between ___ and ___ pounds.

Variation E: Big or Small

Big or Small is a routine to help students develop understanding for the magnitude of number in context of real-world situations (SanGiovanni, 2020). It offers great potential as a variation of this routine. To do this, create some statements like those you see in the example. Then, have students work through one at a time telling if the number is too big or too small for the statement. For the first statement, 80 is too big. There's no way a normal bookbag can hold 80 books. For the second statement, 20 is also too big. Bikes are usually about 4 feet long, maybe a little longer but certainly not 20 feet. Note that the statements are labeled with letters, which can help facilitate the discussion as mentioned in More or Less (Routine #14). Also note that this is a great opportunity for students to create examples for you. After all, they don't have to be accurate. You simply need objects, contexts, and numbers. That is something they can easily provide.

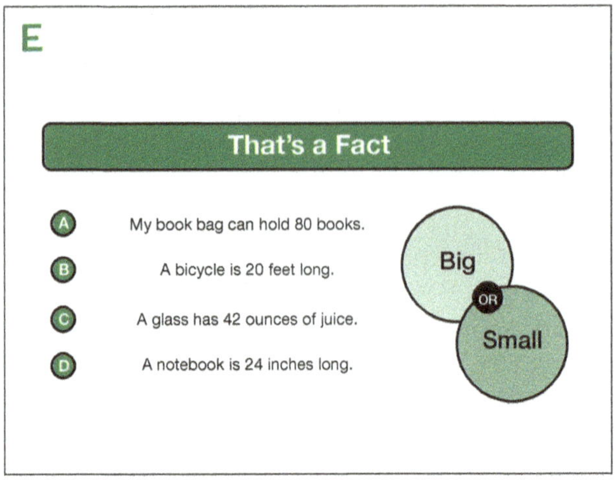

Variation F: Mix It Up, Anything Works

These last two examples are shared to encourage you to be creative with this routine (and all others). The example on the left is similar to an experience our friend and colleague Dr. Honi Bamberger shared with us many years ago. It provides some statements and more numbers than blanks. Some numbers can be canceled rather easily while others seem like they could satisfy more than one statement. The point is not for students to get each one correct but rather to engage them in thinking, reasoning, talking, and estimating measures! The example in F2 is possibly the version reserved for when your students need a really good challenge. Here, there are no numbers to call on. They must generate the estimate on their own before exacts are shared. Also notice the statements. They are real-world statements but aren't topics that many students will be familiar with. In fact, you might have difficulty with some yourself. When you get to this level (variation), you know that you and your students have made tremendous progress. At that point, you can even start to put in your own wonderings to explore with your kids, like "How much does a horse really weigh?"

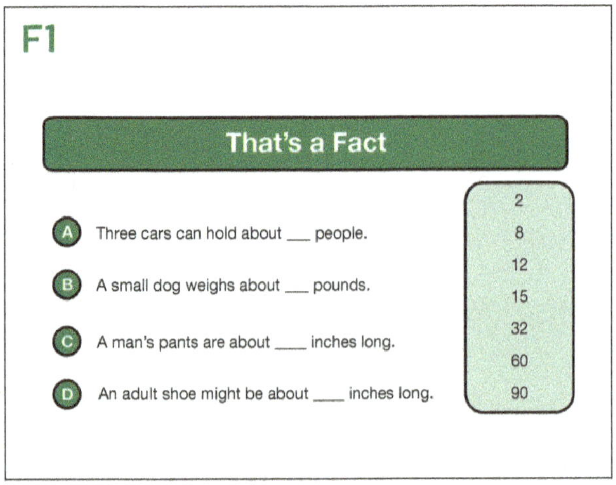

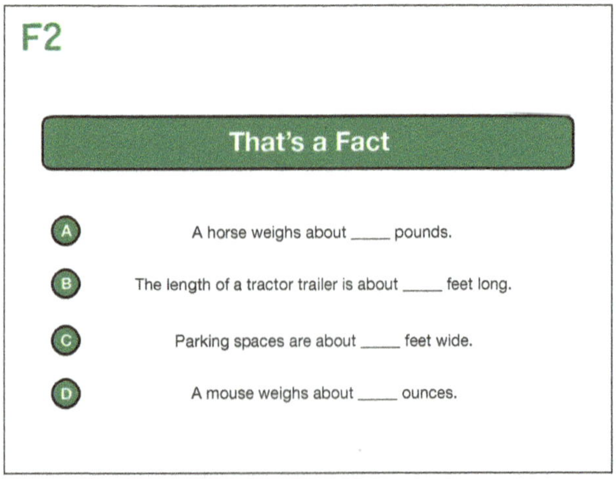

ROUTINE 11

VOLUME QUICK IMAGES

ABOUT THE ROUTINE

In recent years, Quick Image or Quick Look routines have become a staple of primary math classrooms. In these routines, the teacher flashes a quantity and has students talk about the amount they think they saw. Often, the routine features arrangements so that students can subitize the amount, but the routine can also be used for number decomposition, combinations of 10, and other skills related to computational fluency (Bay-Williams & SanGiovanni, 2021; Young Mathematicians, n.d.).

Volume Quick Images is a take on that classic, swapping out dots, ten frames, and base ten blocks for images of regular and irregular figures. In this routine, you display, or flash, an image like the one shown for 3 to 5 seconds before students decide what the cubic volume of the figure is. Determining the volume of a figure may be more challenging than subitizing dots. Consider extending the length of time you display the image—especially for more intricate figures. You can begin to reduce the time as your students' experience and strategies grow.

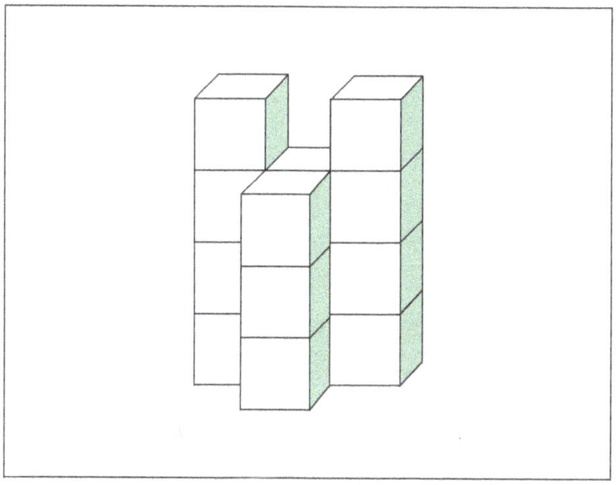

As students share their thinking, listen to how they decompose a figure. Ask them to identify how many columns they see, how many cubes are in a column, or how one column compares to another. In some cases, you might ask them to describe the regular figures within the figure you showed. In this example, you might ask them how many rectangular prisms they saw. This is a slightly different question. In the featured example, a student might say they saw two identical prisms of four cubes on the outside of the figure and one prism of six cubes in the middle of the figure.

Before working with this routine, you want to provide an experience for your students to compose irregular figures with inch cubes and other manipulatives. Consider making this a center where you provide physical models or images taken with your phone of irregular figures for students to work with. Most importantly, ensure that early experiences with this routine feature rectangular prisms as described in Variation A.

online resources All routines can be downloaded for your use at **https://companion.corwin.com/courses/jumpstartroutines-geometry**

HOW THIS ROUTINE HELPS

This routine deepens understanding of measurement by providing opportunities for students to

- practice finding volume through engagement;
- mentally visualize and manipulate three-dimensional figures;
- estimate and determine reasonableness;
- compose and decompose irregular figures;
- develop strategies for finding volume of irregular figures;
- better understand how an irregular figure relates to a regular figure;
- listen to strategies of others to acquire new strategies or refine their own (MP3); and
- give feedback to others about their ideas (MP3).

WHAT TO DO

1. Create an image of a regular or irregular figure. Examples are available from the online resource as well as a template slide for creating your own examples.
2. Flash an image of a regular or irregular figure.
3. Ask students to determine how many cubes are in the figure.
4. Give students a moment to identify the volume and share their answer with a partner.
5. Bring the group together and solicit a few different numbers.
6. Ask students to share how they determined their guess.
7. Display the image again to talk about it. As the image is displayed, allow students time to determine the actual volume. Discuss how they counted or composed/decomposed the figure.
8. Compare student predictions (from #4) to the actual volume of the figure.

SOMETHING TO THINK ABOUT: USING CENTERS TO REINFORCE CONCEPTS AND ROUTINES

Finding the volume of figures is a perfect center experience. You can build a physical model for students, or you can provide an image of a model you build for students to re-create as shown. You can differentiate the experience by building models with different colors to give students ideas about how they might decompose them. You could even make this modification in your Quick Image experience. With the featured example, one column might be displayed in green, another in red, and so on. A fun exploration for students might be to have them build a figure with a certain amount of green, pink, and white cubes. Then, have them compare and contrast the figures built and convenient ways to decompose those creations. There is no wrong way to take a routine and turn it into a center or homework assignment. The overarching idea is that you want to immerse your students in many, many quality practice experiences. Routines, paired with centers and homework, are a way to do this. So, as you explore other routines in this book, think about how you can tweak them in some way so that they become a practice opportunity outside of your opening routine.

VOLUME QUICK IMAGES (VARIATIONS): MAKING CONNECTIONS

Intentionally sequencing routines can help students develop the skill to see patterns, relate to benchmarks (or more thought-friendly shapes and numbers), and solve problems. You can do this by doing a routine with a given topic on one day and then the following day do the same routine with the same topic with slightly different numbers or a different prompt. You can also sequence the experience within the same routine and debrief the relationship with students as you'll see in these variations.

Variation A: Rectangular Prisms

Rectangular prisms or regular figures are a recommended starting point for this routine. Use images like this one to help students find a foothold with the concept of volume, how they might find it, and estimating volume. Start with manageable numbers for each dimension. Listen for your students to talk about all three dimensions (length, width, and height). Be careful to avoid a specific order of dimensions. You want students to be aware and on the lookout for them in general, and the order of the dimensions is not nearly as important. Requiring a specific order of dimensions can create undue pressure. Consider coloring your rectangular prisms as shown to help students develop a sense of decomposition.

A1

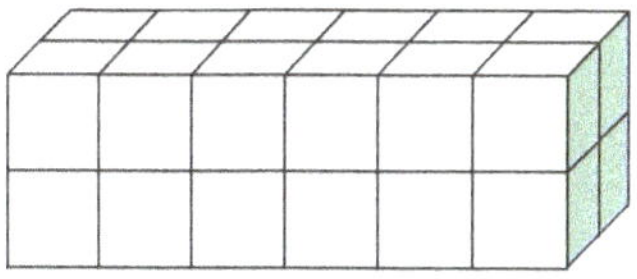

A2

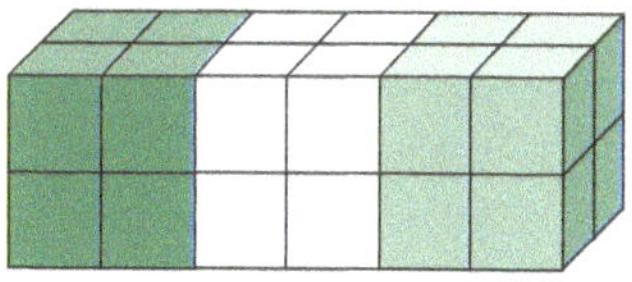

Variation B: More or Less

A natural way to develop skill with estimation is to help students identify and consider benchmarks. With numbers, students might think about relationships to benchmarks or finding convenient, compatible numbers to estimate solutions. You can use that idea to help them estimate and eventually determine the volume of an irregular figure. Here, you begin by flashing a regular figure like the cube shown in B1. Have students suggest the volume and how they found it before determining the actual volume. Then, flash a related figure like the one shown in B2. Before students determine its volume, simply have them determine whether the volume is more or less than the cube and how they know. Then, flash it again for them to make a better estimate before ultimately examining it as described in the opening directions.

B1

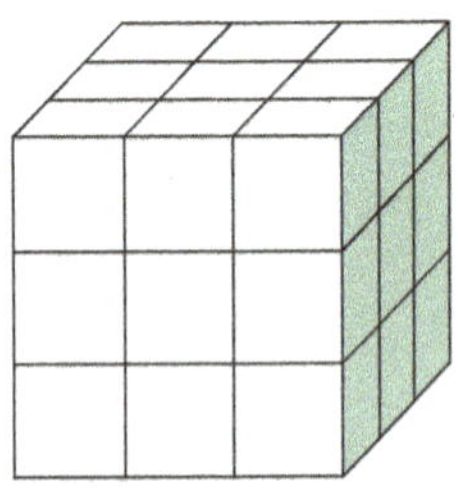

B2

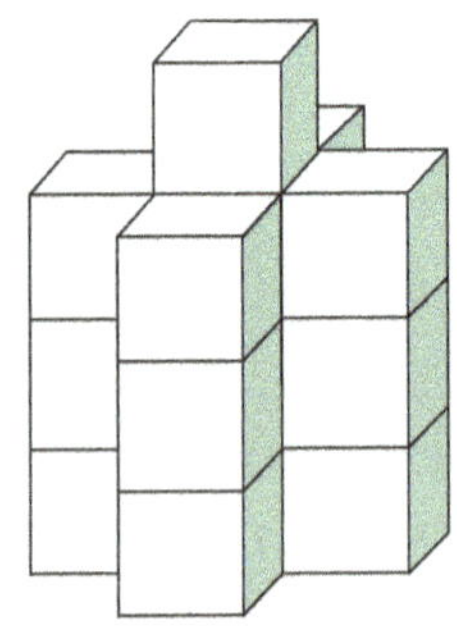

Variation C: How Many More?

In this variation, you want students to determine how many more cubes it will take to create a given volume. For the left example, you would say, "I want a prism that is 12 cubic units." Then, you flash the image. Students then talk with a partner about how many more cubes are needed to realize the goal of 12 cubic units. You solicit their answers and then discuss how they found them. In this example, students might talk about figuring out the volume of the figure and subtracting it from 12. Someone else might talk about "seeing" a prism of 12 overtop of the image and thinking about the missing 4 cubes. To help this visioning, you could first flash that exact prism and determine its volume of 12 before flashing the image in C1 and asking how many more are needed to get to 12. The image in C2 is simply just another example of the variation. There is no wrong way to carry out this routine but it's important to recognize that this variation is more cognitively demanding than the others.

C1

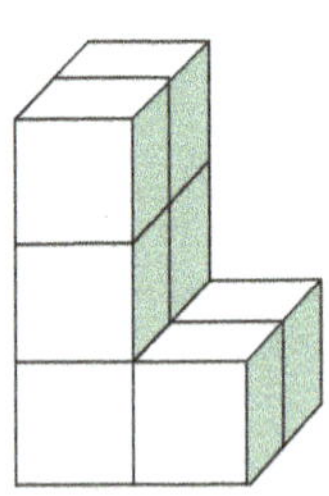

C2

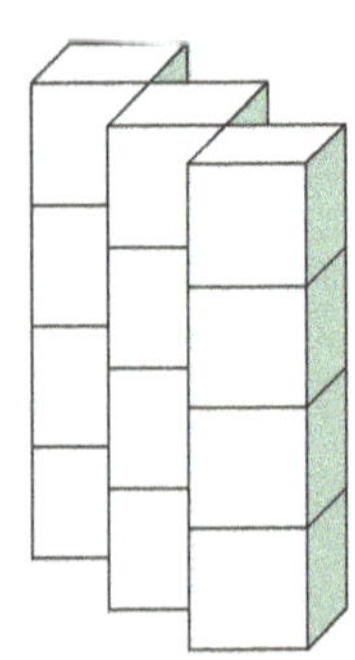

Variation D: Sequencing

Sequencing images is a good way to help students think about composing and decomposing numbers. For example, a first-grade teacher might flash 8 dots in a configuration of two groups of 4. Then, they might flash 9 dots with a group of 4 and a group of 5. This sequence helps students think about using 8 to find 9. The same can be done with this routine as mentioned in the introduction and Variation A. In this example, the volume is decreasing from one figure to the next and to the next. Take your time with debriefing the first image to be sure that students agree on the volume (e.g., 45). Then, flash the next image. Expect and allow students to describe finding the volume by seeing a 3 x 3 x 4 prism attached to a 1 x 1 x 3 prism. But be sure to listen for or explicitly call out how simply two columns of 3 were removed from the original. Talk about how the two figures are related and how knowing one can help you find the next. After confirming the volume of the second figure, pose a third. It's important to note that you can easily sequence the experience so that subsequent figures build or add on from the previous one. That is a fine place to start but you also want to have students work with decreasing volumes as described.

D1

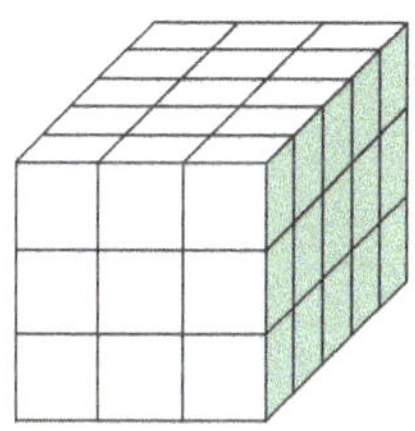

D2

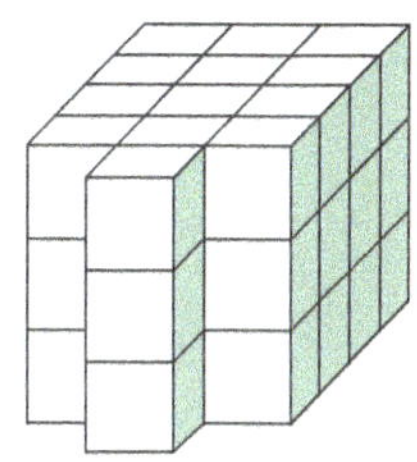

D3

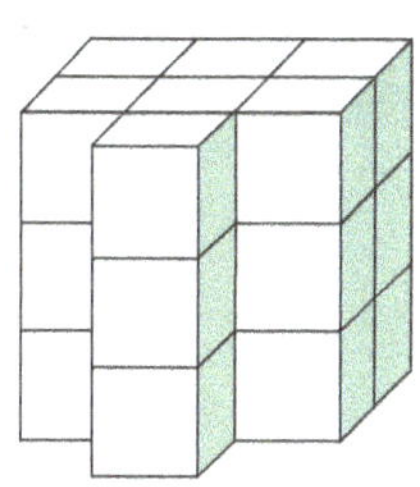

Variation E: Area

This routine is perfect for practice with area and even perimeter. In this variation, you can flash rectangles as shown in E1. Have students determine the area and discuss their thinking. You can transition to irregular figures by shading portions of the figure as was shown in Variation A. This can help students envision "regular" components of the larger figure. After discussion with these colored examples, you can ask students if they have different ideas about how it might be colored. In Example E2, the top 2 x 5 rectangle could be gray while the lower 2 x 1 rectangle could be left white. E3 is a simple example of an irregular figure that you could flash all by itself or after work has been done with the first rectangle.

E1

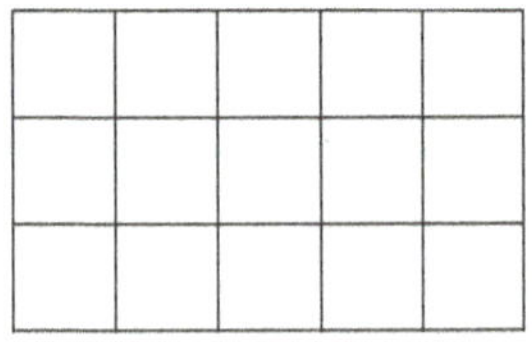

E2

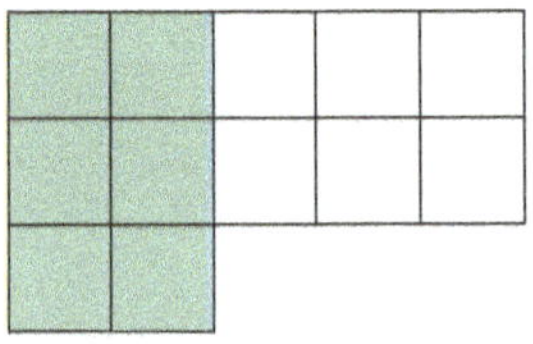

E3

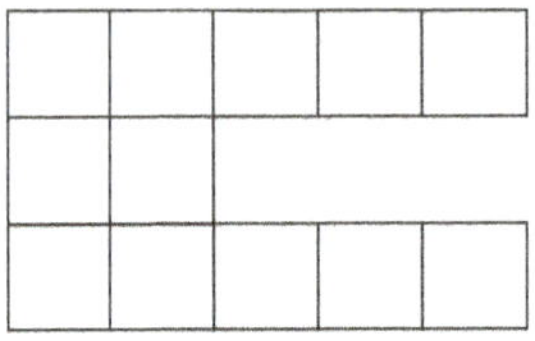

ROUTINE 12

CLOSE, FAR, BETWEEN, AND MORE

ABOUT THE ROUTINE

Time is a measurement of duration rather than the attribute of a physical thing. Shorter durations are typically measured with seconds, minutes, and hours whereas longer durations are typically measured in days, weeks, and years. Learning about time begins with telling time and it can be quite challenging for students. It can be hard to find success because there aren't a variety of ways to teach it. Often it isn't much more than a direct lesson or demonstration of how the clock works, how the hands are different, the meaning of the numbers on the clock, and what the tick marks around the clock mean. Teachers restate these things when students are unsuccessful but there is little more to reteaching it than just that. Students really need quality, engaging practice and lots of repetition. This can be hard to realize when time is a part of a unit toward the latter part of the year when, well, time is running out.

But what if a mini lesson or two were done earlier in the year and then students had bursts of practice through routines? Close, Far, Between, and More is a routine that can help you do just that and more! It is an adaptation of a whole number experience for learning about proximity of numbers (Van de Walle et al., 2023). It is a higher-level experience because

students do more than just tell time on three different clocks. They also have to reason about the relationship or proximity of the times shown on each clock. So, after identifying the times, they tell which two clocks show times that are closest, which two show times that are farthest apart, and which one time is in between the others.

And thinking during this routine doesn't stop with comparing times. After students share their ideas about the relationships of the clocks you

online resources All routines can be downloaded for your use at **https://companion.corwin.com/courses/jumpstartroutines-geometry**

show, you then have them generate a new time that is close to, far from, or between the clocks you present. In this example, students should say that clock B (9:45) and clock C (9:40) are the closest of the three. Then, one might say that 9:44 would be close to clock C or that 9:20 is close to clock A. Speaking of clock A, a student could say that it (9:15) is the farthest from clock B and that 9:05 or even 8-something is even farther from clock A.

Keep in mind that you can but don't need students to generate a new time for each condition (close, far, between). In fact, you don't need to have them generate anything at all. You might first use this routine to simply compare the times you present without them generating anything new. Then, in time, you can begin to ask them to create something that is close or far from one of the clocks. Also note that this example shows time within the same 9 o'clock hour. That is a fine option but so is presenting times across the day using AM or PM for all three clocks or labeling them differently (note that AM and PM are not labeled in this example).

HOW THIS ROUTINE HELPS

This routine deepens understanding of measurement by providing opportunities for students to

- practice telling time with analog and digital clocks (MP5);
- reason about proximity of time shown on clocks;
- begin to think about time passing or elapsed time;
- represent time on an analog clock (see Something to Think About) (MP5);
- develop strategies for determining how much time has passed (MP1);
- listen to strategies of others to acquire new strategies or refine their own (MP3);
- give feedback to others about their ideas (MP3); and
- become comfortable with the notion of more than one right answer.

WHAT TO DO

1. Prepare three different times shown on analog clocks. You can do this with a drawing, drawing on the downloadable master PDF, using the downloadable clock template slides, screenshots of a virtual manipulative/clock, or by taking a picture of a real-world manipulative and inserting it into a slide.
2. Display the three clocks. Ask students to identify which two clocks show times that are closest together, which two clocks show times that are farthest apart, and which one clock shows a time between the other clocks.
3. Have students discuss their thinking with a partner.
4. Bring the class together. Ask them to identify which are closest.
5. Record their ideas (e.g., clock A and B or clock A and C, etc.). After recording their ideas, ask students to justify their offerings. Note that during the discussion you might find it helpful to record the digital representation of each clock. You can do that first by having students tell you the time for each. Then, to discuss which are the closest you can ask questions like the following:
    - How did you think about the clocks?
    - What did you do first as you were comparing the clocks?
    - How did you know clock ___ and ___ are closest?
    - What time did the other clock show?
    - How much closer is clock ___ than clock ___ to clock ____?

6. Repeat the discussion for the other two comparisons (i.e., which two times are farthest apart and which time is between the others?)
7. Then, ask each student to think of a new time that is close to one of the clocks, far from one of the clocks, or between two of the clocks.
8. Once they think of a new time, have them share their idea with a partner.
9. Solicit a few new ideas from the group for any or all of the three conditions. It's possible, if not likely, that the initial discussion about the three clocks you present may take all of the time you allotted for the routine—especially when your class is first starting to work with telling time. If this happens, you can use the same clocks the next day and have students create new examples, carrying out the routine across two different classes.

SOMETHING TO THINK ABOUT: USING MANIPULATIVES DURING A ROUTINE

The routines in this book, along with most number routines, including Number Talks (Parrish, 2010), are intended to be mental exercises for good practice after students have shown understanding of a skill or concept. In most cases, students shouldn't be writing things in a journal or using manipulatives. That being said, this is one routine where passing out Judy Clocks or similar time manipulatives makes good sense. This is especially true during the "and More" portion of the routine where students create a new time that is close, far, or between the other times presented in the routine.

CLOSE, FAR, BETWEEN, AND MORE (VARIATIONS): KEEPING IT FRESH

One feature of quality practice is that it is varied (Bay-Williams & SanGiovanni, 2021). Varied practice means that students practice skills, concepts, and procedures on paper, they play games, they work with centers, and they engage with routines. And though these experiences or formats are varied, there is little question that changing the format alone satisfies the different challenges the human brain craves. This is a good move when a routine isn't especially high in terms of cognitive demand. It's a good move when you don't seem to be getting much "bang for your buck" with a routine. But, even when a routine proves to be a class favorite, don't be afraid to modify it a bit. Close, Far, Between, and More can be varied in quite a few ways like those shown here.

Variation A: Four Options

This first variation highlights two different ideas. The most obvious is that you can present more than three clocks for your students to consider. Offering a fourth clock opens the door to multiple right answers and potentially much livelier discussions. But this variation shows time across different hours as mentioned earlier. While the initial example used clocks within the 9 o'clock hour, the clocks here range from the 12 o'clock hour (clock B) to the 7 o'clock hour (clock C) assuming they all are within AM or PM. Again, that label is missing from these examples, but it can be easily added when needed. We choose to leave the AM/PM designation off for different reasons. First, students might learn to tell time before AM/PM is introduced. Second, it can "muddy the waters" when we're just trying to tell time on the clock. Yet, if you leave them off, you'll find at some point a student will raise the question themselves signaling to you that they're ready for the discussion of AM or PM. Also note that by leaving it off, even more answers are possible. For example, 8:30 AM is 8 hours from 12:30 AM (possibly farthest) whereas 8:30 AM is only 4 hours from 12:30 PM.

Variation B: Two and You

Just as you can add a clock to create more possibilities, you can take a clock away to narrow focus and lessen the rigor of the experience. Doing so doesn't lessen the value. It's a perfectly fine place for students to begin. In this variation, students still have to consider more than one possibility for near or far from clock A or B. The difference, of course, is that there is only one between time. And even with just two clocks you can still have students create new times that are near or far from one of the clocks.

Variation C: Mixed Clocks

This variation amps up the challenge a bit by mixing up digital and analog clocks. The value here is that students practice both representations at the right time. It creates a different experience. In using this variation, it will be interesting to see if students gravitate toward one representation or the other and it's fine if they do. After all, digital clocks are easier to read. But before you pose mixed representations with your class, you might find it beneficial to do all analog examples (like in the opening), then all digital (no examples given), before mixing like shown here. An interesting experience could be to present three analog clocks on one day and then three digital clocks the next day that have the same times as the analog clocks from the day before. Would students recognize that they're the same? Would they identify close, far, or between more quickly? Would they find it less challenging to think of new times?

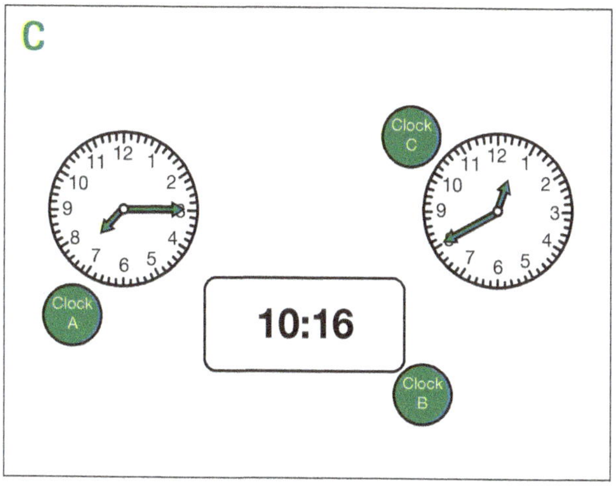

Variation D: Converting and Comparing

Other routines have talked about converting between measurement units, such as The Truth (Routine #6). This variation does that with units of time. Converting and comparing is certainly much more rigorous than the previous examples. An entry point into this experience would be to provide two or three times with the same unit (e.g., minutes) and one or two times presented in another unit (e.g., hours). Mixing the units (e.g., minutes, hours, days, etc.) within the same experience is probably the most difficult version though not necessarily. In this example, you would expect students to share that 90 minutes and 75 minutes are close together but that 3 hours (180 minutes) is close to 200 minutes too. Notice that the amount of time in each circle isn't labeled in this example. Remember that you don't have to label your clocks or times but that can make the group discussion easier to facilitate (see Something to Think About: Lettering Options in Routine #6).

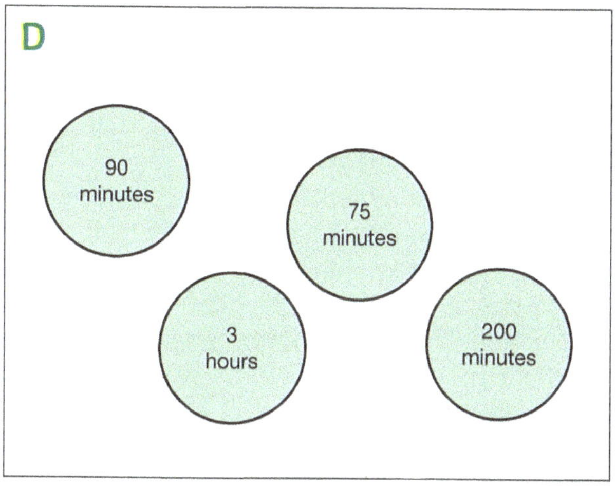

Variation E: Time in Later Grades

This variation shows multiple units of time (weeks, months, years). It would be a fine challenge for upper elementary school students. As mentioned with other conversion routines, it is a good idea to provide an anchor chart or conversion table. Ample exposure to these conversion tables helps students master them. It also lessens the cognitive load for comparing the durations in each circle. At first, it's wise to make the durations somewhat obvious so that students get comfortable. For example, you might use 2 weeks instead of 84 weeks in this example. That would be a good place to start because most students will almost instantly recognize that 2 weeks isn't close to 2 years. After they get comfortable with the experience, you can begin to make the durations more challenging.

E

Time	
1 year	365 days
1 year	12 months
1 year	52 weeks
1 week	7 days
1 day	24 hours
1 hour	60 minutes
1 minute	60 seconds

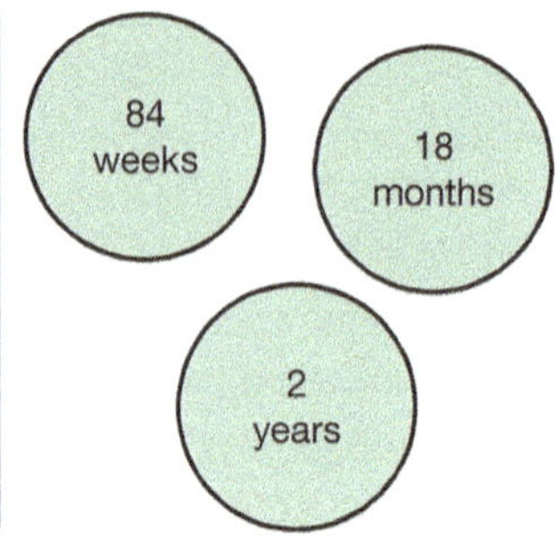

Variation F: Other Comparisons (With Conversions)

Close, Far, Between, and More is perfect for other types of conversions too. This example shows conversions with liquid volume. The measurement of 9 cups is far from 3 gallons, 15 quarts is close to 3 gallons, and 15 quarts is also between 3 gallons and 9 cups. But there's one other twist here that you might notice. The black circle is for the "and More" or created measurement. It requires a specific unit of cups. It's an intentional twist offered for a few reasons. First, you might find that your students always create a close, far, or between of a certain measurement unit. When this happens, you can tell them which unit they must use, in this case cups. Also be on the lookout for students to give a simple tweak to their earlier thinking (e.g., 3 cups is far from 3 gallons because 9 cups was far from 3 gallons). It's ok if they approach it in this way. If they do, start to think about how you can increase the challenge (e.g., give all measurements in cups, quarts, and gallons as shown but require the new measurement to be in pints.

F

Capacity	
1 cup	8 fluid ounces
1 pint	2 cups
1 quart	2 pints
1 gallon	4 quarts

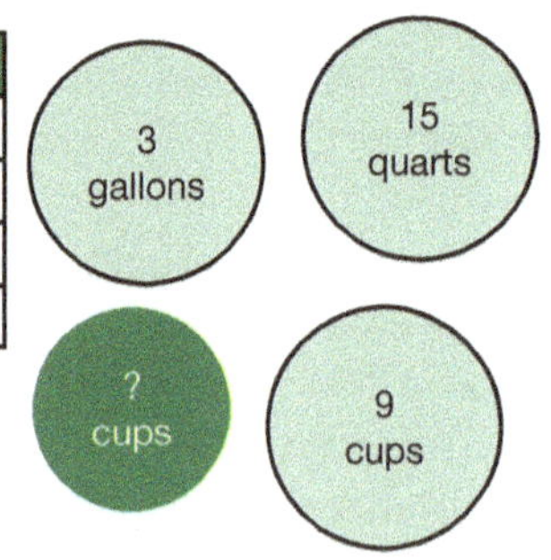

Variation G: Mass

This variation provides practice reading a scale to determine and compare the mass of objects. Reading scales like the ones shown asks students to use the same kind of reasoning as when they use a number line. You can begin with whole number intervals like these, where students have to figure out that there are 10 sections between each multiple of 100 and then use that to identify the weights as 280 grams (block A), 450 grams (block B), and 140 grams (block C). When first learning about grams, consider pulling out a digital scale and weighing some familiar objects, such as a pencil or notebook, to get a sense of what 280 grams feels like if measured in hand.

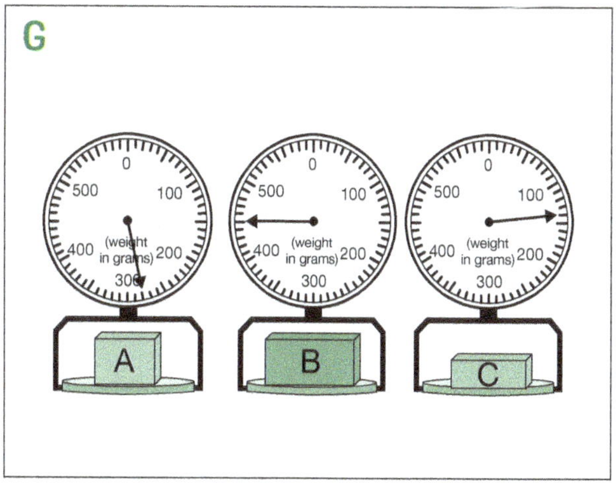

Variation H: Volume in Graduated Cylinders

As students learn to measure the mass of objects, they also learn to measure the volume of liquid using tools like measuring cups and graduated cylinders. This is often their introduction to liters and milliliters, units that students may rarely encounter in their day-to-day life, and even then in only the occasional science lesson. This variation allows students to examine graduated cylinders and use the scales on them, which are essentially vertical number lines. As with other routines, be sure that your students first explore real measuring cups and graduated cylinders to help them develop a mental image of what a milliliter, liter, cup, or ounce is like, which can be used to aid their ability to estimate liquid volume.

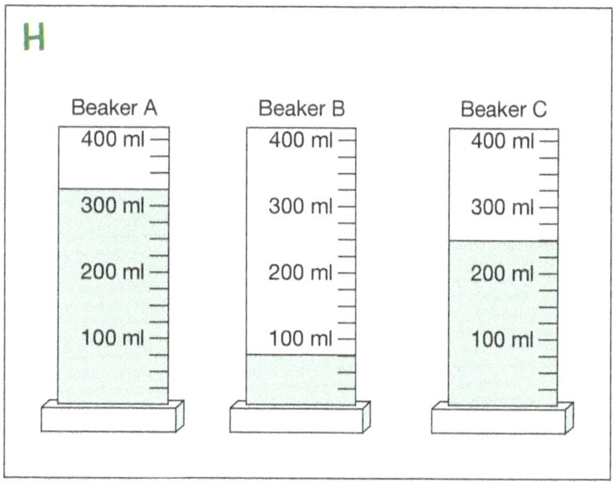

Variation I: Angles

Close, Far, Between, and More is good for building understanding of angles and angle measurements. Often, instruction emphasizes angles as a static representation, a geometric figure formed by a pair of connected rays, which fails to develop the idea that angles are dynamic. "Angles are created by a turning motion, that the amount of turning is connected to the number of degrees in the angle measure, and that an angle is related to part of a circle" (Gay et al., 2022, p. 560). This variation presents angles inside of circles and uses the knowledge that a circle measures 360° to estimate and compare the presented angles. It can also provide an opportunity to connect fractions and angles, such as with angle A. Students may first "see" angle A as part of a circle rather than a number of degrees. In other words it looks like it is about one-third of a circle. Using that idea, they can divide 360 by 3 deducing that angle A is 120 degrees.

I

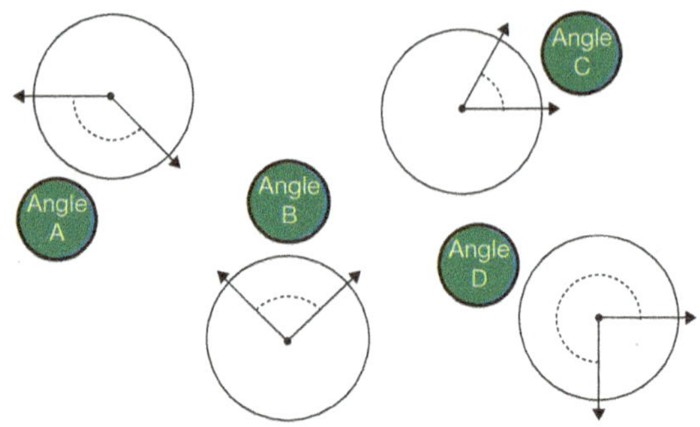

ROUTINE 13

IT'S ABOUT

ABOUT THE ROUTINE

Estimation should be a daily feature of mathematics class. To make this happen, teachers create estimation jars and use quick images for students to practice estimating quantity. Teachers ask students to estimate results before calculating. Teachers have students estimate length, weight, elapsed time, and capacity. Estimating area is a great option too, and a routine like this one is great for doing it. A nice thing about this routine is that your students don't have to "master" area to work with it as the routine itself naturally reinforces the concept while building skill with estimation and reasoning.

Start with rectangles, especially as students first learn about area. The rectangle in this example is 72 square units. It might be a bit too large for the first few experiences with the routine. Instead, you might use rectangles that are 5 x 6, 5 x 3, or even 3 x 4. Those smaller rectangles should be easier to estimate and will certainly be easier to count or calculate at the end.

To implement the routine, pose a rectangle with one square unit as shown. Ask students to estimate how many square units it would take to fill the space inside the large rectangle. Have them share and then solicit a few estimates from the group. Then, reveal a bit more as shown in the left example. Have students revise or stay with their estimate. Confirm their ideas before showing a bit more of the area, with a full row and column, as shown in the example on the right. While there is no limit to how much you should show with each new reveal we suggest starting with parts of each row and column before showing them fully. But feel

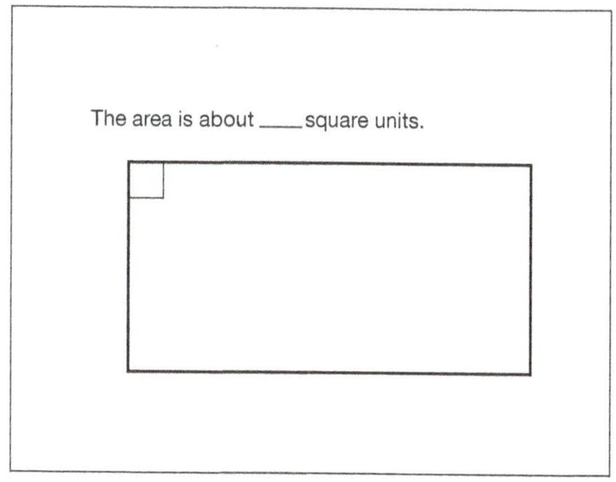

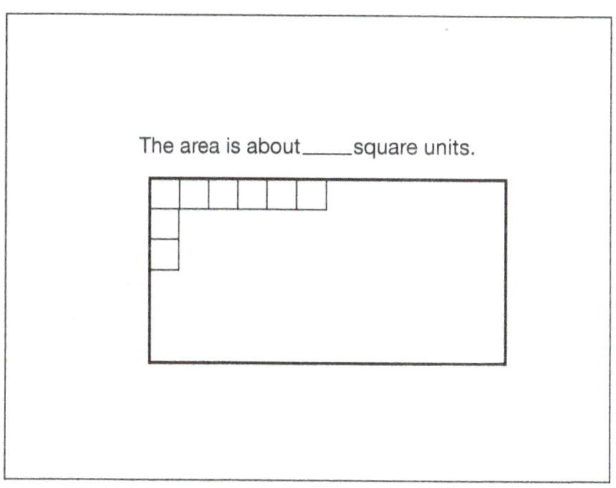

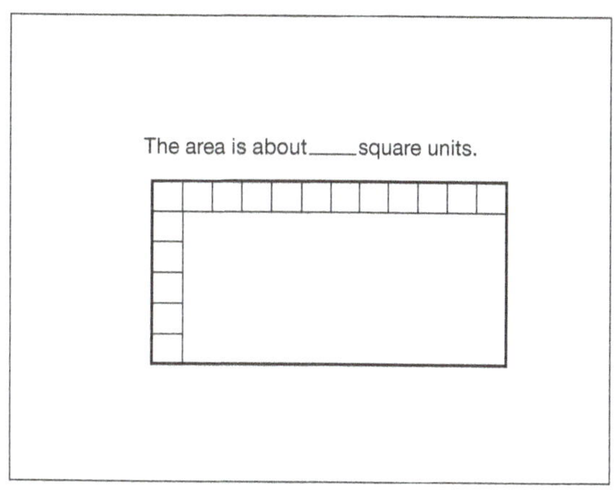

online resources All routines can be downloaded for your use at **https://companion.corwin.com/courses/jumpstartroutines-geometry**

free to adjust as you like. Also note that you don't have to share the top row and leftmost column though they are good starting points. In time, you might feature a center row or a far right column.

Listen to the strategies students use for their estimates, especially with the beginning image and the first reveal. For example, they may talk about the number of rows and columns. Some might speak to multiplying the rows by the columns or vice versa even if you haven't formally introduced that idea yet. Others might look for chunks within the rectangle. For example, they might imagine how much space four squares (2 x 2) take up and then build from there (this strategy is featured in Variation C).

Show the fully gridded rectangle after you and your class have discussed strategies, estimates, and revisions for one or two reveals. You can count the number of units together if it is a reasonable size. For larger examples, like the one shown, you

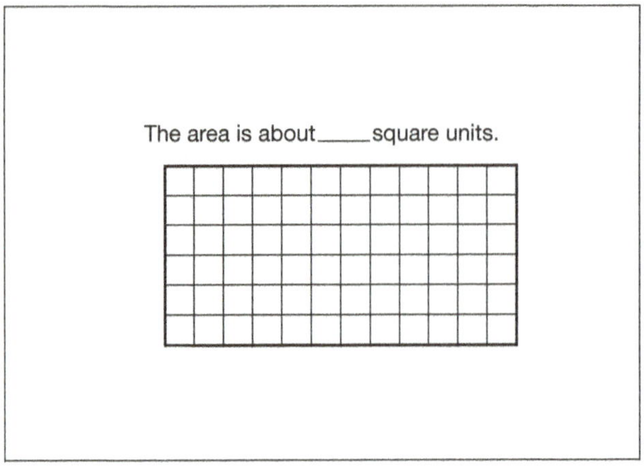

might choose to simply tell them that there are 72 units in the rectangle. Telling them, especially with larger rectangles, helps you make the most of your instructional time. Regardless of how the exact total is shared with students it must be shared to help them grow their estimation skills.

HOW THIS ROUTINE HELPS

This routine deepens understanding of measurement by providing opportunities for students to

- reinforce the concept of area;
- develop comfort and confidence with finding area;
- find area by counting (or tiling) and computing;
- estimate the area of figures (MP2);
- develop strategies for estimating area (MP2);
- determine reasonableness of estimates and exact values (MP2);
- construct and critique arguments for strategies and solutions (MP3); and
- think strategically and critically to solve problems (MP1).

WHAT TO DO

1. Create rectangles with one square unit showing and rectangles with parts of a row and column, full rows and columns, and fully tiled. Read about how to do this with or without technology in the variations section that follows.
2. Pose the first rectangle with one unit showing. Ask students to estimate the area of the rectangle with this one grid.
3. Have students share their estimates with a partner and then solicit some from the whole class. Record estimates on the board. Briefly discuss the strategies students use for making their estimate.
4. Show a new image that reveals some of the rows and columns. Have students revise their estimates, if they would like. Record some new estimates. Underline, circle, or check estimates that students do not want to revise.
5. Repeat #4 with a new image that shows a full row and column.
6. After the last partial area is shown and estimates are in place, show the fully tiled area. With smaller rectangles, count the units to find the total area. With larger rectangles, simply tell students the area.

7. Once the exact area is known. Ask students questions like the following:
   - How did our estimates compare to the actual area?
   - Does the actual area surprise you? Why?
   - How did your estimates change as you learned more about the number of units in a row and column?
   - Which estimates would you say were good estimates? What makes them good estimates?

SOMETHING TO THINK ABOUT: ROUTINES IN THE BUILDING THINKING CLASSROOM

Mathematics classes should be thinking rich environments where students engage with each other to solve problems and communicate their ideas, strategies, and solutions (Liljedahl, 2020). Routines are the perfect complement to daily lessons in a thinking classroom. When used to start class, they set the stage and expectation for what you want your students to do throughout the full, focus lesson for the day. Routines require students to engage, discuss, and think! Routines position students to be the doers of math. Your work is to pose a prompt, facilitate the process, ask good questions, and clarify what they share. You want to withhold your strategy or solution path until they've had a good chance to do the math on their own. Executing a routine (and lesson) like this is the perfect way to reduce mimicry, building toward student agency and understanding.

IT'S ABOUT (VARIATIONS): HOW TO MAKE IT

There are a few different ways to make the figures and images for this routine. One option is to make a square in a PowerPoint slide that you copy and paste repeatedly to make a larger figure. Then, use dark lines to trace the outer edge of the figure before deleting some of the "inner" squares that form the grid. When you do this, be sure to copy a few slides so you have images to reveal along the way. A low-tech alternative is to use graph paper or centimeter grid paper with the latter likely being the better option due to the size of the grids. There are different ways to create a figure. One is to create a figure on grid paper and cut it out. Then, trace that figure on a piece of construction paper or something similar. You can add a square, row, or columns to the construction paper for students to make their estimates with and then show the figure cut from graph paper to know the exact area. Also, you can reuse a figure by simply changing the size of the square units to estimate as shown in Variation D.

Variation A: Be Clever

This variation is shared to give you some ideas about how you can cleverly dismantle misperceptions or make connections and build relationships. First, this variation doesn't offer just one unit. There is a full row and a full column for students to consider. You might think they'll simply multiply the two rows but that isn't needed. One could think about counting by 8s (i.e., the columns) or by 5s (i.e., the rows). In other words, it's a misperception to think they have to know the formula to estimate or find the area. But, there's more. Often, rows and columns are shown on the left (column) and top (row). In A1, the left column is used but a middle-ish row is provided. While this shouldn't be that big of a difference, you may find that your students have made some generalizations that are disrupted by this subtle shift.

The reveal for revising estimates changes in this variation too. It doesn't show any full columns, but it does show half of the full rows. Showing this much might be a nice way to help students as they find their footing with estimating area. It's also shared to show how connections or relationships can be developed through a routine like this. It would happen after the last image is shown, and the actual area of 40 is shared. Then, you can point out that the reveal showed half of 40 or 20. You can also point out that 4 rows of 5 made 20 (a basic fact students have likely experienced) which was half of 8 rows of 5 (a basic fact students might have trouble recalling). Don't feel compelled to do a mini lesson on examples of connections like this. Simply point them out and keep moving.

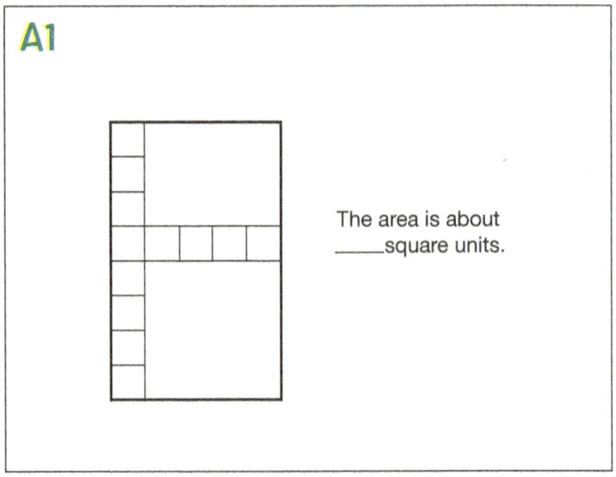

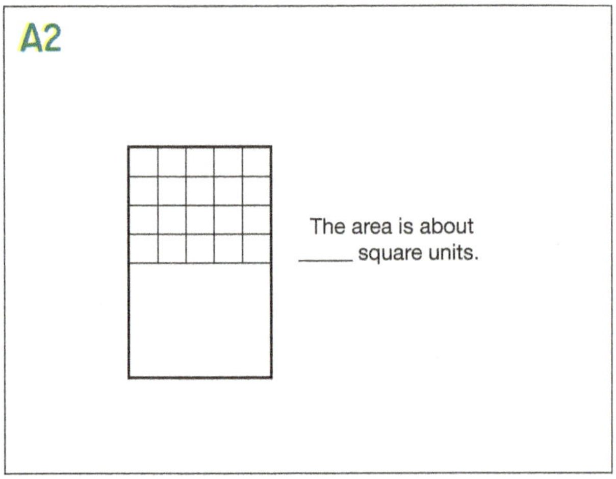

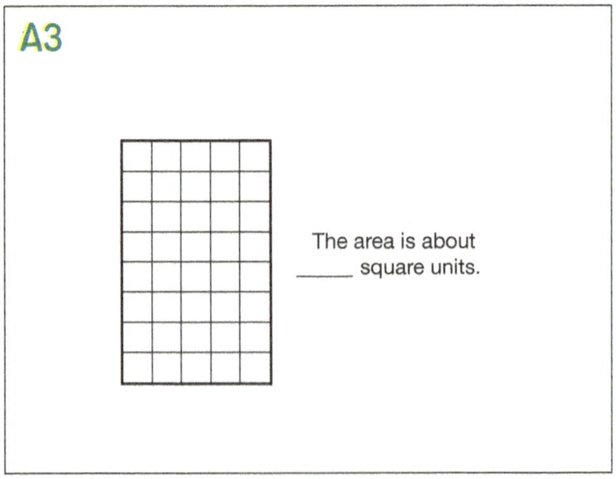

Variation B: Irregular Figures

Irregular figures are perfect for this routine too. In this example, a long row of 8 square units is shown across the top for students' initial estimates. The reveal, shown In B2 might be a nice option. Here, the column is on the right to help students estimate the parts more easily. Remember, composing the two rectangles is one approach to finding the area of the irregular figure. Some students prefer to find area of irregular figures by thinking about a large area and then taking away a missing space. You can even provide reveals that help students "see" those missing pieces. An example is shown in B3. We don't suggest using both the upper-right and lower-left reveals at the same time but rather just one. They're offered to give you more ideas about what you might reveal and why.

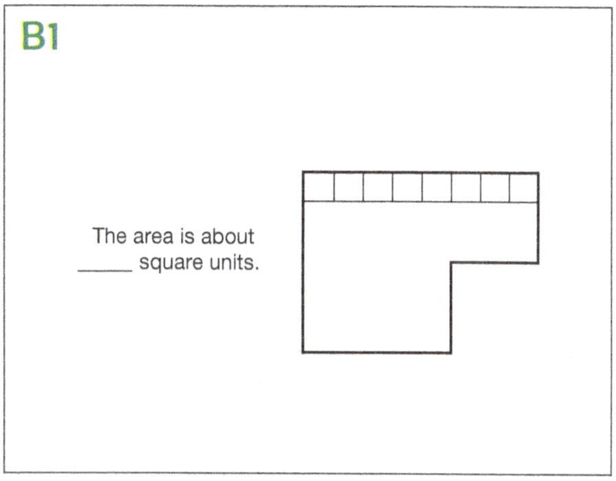

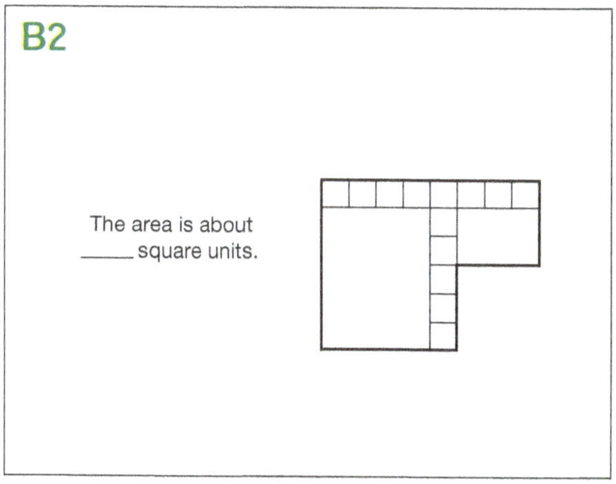

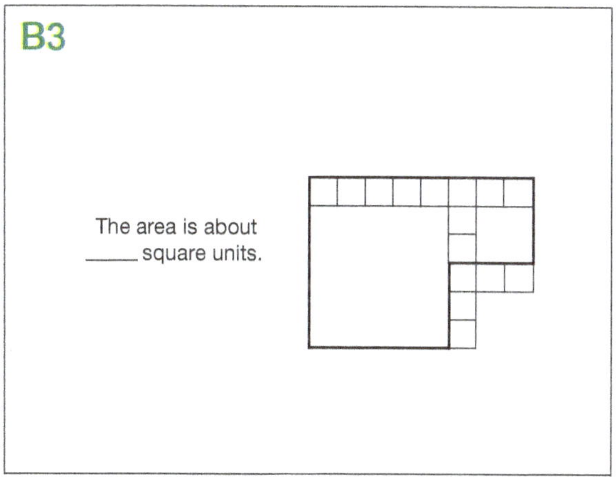

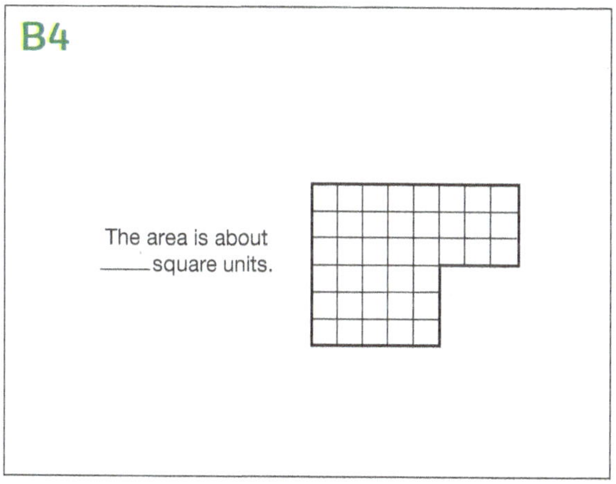

Variation C: Chunks and No Reveals

Variation C has two distinctions from previous examples of the routine. An irregular figure is posed with a known chunk of 6 square units. This chunk is convenient because it is the same size as the missing pieces from the larger rectangle. More importantly, the larger figure is made up of those chunks. They serve as a good reference for making an estimate. Students can think about how many of those 6 square unit chunks are in the entire figure. There are 8 chunks of 6 so the actual area is 48 square units. Know that students might at first think there are 6 chunks which is totally fine! Also note that in this variation, there is no reveal. The chunk of 6 is the only amount given to students. There will be no revising of estimates. Removing the reveals when using chunks seems to make the most sense but you certainly could use them if you like.

C1

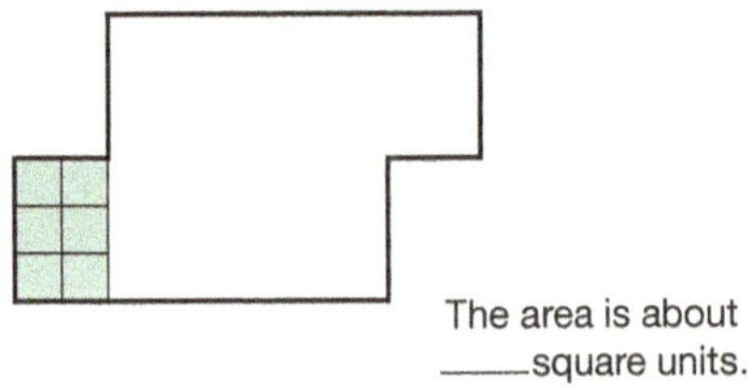

C2

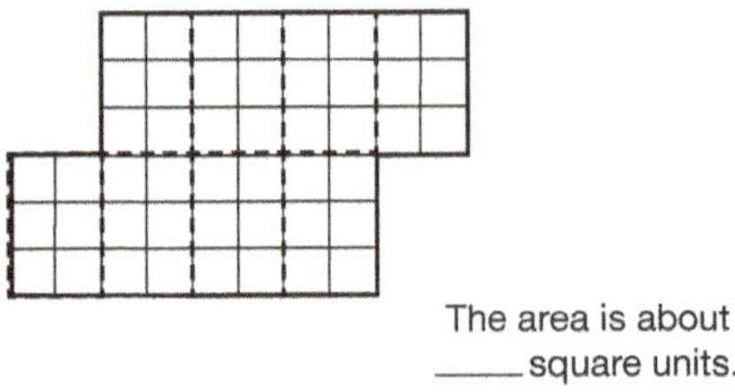

Variation D: Different Square Units

Asking students to estimate the number of two different-sized square units is an advanced variation of this routine. This variation is good for students who have had lots of estimation practice. So much so, they can reason with different sizes. They may estimate the number of larger square units (14) and then think about its relationship to the smaller unit (i.e., 4 times larger) rather than thinking about the entire figure all over again. You can help them start to do this by telling them that the larger square is equal to four smaller squares. But we suggest you don't do this. Instead, give the variation some time and see if any of your students come up with this suggestion on their own first. Also know that if you are using this advanced version, it's unlikely that you need to provide reveals any longer, hence none are shown.

D1

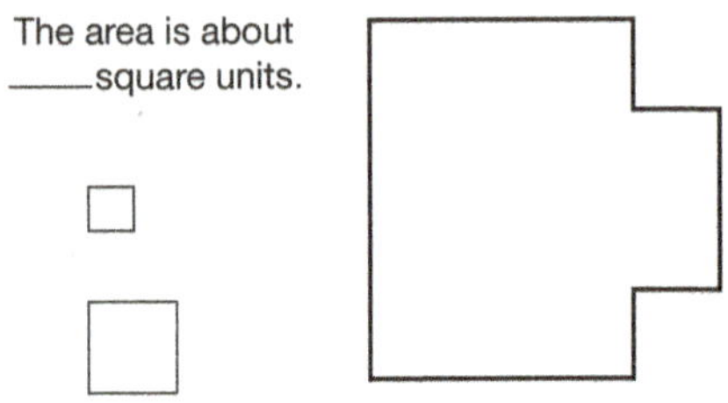

D2

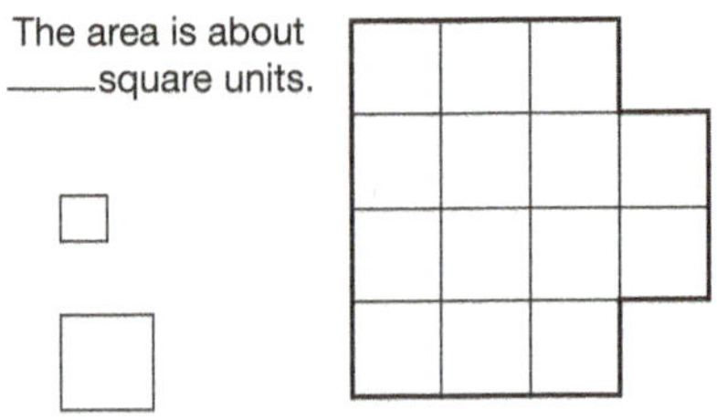

D3

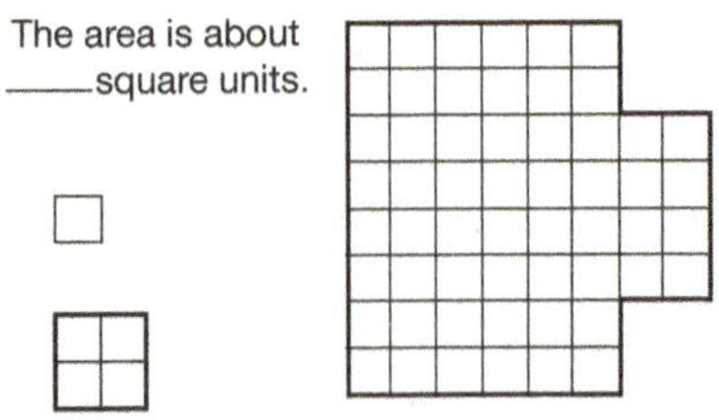

Variation E: Linear Measurements

Area isn't a measurement standard in primary grades but measuring length is. This variation shows how this routine can be changed to feature linear measurement in those primary grades. It starts with a line and a cube. Students estimate how many cubes long the line is. Then, more cubes are revealed (images E2 and E3) so that students can revise their estimates. E4 shows a neat twist after the exact length is found. In it, you see a cube and a paper clip. Let's say the line turns out to be 20 cubes long. Then, students would have to estimate how many paper clips. They may try to offer an exact number, but you should also encourage estimates like "a few more than 20" because the paper clip is a little longer. And though this example shows objects made with technology, you can just as easily implement this routine with a piece of string, real cubes, and real paper clips. Keep in mind that this example features nonstandard units but most manipulative cubes are 1 inch long, meaning they're the perfect bridge to standard units.

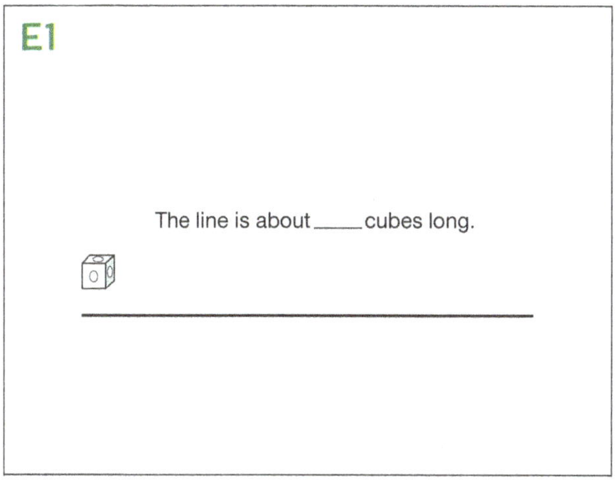

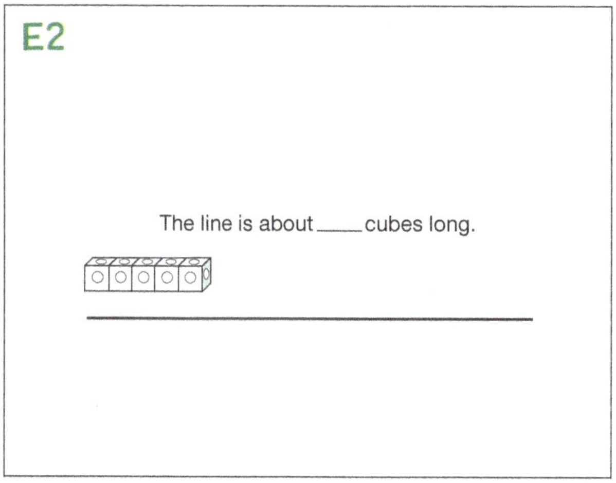

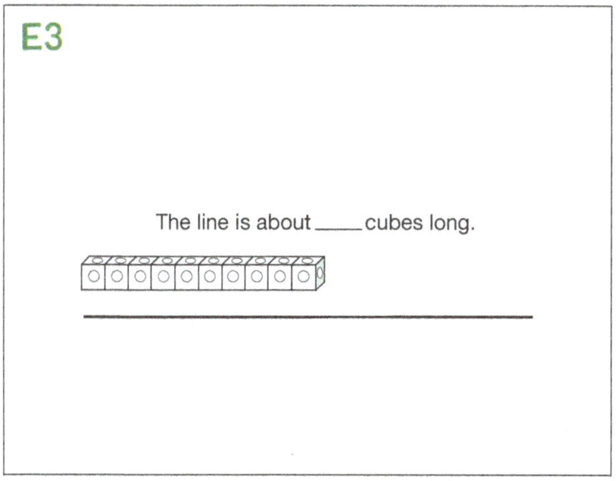

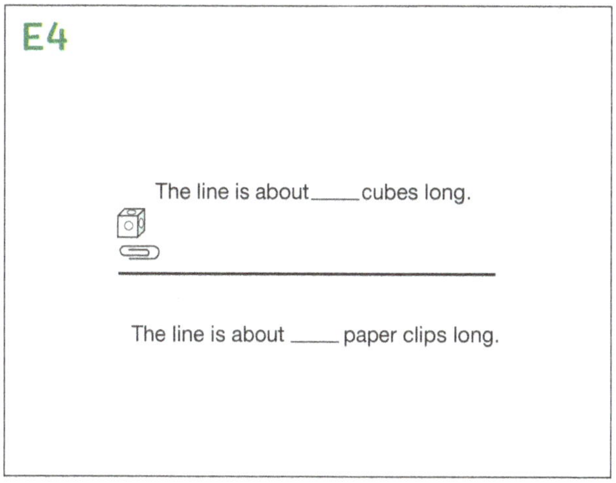

Variation F: Volume

It's About is a good routine for estimating volume. As with area, it starts with a figure and a single cubic unit. Students make an estimate with that much information before more information is revealed (image F2). Students revise their estimates, if necessary, before more is revealed (image F3). Remember, there is no one right way to carry out this or any other routine. The reveals shown here highlight the dimensions of a prism. You could just as easily reveal a few more columns across the back of the image or a small chunk for students to use as a reference for finding the volume like the idea in Variation C.

F1

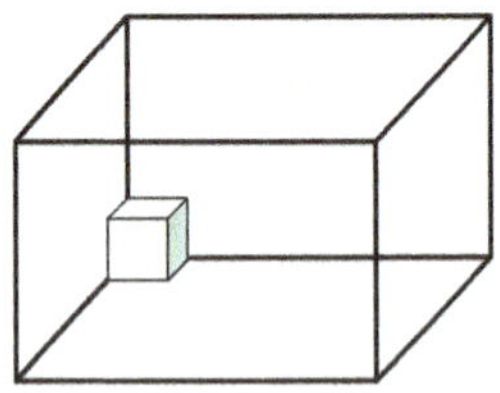

The volume is about_____cubic units.

F2

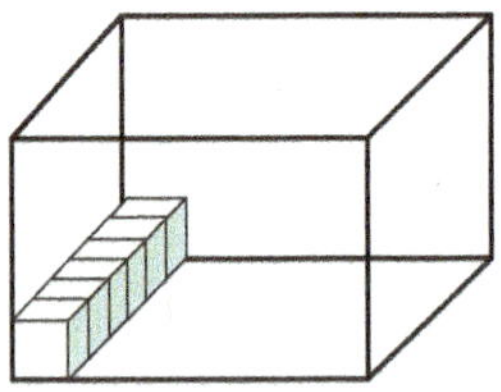

The volume is about_____cubic units.

F3

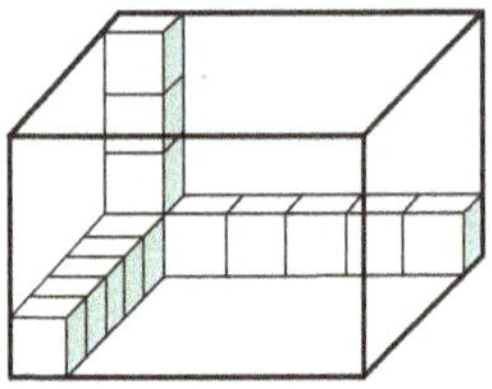

The volume is about_____cubic units.

F4

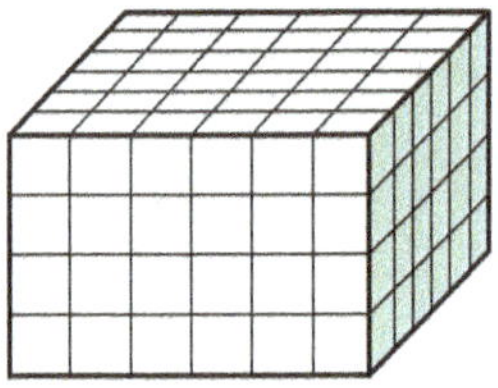

The volume is about_____cubic units.

Variation G: Angles

Estimating angles is another option for this routine. It would be hard to leverage the idea of revealing more information for students to revise their estimated measures of the angles. But there are other options to help students. The angles in G1 show one way. In each of them there is a light gray reference for 90 degrees. Students can use that to estimate how far the angle has opened. The left angle is just over halfway so students should reason about a number just over 45 or half of 90. The angle on the right is a little more so an estimate of 110 degrees or so is perfectly reasonable. The image in G2 shows another way you might go about estimating with angle measures. In this example, you would tell students the angle measure of the solid angle and then have them use that information to estimate the dotted angle. The angle on the left is 86 degrees so the dotted angle is about half, or 43 degrees. That also matches up well with the light gray, 90-degree reference. The angle on the right works a little differently. The given information here is that the dark angle is 20 degrees, and the dotted angle is obtuse. That can help with the dotted angle because both seem to be about the same. So, one could estimate that the dotted angle is about 160 degrees or 20 degrees less than 180.

G1

G2

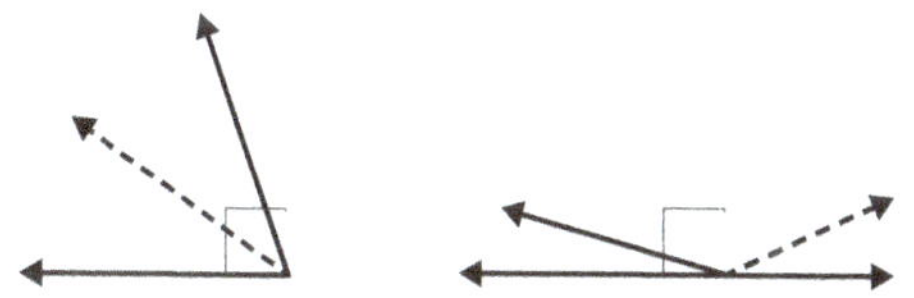

ROUTINE 14 MORE OR LESS

ABOUT THE ROUTINE

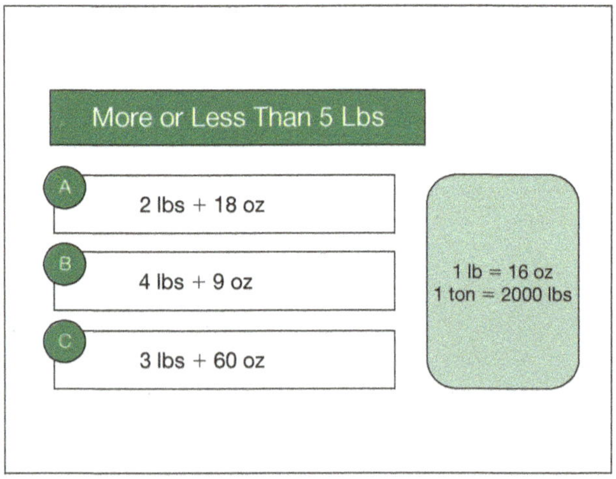

More or Less (Bay-Williams & SanGiovanni, 2021; SanGiovanni, 2020) is a routine where students determine whether an expression (e.g., 27 × 4) is more or less than a benchmark or target (e.g., 100) using estimating and reasoning (e.g., 25 × 4 is 100 so 27 will be more) rather than exact calculations. The routine provides practice with estimating and mental math so that students develop number sense and fluency. This routine takes that experience and blends it with converting between measurement units. The latter is a measurement standard that can baffle students and even challenge adults as they try to remember the number of ounces in a cup or pint when buying something at the grocery store. Conversions present a significant challenge because they are typically all wrapped into a single standard addressed through one, possibly two lessons. Realistically, remembering conversions and skillfully moving between them doesn't come from those lessons but rather lots of quality practice like with this routine.

One thing you'll notice right away in this anchor example as well as the variations that follow is that the unit conversion is provided on the slide. This is done with intention. First and foremost, it is an aid for students who can't remember the conversion rate. Second, many (if not all) state assessments provide conversion and formula tables to students while they take the test. After all, the point of the standard is to understand how to convert and when to apply it, though it can often be misunderstood as memorizing the conversion rates. The third reason for providing it is that as students see (and use) the conversion table over and over again they are more likely to actually remember the conversion rate; at the least they become comfortable with the idea of conversions, know how the information in the chart works, and can use such a tool on the assessment when they can't remember.

Another thing you'll notice is that each comparison statement (e.g., 2 lbs + 8 oz) is labeled with a letter. This is done intentionally to support discussion. It is easier and clearer to direct and redirect students to "statement A" rather than saying "2 pounds plus 8 ounces" over and over again. Labels are also helpful for simplifying the discussion, especially when so many numbers are at play, or for pointing out similarities between two statements. For example, you might say, "The number of ounces in C is like A because they are both more than 1 pound."

Also notice that there are three comparisons in the example. Three isn't a magic number. You can provide fewer if you like. But it is a good idea to

online resources All routines can be downloaded for your use at **https://companion.corwin.com/courses/jumpstartroutines-geometry**

offer more than one because you can allow students to choose between the statements they want to compare and then give them a choice about which one they want to discuss first. We have found that three is usually a good number to offer. We have also found that sometimes three can cause great discussion but also eat up a lot of instructional time. Remember, these routines are to be brief bursts of practice. When time begins to slip away, pause the experience and resume the discussion the next day. However, it's understandable if you want your students to engage with all of the statements you provide. If so, you should give one statement at a time because providing all three can be overwhelming to some students and distracting to others.

HOW THIS ROUTINE HELPS

This routine deepens understanding of measurement by providing opportunities for students to

- practice converting between units of measure;
- practice using conversion tables or tools (MP2);
- estimate sums, differences, products, and quotients (MP2);
- ask themselves if a conversion or solution is reasonable (MP6);
- determine efficient strategies for computing and converting (MP2);
- compare estimates with actual results;
- determine whether their computations are accurate (MP6);
- defend their reasoning and consider the strategies of others (MP3); and
- give feedback to others about their ideas (MP3).

WHAT TO DO

1. Present a conversion table or chart on the slide or with an anchor chart.
2. Present two or three conversion statements for students and a comparison number.
3. Have students choose a conversion statement and compare it to the "More or Less" number. Alternative: Present the first statement for students to compare.
4. Have students determine whether the statement is more or less. They should be asked to do this mentally unless a specific accommodation is called for.
5. Have students share their ideas with a partner before having a whole class discussion.
6. Hold a whole class discussion about the statements. Ask students to share how they made their decisions. As students share their thinking, it is important that we probe thinking and ask clarifying questions rather than ask questions to establish how we thought about the expression. Questions might include the following:
   - How did you determine your comparison?
   - How did you estimate?
   - Why did you think about the numbers in those ways?
   - How did your estimation compare to the given value?
   - Why was it easier to start with the ___ and convert the ___ instead of the other way around?
   - Might there have been another way to compare? Why was your approach more efficient for you?

- How does your thinking compare to (another student's)?
- How are the different strategies similar?
- What is a strategy you might use next time? Why?

7. Honor and explore both accurate and flawed reasoning.
8. Consider providing exact values after discussion so that students can compare and confirm their more or less estimates.

SOMETHING TO THINK ABOUT: ANCHOR CHARTS FOR CONVERSIONS

As mentioned in the opening, this routine features conversion charts and tables for students to use as they compare statements. You can provide them in the slide deck, or you can create an anchor chart and display it near the routine. Before students work with this routine, they must first learn about conversions, which can be done in a few lessons. Anchor charts that capture the experiences of those lessons are powerful tools for students to use during the routine. In fact, creating the chart with students rather than purchasing one to display is better instructional practice altogether (SanGiovanni et al., 2023).

MORE OR LESS (VARIATIONS): ALL SORTS OF CONVERSIONS

When you think about it, there are a lot of conversion rates to remember across measurement attributes (e.g., linear, mass, etc.). Some attributes, like liquid volume, have a bunch of conversions within them (e.g., cups to pints, gallons to cups, quarts to gallons, etc.). It's no wonder that students and adults are challenged to remember them all. This is where a routine like this one can help. Remembering the relationships will get a boost when they are all practiced across the year. In order to do this, you'll need a collection of variations like those shown in the following examples.

Variation A: Sequence and Support

Before we get into the different conversions you can practice in this routine, we want to spotlight some other things you might consider to support and grow your students' skill, reasoning, and efficiency. In this variation, you see the pounds are constant while the ounces change. What's done differently here is that all students would work with statement A while the other statements remain hidden. The reasoning is discussed and a conclusion is made (e.g., 3 pounds and less than a pound don't make 5 pounds). Then, the next statement (B) is shown. The goal here is that students don't have to give it much more thought because they build off the reasoning from the first statement. Then, a third statement is given and they again build on the established reasoning. Sequencing in this way can help galvanize student thinking. It can also help expedite the routine because each new offering isn't a new problem altogether.

There's another important aspect of this variation that you surely noticed. On the right side, there is a function table that offers exact calculations. Sure, a table like this won't be on a state assessment but this routine is about practice. Even with the chart students have to think! Look at statement C. There is no exact conversion; however, students can reason that 75 ounces is between 4 and 5 pounds and that statement C should total something between 7 and 8 pounds, which is more than 5. When you use a function table like this, consider building it briefly with students before you show the statements. In other words, before showing the three statements offer a blank table with pounds and ounces. Tell them that 1 pound is 16 ounces. Then, ask how many ounces two pounds equals. Try not to linger. Give them a moment to think and then tell them or model using a calculator to establish the total. Build the chart together and then use it to make the comparisons.

A

More or Less Than 5 Lbs

A. 3 lbs + 9 oz

B. 3 lbs + 21 oz

C. 3 lbs + 75 oz

Pounds	Ounces
1	16
2	32
3	48
4	64
5	80

Variation B: Miles and Miles

Remembering the number of feet or yards in a mile for adults can be hard. Now, imagine that you're 9 years old and don't have much experience with lengths like miles because you don't drive a car. Then, to complicate matters the conversion rates are not nice, neat numbers. That's where this version comes in handy. Here, students compare yards to miles (statement A), feet to miles (statement B), and a combination of the two (statement C). You could provide them with a calculator to make the work quick, simpler, and (hopefully) more accurate. Or you might help them reframe the conversion rates in the provided chart as "about" statements. In other words, 1 mile is about 2,000 yards or about 5,000 feet. Thinking of a conversion in this way can help you determine whether your work is reasonable. A most powerful way to do this is to first estimate the conversions, evaluate the statements, and then use a calculator to see how everything checks out.

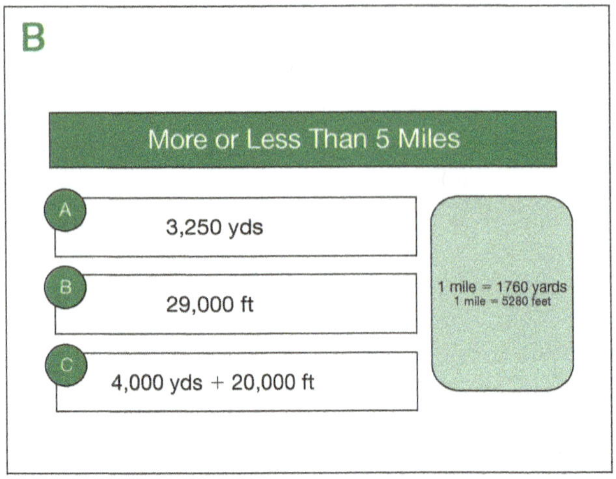

Variation C: Liquid Volume

Conversions with liquid volume is another natural choice for this routine. In this example, a full chart of conversions between the different units is provided. Offering such a chart helps students practice sifting through all lines and finding the one they need for the statement they are considering. Like Variation B, you see that you can provide simple comparisons like the first two statements or combinations of units that have to be converted and compared. The first two allow for different solution paths. For example, students might multiply 4 (gallons) by 4 quarts to establish that A is more than 12 quarts. Alternatively, a student might argue that 12 quarts divided by 4 equals 3 gallons which is less than statement A. As you know, both are accurate approaches but sometimes students fall into traps of thinking that there is only one way to work with conversions and comparisons. Your students will benefit from exposure to both. And, if it doesn't come from the group, you can offer an alternative for them to consider. Just remember that you don't want to insinuate that one approach is "the way."

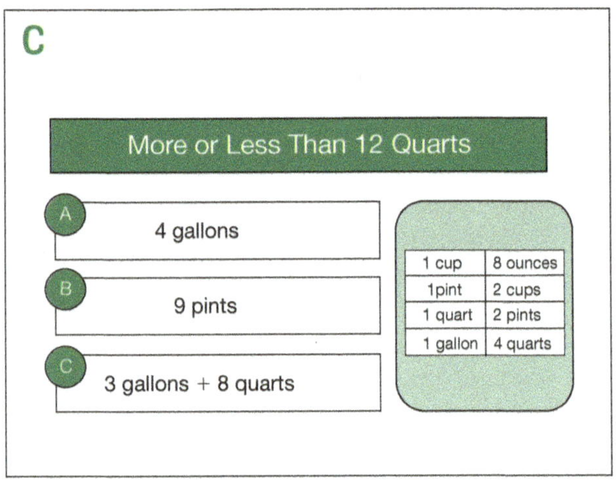

Variation D: Comprehensive Chart With Focused Conversion

Variation D is closer to where you might want to get to, but it certainly isn't the place to start. Assuming your students have worked, in isolation, with all of the conversions highlighted in this variation you then want to begin to mix up ideas. Granted the target comparison (10,000 pounds) and the comparison statements all go after pounds and tons; the chart on the right brings in every comparison students have experienced. It can seem overwhelming if they haven't had time to work with all of them. And though the resource on a state assessment might not be as condensed as what you see in the image, all of these conversions are presented in the same space meaning students have to find the right attribute, the right conversion, and then work from there. This variation can be a bridge to the next variation.

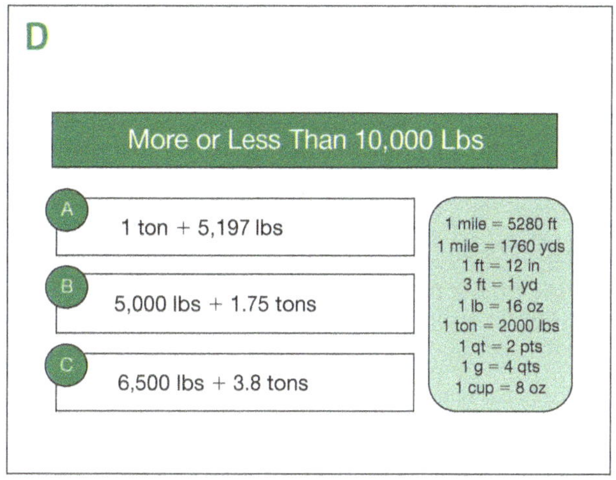

Variation E: All Mixed Up (Same Attribute)

This variation can be a relatively challenging experience for elementary students who rush to calculate exacts without pausing to think. Here, they have to compare a variety of different units within a measurement. But the challenge is offset with some hopefully obvious comparisons. Take for example comparison E. There's no calculation needed at all. Yards are longer than feet and there are the same amount of both. In C, miles are very much longer than feet so C should take almost no time to consider. And yes, there are six comparisons to make which could seem daunting to a fourth grader but as they talk about the different comparisons you can debrief the feelings of angst when presented with so many things to consider. Point out that sometimes things aren't as complicated as they seem. Also encourage them so simply start somewhere and chip away at the work.

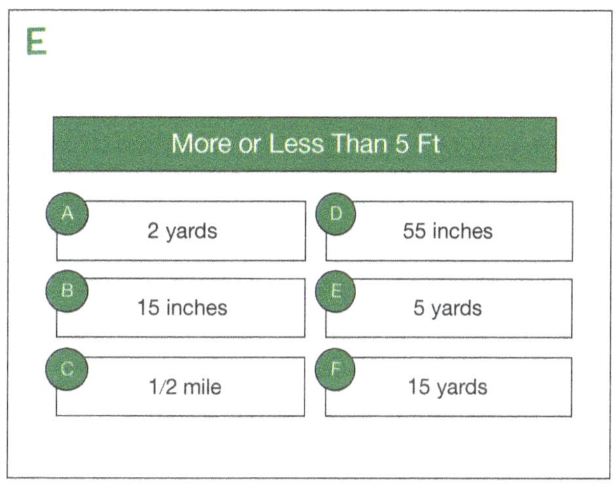

Variation F: Elapsed Time

It may seem like there is never enough time to practice time (bad humor intended). In reality, we can use these routines to do just that. Variation F shows how elapsed time might work with More or Less. A nice thing to practice is the use of common elapsed time chunks like 45 minutes, 75 minutes, and 90 minutes because they come often in our lives. But, the place to start might be simple conversions of hours and minutes. For example, you might ask students to compare an elapsed time to 60, 120, or 180 minutes. That might be something like comparing 180 minutes with 3:25 to 5:25. In time (bad pun intended), you can combine hours (multiples of 60) and a half hour. There is no wrong way to do it. Start simple, find success, and amp up the challenge.

F

More or Less Than 75 Minutes

A. 12:40 to 1:15

B. 9:20 to 10:15

C. 3:05 to 4:35

Variation G: Other Measurement Topics

As you might imagine, there is no end to the estimations and comparisons you can feature in this routine. Here are two last variations that fit perfectly with the content in this book. In G1 you see volumes for students to compare. Understandably, some students will try to find exact answers but that isn't necessary. Look at the prism in option A. An exact isn't needed. 4 × 10 = 40 and 40 × 10 = 400. The width is more than 10 and the depth is more than 10 so the volume of the prism will be more than 400 cubic units. Similar reasoning can be applied to the other figures as well as the areas of the rectangles in G2. You will have students who find one and then "eyeball" the others. Push back on that thinking by focusing on the numbers. For example, figure C has an area of 24 ft^2 because 4 × 6 is 24. By the way, this is also a good way to reinforce fact practice.

G1

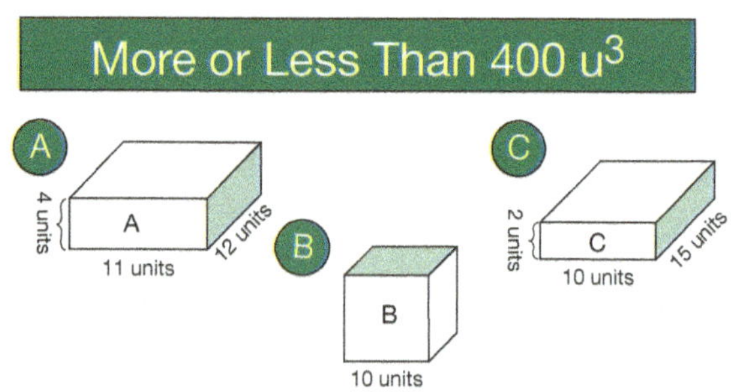

G2

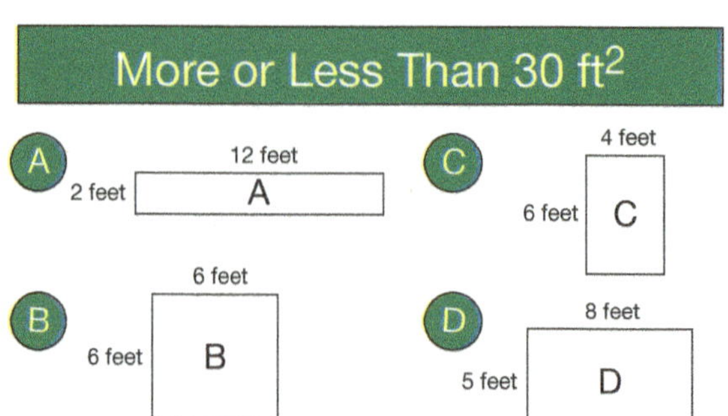

ROUTINE 15

THIS OR THAT?

ABOUT THE ROUTINE

There are few, if any, people who haven't played the game "would you rather?" Often, it's played with outlandish choices causing one to consider which is truly the better choice. Players quickly defend their thinking with reasoning that is sometimes rational and sometimes not. There are mathematical versions that ask students to pick one group of base ten blocks over another or to tell which basic fact is greater than another. Often, the choices are rather mundane and the reasoning in these versions is nothing more than recall. This or That? is a take on would you rather in which students have to determine whether they would want one thing over another by comparing measurements. Like the number sense routine of the same name (SanGiovanni & Milou, 2018) these comparisons are grounded in reasoning about number and conversions. In some cases, students will estimate. In other comparisons, students will have to calculate exact values. There will be times when exacts are perfect and other times when exact calculations are simply inefficient for making a choice.

The featured example compares conversions of liquid measurements. In the "ancient" past, teachers used hokey gimmicks, like "gallon man," so that students would remember the relationships. Practicing them repeatedly, buoyed by a conversion anchor chart, like the one shown in the example, is probably the better approach to develop and retain skill with relationships between these measurement units.

This or That?

Your Favorite Juice

THIS	THAT
3 cups	2 pints
13 quarts	3 gallons
16 ounces	2 quarts

Volume
1 cup = 8 fluid ounces
1 pint = 2 cups
1 quart = 2 pints
1 gallon = 4 quarts

This example shows three rows of comparisons. Students must determine which value (This or That) is the better choice. In the context of favorite juice, students would want more but there may be contexts where students would want less. You might give one comparison at a time or offer all at once. As mentioned, students can and will use different strategies for finding their preferences. In the bottom row, someone could say that 16 ounces is 2 cups, and 2 quarts is way more than 2 cups. Another student might rely on the idea that quarts are much more than ounces. While that gets them to a solution in this example, it might not always work. When ideas like this are offered be sure to talk about them with students so that they don't rely on faulty approaches that work in one situation but won't always.

online resources All routines can be downloaded for your use at **https://companion.corwin.com/courses/jumpstartroutines-geometry**

HOW THIS ROUTINE HELPS

This routine builds measurement skills by providing opportunities for students to

- practice converting between units of measure;
- practice using conversion tables or tools (MP5);
- estimate quantities (MP2);
- ask themselves if a conversion or solution is reasonable (MP6);
- determine efficient strategies for computing and converting (MP2);
- compare estimates with actual results;
- determine whether their computations are reasonable and accurate (MP6);
- develop confidence in their reasoning and computations;
- defend their reasoning and consider the strategies of others (MP3);
- give feedback to others about their ideas; and
- look for and make use of number relationships and patterns within operations (MP7 and MP8).

WHAT TO DO

1. Select two or three sets of measurements to compare. Take a moment to compare each to anticipate what students might do.
2. Direct students to compare each row of measurements, deciding whether they would prefer "this or that" (determine which measurement is greater). Consider posing one comparison, or row, at a time.
3. Remind students about anchor charts for conversions and that exact answers aren't required though they can use exact figures if they are able to find them.
4. Provide time for students to reason and compare.
5. Direct students to share their findings and reasoning with a partner.
6. Facilitate a discussion about how students compared the expressions to make their decisions about this or that. Some questions to ask include the following:
    - How did you know the measurement was greater than the other?
    - Did you find an exact amount, or did you find an estimated "about" amount?
    - How did friendly numbers help with this comparison?
    - Did you use the conversion chart? How did you use it?
    - Did you notice a pattern? Does this pattern always work? When might it not work?
    - Can you think of another measurement that would be greater than _____ or less than ____?
    - Did anyone compare the measurements differently?
7. Optional: Record student strategies on board, white board, or document camera. Doing this can help other students "see" classmates' reasoning.
8. Honor and explore both accurate and flawed reasoning.

SOMETHING TO THINK ABOUT: WHY SO MANY ROUTINES?

As you read about the different routines in this book, you may ask yourself, "Why are there so many routines?" It's a good question with a few different right answers. First and foremost, you want geometry, measurement, and data practice to be dynamic and vibrant. You want (and need) your students to be enthusiastic and engaged. The same routine done every day loses its luster. When overdone, even the best routine becomes boring and played out. Having a large collection to choose from alleviates this challenge.

Second, a routine like This or That?, which features measurement conversions can be complemented by a routine like More or Less (Routine #14). Because geometry, measurement, and data topics require more than simple recall, it's important to practice reasoning and thinking in different ways. Third, students are different. One routine might serve them well whereas another might not. Fourth, teachers are different too. You might prefer certain routines while colleagues prefer others. The intent is to give you many options to meet the needs of your students through the approaches that are most comfortable and engaging.

THIS OR THAT? (VARIATIONS): CONTEXTS FOR COMPARISONS

This routine is great because there are so many fun, interesting contexts for students to compare. Knowing your students well can help you think of topics that they are interested in or at least familiar with. This is one small way to make math relevant to students. That said, it can still be hard to think of topics even when you know your students well. An easy way to get ideas is to ask them to create a list of things in their everyday lives that they measure or things that they want more of. Collect their lists and look for topics that work well with different types of measurement. You will see contexts that are probably familiar and relevant to your students but if they aren't you can swap those contexts with those from the lists your students create.

Variation A: Starter Conversions

This variation is called "starter conversions" but it's really about unit conversions or knowing how many of something is in one of something else. It is the groundwork of converting and thus a good starting place. Using this variation helps students gain hold of conversion rates, which can be especially helpful for liquid volume that has multiple units. You might think including the conversion anchor chart will shorten or lessen the value of the practice but including it, especially in the early experiences with volume, is crucial. The chart provides support and an extra dose of practice or reminder each time students access it, ultimately lessening the need to use it. More importantly, you want your students to be comfortable with it assuming something similar is a tool on your state assessment. And simply providing it doesn't answer the questions because the direction of the relationships should vary during the practice. In the first row for example, pints are on the left with quarts on the right whereas the anchor chart shows the opposite.

A

This or That?

Chocolate Milk

THIS	THAT
6 pints	1 quart
1 gallon	3 cups
7 quarts	1 gallon

Volume
1 cup = 8 fluid ounces
1 pint = 2 cups
1 quart = 2 pints
1 gallon = 4 quarts
Volume (Metric)
1 liter = 1,000 mL

Variation B: Length and Context

You would think that some contexts are familiar to everyone but that's not the case. Unfamiliar contexts can muddy the "math waters," challenging a student's ability to reason or make sense of what they're doing. This variation is a good example of that. Licorice might be familiar, but "Twizzlers" might not be. Regardless, adding an image can help provide context for all and additional support for multilingual students. But know that certain contexts may create solutions opposite of what you expect. For example, if one doesn't like licorice, they would want 1 foot of rope rather than 16 inches. You may also notice that this variation compares length and the same two units. It also omits a conversion chart. The reason for the latter is that this is an example where a class has only been working with one conversion (inches and feet). They have shown mastery of the conversion rate so the anchor chart has been removed.

B

This or That?

Twizzlers Ropes

THIS	THAT
16 inches	1 foot
26 inches	2 feet

Source: istockphoto.com/bhofack2

Variation C: Reasoning Without Calculation

Comparisons don't always require precise calculations. This variation spotlights that notion by posing two measurements that aren't relatively close to one another. Some students will try to calculate but the most efficient approach for these is to pause and think about the relationships. For example, 1,200 inches would be the same as 100 feet. 100 feet and 100 yards is an easy comparison. In the middle row, 5,500 inches seems like a lot until compared with 1 mile. Knowing that 5,500 is close to the number of *feet* in a mile makes for a quick deduction that 5,500 inches aren't even close. Experiences like this are a good way to practice estimating and reasoning with comparisons. It can be a good place to begin before work with more precise calculations. Doing so, creates a "process filter" of sorts where students first look for an easy way to compare (like thinking about the number of units being compared), determine whether that works, and then move to another process (like finding an exact conversion).

C

This or That?

Bike Ride

THIS	THAT
100 yards	1,200 inches
5,500 inches	1 mile
5 feet	4 yards

Length
1 foot = 12 inches
1 yard = 3 feet
1 mile = 1,760 yards
1 mile = 5,280 feet

Variation D: Money

This variation frames coins in a piggy bank. The idea of a piggy bank might be dated or unfamiliar. If so, remove it and don't feel obligated to replace it. After all, money makes for a natural comparison that needs no additional context. Using it in this routine is a great way to practice coin identification and counting mixed coins. This example includes both sides of each coin along with their names. This is good to include until students show mastery. As with other examples, there are different strategies for comparing. The first strategy is to find the total value of the two cells within a row to compare. In the top row, This has a value of 57¢ and That has a value of 50¢. Another strategy is to find the value of one and then check to see if the other is close. In the top row, That is 50¢ and This has 2 quarters and some more coins meaning it is greater than 50¢ so the total value isn't needed. Be prepared for students to gravitate toward the side with more coins. In the bottom row, you see eight coins in the This cell but only 36¢ whereas the fewer coins on the right have a greater value. The online resource for this routine includes a slide with master images of coins. You copy and paste them in cells. You might need to shrink the size of coins so that a collection fits in the cell. If so, be sure that their sizes aren't equal (e.g., the size of the dime should be smaller than the size of the quarter).

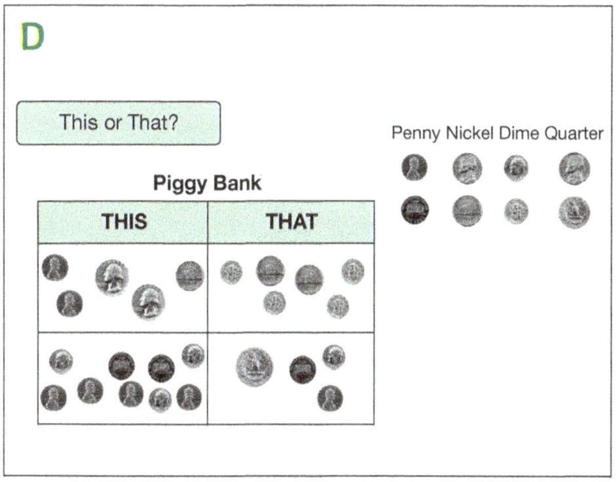

Source: istockphoto.com/filo

Variation E: Calculators and Estimation

This highlights a few things that make it a good choice for later grades. First, it mingles measurements. That is, the first row compares pounds and ounces, the middle compares inches and feet, and the bottom row compares hours and minutes. This is the first variation to mix in this way, as others focus on one type of measurement. This mixed set should be reserved until students show some level of competency with most, if not all, conversions. That's one reason it's better suited for fourth or fifth grade. Another highlight is the calculator icon in the upper-right-hand corner of the slide. This is included because students typically have access to calculators on standardized assessments but may not have much experience using them. Using a calculator with this routine and others can give them valuable experience for use on those assessments. If you include calculators, also be sure to have students talk about when to use them. For example, the middle row probably isn't a time to use a calculator because 2 feet is the same as 24 inches or 2 x 12. Another good idea is to have students estimate what they think a value is before using the tool. For example, in the top row, they might estimate 3 pounds to be less than 60 because 3 x 20 is 60 and there are 16 ounces in a pound not 20. Having brief discussions like this not only helps with conversions but helps students develop ideas of reasonableness.

E

This or That?

THIS	THAT
3 pounds	50 ounces
26 inches	2 feet
52 hours	3,000 minutes

Conversions
1 hour (hr) = 60 minutes (min)
1 minute (min) = 60 seconds (sec)
1 pound (lb) = 16 ounces (oz)
1 foot (ft) = 12 inches (in)
1 kilogram (kg) = 1,000 grams (g)
1 kilometer (km) = 1,000 meters (m)

Variation F: Mystery Number

This variation takes you back to the routine focusing on a single measurement type. Here, different units of time are compared. An anchor chart for converting between units of time is provided. This may not be needed for your students, but it doesn't hurt to include it. The main difference in this variation is that they aren't comparing two amounts. Instead, they are given an amount in the This column, and they are to create an amount that is greater. But the greater amount is in a different unit. In the top row, 240 seconds is 4 minutes so any value greater than 4 would be fine. Know that some students will use a really large value to be silly, for convenience, or both. If this happens, put a limitation on their creation. For the top row, you might say create minutes within 120 seconds of 240 or something like that. But don't start with the limitation. Wait and see what they do before you consider adding it.

F

This or___?

Time
1 minute = 60 seconds
1 hour = 60 minutes
1 day = 24 hours
1 week = 7 days
1 year = 52 weeks

Time at Recess

THIS	THAT
240 seconds	? minutes
3 hours	? minutes
27 days	? weeks
100 weeks	? years

Variation G: Metric Conversions

Metric conversions can be a challenge for students because we use Imperial or Customary Units in the United States. Because of this, the terms may be unfamiliar. Metric can also be challenging because moving from one unit to the other calls for a sound understanding of place value relationships. A good way to counter the challenge is to show the relationships between the metric units and to practice them a lot. In this variation, there is no context because you again see mixed measurement types (i.e., length, volume, and mass) in the same offering. The left side of this example shows a truncated conversion table that includes those called for in most curriculum standards. But you could provide a more robust chart that has all the gram, meter, and liter conversions on it. Doing so can help students see relationships between the prefixes and quantities like how kilograms are 1,000 grams and kilometers are 1,000 meters.

G

This or That?

Metric Conversions
1 kilogram (kg) = 1,000 grams (g)
1 kilometer (km) = 1,000 meters (m)
1 meter (m) = 100 centimeters (cm)
1 liter (L) = 1,000 milliliters (mL)

Which is greater?

THIS	THAT
3 m	300 cm
1,500 mL	3 L
4.5 g	4,500 kg
1,200 cm	120 m

Variation H: Volume

This routine can be a nice way to practice volume of prisms. Here, students identify how big a filled treasure chest they would want. The numbers in the dimensions of these prisms might be overwhelming to students. If you use numbers of this size, consider using a calculator as mentioned in Variation E. Again, have them estimate the volume before finding the exact number. Beginning with single digit whole numbers is the obvious starting place but regardless think about using numbers in clever ways to see if students reason rather than simply calculate. For example, the prisms in the top row can be compared by reasoning. Two dimensions (31 inches and 27 inches) are equal in both prisms. Therefore, the volume of the prism or treasure box in the This section is greater because its width is 27 inches, which is greater than 15 inches. A similar reasoning can be applied to the bottom row where two dimensions are again equal (33 inches and 22 inches) so then the prism or treasure box on the left is greater because its height is 45 inches, which is greater than 41 inches.

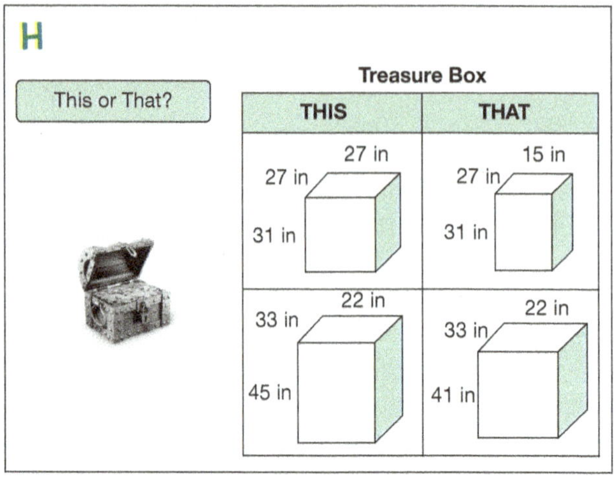

Source: istockphoto.com/koya79

ROUTINE 16

I WOULD SAY

ABOUT THE ROUTINE

Unique data displays or infographics like the one shown here have become a common feature in newspapers, blogs, or social media. They grab your attention, pulling you into the data. They stir thinking and help you generalize or summarize ideas. They can support arguments or disrupt perceptions. Take this infographic, for example. It shows average basketball scores by decade across 7 decades, though the 2020s are not even halfway complete. It's a good piece to show how basketball has changed in the past 20 years. It supports the argument that for a time basketball became slow or boring. It might be used to combat the notion that players from long ago weren't as skilled or athletic because points dropped significantly for many years. And it could be used for a variety of other arguments.

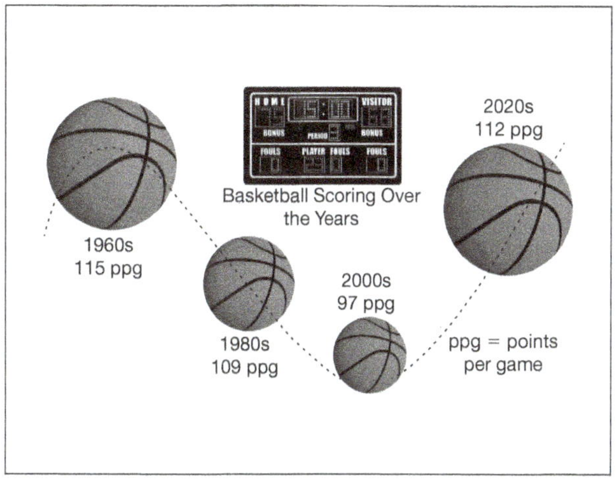

Source: istockphoto.com/GeoffBlack

Encounters with infographics and data displays in general are common. Preparing students to interpret and analyze them is a must. But, like solving word problems, this can't be done with a single acronym, formula, or procedure because data displays, like word problems, come in all sorts of shapes, configurations, and complexities. The act of sense making cannot be done to or for the individual. It cannot be mimicked. It is developed through practice, experience, discussion, observation, and error. You might think of it as teaching reading comprehension to students. That is, you cannot understand a passage for your students. You must arm them with tools and experiences so that they can comprehend what they read on their own.

Like problem-solving, understanding a data display starts with making sense of the problem in one's own mind (SanGiovanni, 2023). That means students must be able to describe the context of the graph. They must be able to identify the data points, the labels, and other features. They should consider what question the data answers and what questions can't be answered for that matter. Retelling or summarizing is a natural way to do all of this. But students don't simply know how to do this. They need to learn about it and practice it. Summarizing isn't just a skill for making sense but it's also a tool for getting unstuck (SanGiovanni et al., 2020). Retelling is a "go to" strategy that every student can use and is one that potentially always works.

Some students take to retelling problems (and stories) naturally while others need lots

online resources All routines can be downloaded for your use at **https://companion.corwin.com/courses/jumpstartroutines-geometry**

of practice. The same is true for summarizing or talking about data displays, including infographics like this one and traditional displays like bar graphs or line plots. This routine provides that all-important practice. You can use it to pose a data display and give students the opportunity to summarize it in their own words. They share with partners and then the whole class discusses. This routine exposes students to others' thinking and perspective. The intent of the routine is not to answer specific questions or solve problems with the data, as doing so can distract from the focus of the routine. This routine is solely about the practice of putting a data display into one's own words!

In this example, students should say that the infographic is about basketball scores over time. They should justify that idea by noting the scoreboard, the "PPG," and even the decades above or below each basketball. You might also expect them to say that scores went down over time but then went back up. They should notice that bigger basketballs represent higher scores. They might even talk about how the ball appears to be bouncing—a novel interpretation that might come up but doesn't require such insight. The simple point is to be able to fully summarize the display. Asking students what they notice or wonder about a graph is a good idea. At first, they might make a simple statement like, "It's about basketball scores." But over time you want to build toward fuller, if not complete, summary statements. The graphic organizers shared in the variations help you find ways to support students' retelling.

HOW THIS ROUTINE HELPS

This routine builds data literacy skills by providing opportunities for students to

- process information about data displays without pursuing answers;
- retell or summarize a display in *their* own words;
- organize their thinking before encountering a problem to solve;
- identify the important information in a data display and consider messages or takeaways about the display;
- distill a display into manageable chunks of information;
- listen to how others interpret and describe a problem in their own words (MP3);
- give feedback to others about their ideas (MP3);
- make sense of data by thinking about it in diverse ways thus growing their agency; and
- determine questions to ask oneself when reading and working through a data display (MP1).

WHAT TO DO

1. Pose a data display (e.g., infographic or traditional graph).
2. Give students time to observe and process the display. At this time, they should begin to think about how they would describe it in their own words. Optional: Use questions or sentence starters to guide student thinking. Recording these on an anchor chart would be a good idea. Some questions you might use are
    - What is the graph talking about?
    - What is happening in the display?
    - What are the important features?
    - What is the title? What are the labels?
    - What do the data points (i.e., numbers) describe? How do I know what they describe?
    - Does anything surprise me about the data? Why?
3. Have partners describe the display to each other.
4. Bring the class together to share ideas. Have students listen carefully to how others describe the data. Have all students signal that they agree (thumbs up) or have questions (thumbs down) about summaries.

5. Optional: Share your own summary of the data. Note that you should share last so that you don't influence student thinking or suggest there is a correct summary or retelling.

Each time a student shares, reinforce the big ideas that their summaries have in common with a classmate's summary. If conversation is stalled, refer to the questions or sentence starters you used to prompt independent thinking. Be sure to avoid going over a specific "math" questions like, "How many more points were scored in the 1960s than the 1980s?" You want the sole focus of this routine to be about summarizing and nothing more.

SOMETHING TO THINK ABOUT: GRAPHIC ORGANIZERS

Graphic organizers help thinking by providing organization and structure. To be effective, they must be simple and clear (Egan, 1999). The act of summarizing and retelling a problem, task, or data display can be developed through different graphic organizers highlighted in a few of these variations. There are different organizers because there are different things to consider when examining data. Avoid using graphic organizers procedurally and use them to temporarily scaffold student entry points into retelling. Each organizer is available as downloadable content. Creating anchor charts or just sketching them freehand on the board would be good supports for whole class discussion.

I WOULD SAY (VARIATIONS): SUMMARIZING ALL SORTS OF GRAPHS

Making sense of data displays through infographics in the introduction (basketball scores) or like those in the first two variations is probably not in your curriculum. That doesn't mean you can't, or shouldn't, spend a little time with them over the course of the year. We don't propose doing so to give you "one more thing to do." Using these displays is suggested because they are everywhere. Spending a little time with them helps prepare your students for everyday life. You help them become data literate in the 21st century. It can be a nice way to get students excited about math because they are so interesting. Other ideas about how to use them along with summarizing traditional, curriculum-based graphs are unpacked in these variations.

Variation A: Questions

Infographics come with a "wow factor" with interesting images and clever titles or statements. They make data more appealing drawing readers into it. In this example, the tiny trees sandwiched between the really big trees are impossible to miss. The placement of the title "centers" your attention on a popular topic and it communicates the measurement unit because the numbers don't have labels. These displays also spark questions. Embrace that! You want students to summarize data, but you also want them to analyze, interrogate, and think critically about it. Just telling that this is about the size of national parks, that Mammoth Cave is tiny (though 54,000 acres is not tiny), or that Yellowstone is enormous isn't good enough for interactions with data in today's world. After you summarize, encourage them to ask questions. You can even use questions, or wonderments, as an entry point to summarizing. And there are no wrong questions! A good question for this example could simply be, "How big is an acre?" Another good question is, "Are the trees the right size for comparing with each other (i.e., are they proportional)?" Students could ask about why these parks were selected of the 62 national parks there are or why did the designer use evergreen trees. Some questions, like the latter, aren't necessarily as important, but still have value. So, with infographics or traditional, standard graphs, encourage questions about displays, organization, labels, units, values, and anything else.

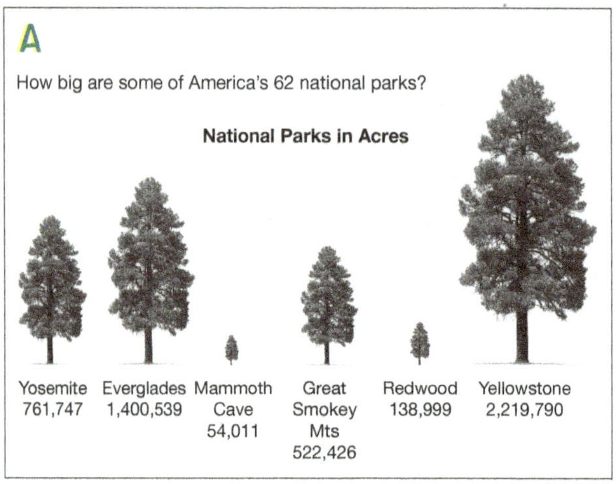

Source: istock.com/DNY59

Variation B: Be Critical, Be Curious

Whoa! Boys have really grown a lot over the years. Or, at least, this display might lead you to think they have. Yes, the average height of a male at age 18 has increased every 20 years over this period. But what was their height in 1894? Is that data available? Why wasn't it included? How big is 10 centimeters? After all, that is the amount of change over 80 years. It turns out to be about 4 inches. That is a good bit, but the chart seems to suggest a much greater change. The point of this variation isn't that you do something different with the routine necessarily. You still want students to summarize. After they do, you want them to react to the summary. This is where you emphasize questioning. You want to help them begin to critically analyze the data displays they encounter. This might happen organically, or you might have to introduce it as an additional feature of a summary. It can sound like, "I noticed that the pictures of the boys seem to get much, much bigger. That made me wonder how much the heights are really changing." You can also introduce a different layer of inquiry and conjecture saying things like, "I wonder why that is" and so on.

B

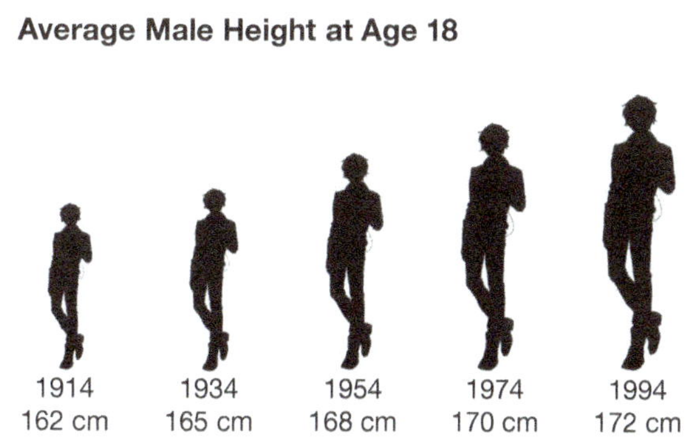

Source: istock.com/Yurii Karvatskyi

Variation C: Graphic Organizers for Summaries

The first thing you probably notice in this variation is that it uses a traditional bar graph that is likely in your curriculum. It is a display that your students should be comfortable with. They should be able to tell what it is about while pointing out specific features or data points. But learning to do this can be hard for elementary students especially when it might seem like there is a lot going on in the image. A graphic organizer is the perfect tool to scaffold their success. While any organizer will do, we suggest that you keep it simple and focused on the major points. Frayer models, like the examples in C2 and C3, are good options. The one in C2 might be a good place to begin the experience of putting graphs into one's own words. The one in C3 might be reserved for practice with summarizing, drawing conclusions, and asking questions as discussed in Variations B and C. You can use organizers to support summaries as familiar displays become more complex. For example, this bar graph has five categories and a scale of 2. These details would be new in Grade 3 though the concept of a bar graph was learned in previous grades with fewer categories and a scale of 1.

C1

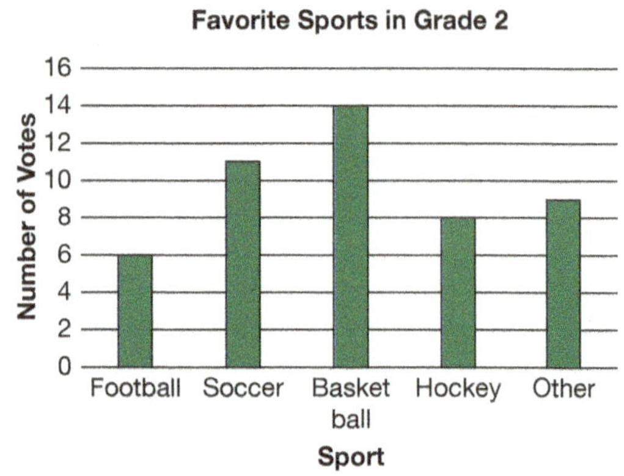

C2

Topic	Important Features
What Is the Graph About?	What Does the Data Describe?

C3

Summary	Important Features
Conclusions	Questions

Variation D: Different Organizers

There is no "right" organizer to use. Consider your purpose, your students' strengths, and experiences with other organizers. A reading comprehension strategy is to identify a big idea and to determine some details. This is a skill useful for summarizing a graph. This variation takes that approach using a concept web (image D2) to capture student thinking. In this example, the big idea is favorite pets. After noting the big idea, one begins to think about details. The details in the problem include the key, the different pets, the number of votes for each pet, and so on. While this seems straightforward, you might find that a student notices a missing detail—it doesn't say who voted! Was it a class, two classes, or just a group of friends? What could you infer? Why? The 3-2-1 organizer in D3 is good for helping students narrow their thinking. It asks them to identify three things they can say about the data, which supports summarization. They wonder, or ask questions, about the data helping them to analyze and potentially spot other details. The third point is an entry point into the mathematical questions one can answer through data.

D1

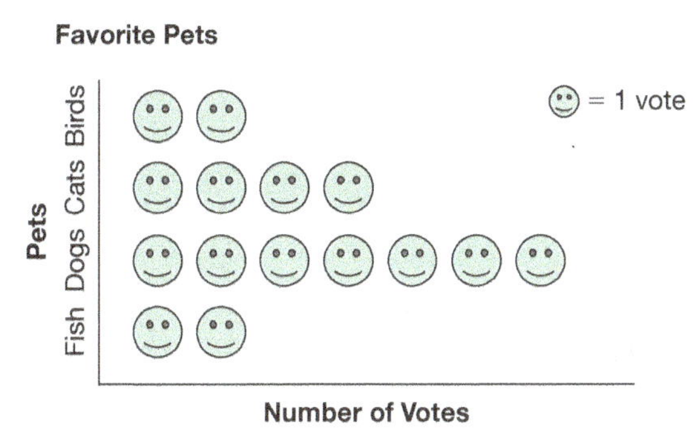

D2

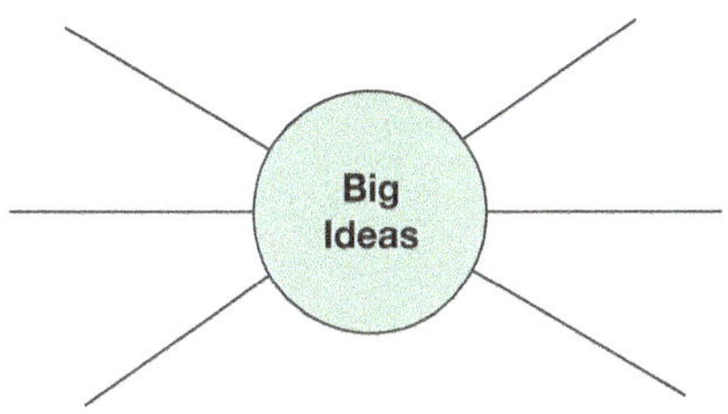

D3

Variation E: Scaffolds With Other Routines

This variation is offered to give you an idea about how you can create an organizer for other routines. Asked and Answered (Routine #17) is a routine that practices identifying questions that can or can't be answered through the data presented. In that experience, you may find that, at first, students have a tough time generating questions. Using an organizer like the one in E2 and mixing it with some wait time will do wonders for student success. You can choose to have them complete it separately, or they can work with partners to generate questions. You can have them do both sets of questions in the same experience or break it up over two days. Though this variation doesn't seem directly connected to the idea of summarizing a graph, it is something students will need to do to generate questions.

E1

E2

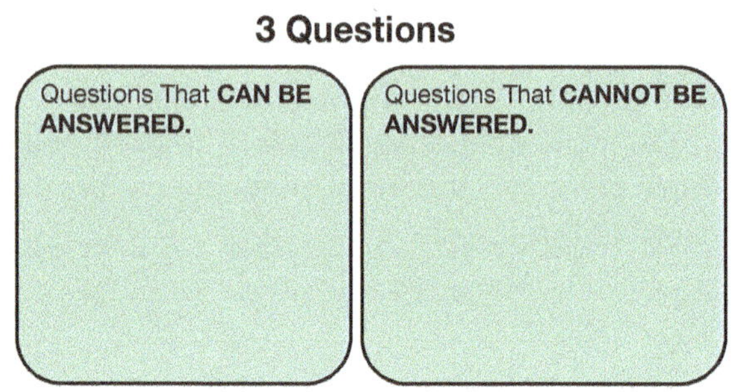

Variation F: "New" Graphs

The line plot and line graph are offered as "food for thought." First encounters with these displays can be overwhelming for students. You can tell them how to read and make sense of them and practice it over and over again. Or, when students begin work with new types of graphs, you can present them and ask them to attempt to summarize or explain what they *think* the displays are communicating. In this situation, you wouldn't do it as a routine per se. Instead, it would frame a lesson about the display that you could then practice later. To do this, you can post different examples of line plots around the room. Students can move from one to the next making observations and writing about what they think is happening or what the graph is saying. Then, the whole class would come together to share observations and ideas. After that, you would explain how the graph works, confirm their accurate conclusions, and clarify misinterpretations. Keep in mind the line plot and line graph are just examples. For your students, the displays might be simple bar graphs or picture graphs.

F1

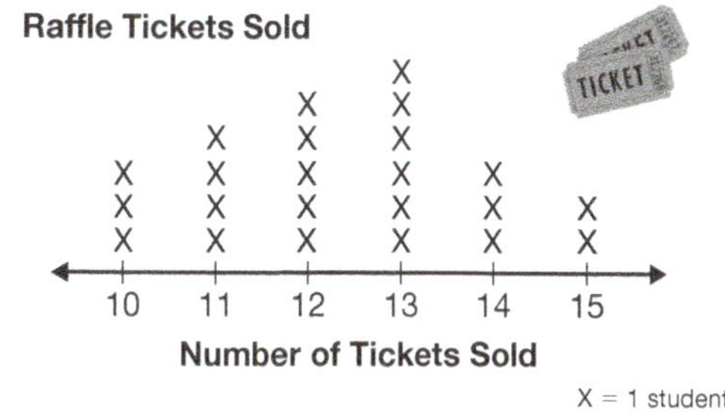

F2

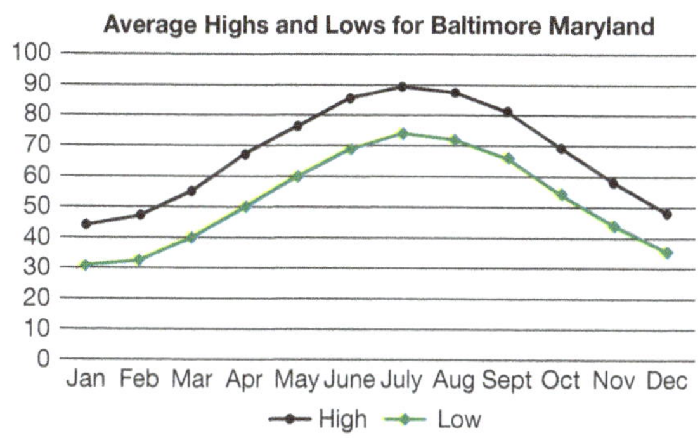

Source: istockphoto.com/hatman12

Variation G: Constructing Graphs

Some curriculum standards still require students to draw or construct bar graphs or picture graphs from provided data or the data they collect. Though software renders the need for this standard moot, there is relevance in thinking about the design and layout of a data display. This can be a subtle, yet valuable, addition to the summarizing aspect of this routine. To do this, have students summarize data tables as shown here. On the left, you see a primary example recorded with tally marks. On the right, you see an intermediate example with somewhat more complicated data. After they summarize, ask them to talk about what type of graph would be good to communicate this data. Consider asking them to imagine what it would look like or to sketch it on a white board. At this juncture, they don't have to be exact. Instead, you just want them to tinker with design. In older grades you might also ask them to think of the need for a key, scale, or other features. Keep in mind they don't necessarily need any formal instruction about how to design the graph, they only need previous exposure to certain graphs. This addition to the routine can be the entry way into that formal instruction. And at the least, it sets them up for future success when they begin to create graphs with software.

G

Favorite Hobby	
Music	𝍸 |
Art	𝍸 |||
Games or Puzzles	|||
Sports	𝍸 𝍸

Race Times	
Jay	36
Kate	32
Dee	17
Li	23
Jax	17
Kendra	18
Jared	22

ROUTINE 17

ASKED AND ANSWERED

ABOUT THE ROUTINE

As teachers, we saw our students "solve" word problems by zooming in on the question, grabbing the numbers, and doing *something* with them. They made assumptions about which operation to use and were baffled when asked if their answer made sense. The experience wasn't relegated to word problems. We had similar experiences with other concepts, including questions about graphs and data displays. When a question was asked, they would home in on a word in the problem, find the data point in the graph, and find a solution. Some did it because they believed first was best in math. Others because they didn't know what to think. We were frustrated that they didn't pause to think about the question or the important information in graphs or word problems for that matter. We overlooked that they might not be paying attention to the details of the word problem, data, or question for that matter.

We learned to start asking questions that couldn't be answered just to see what would happen. We found that some students were paying close attention and they would argue that a question couldn't be answered. Their classmates would have a "solution." We would have a math fight on our hands and that was a good thing! Those discussion helped everyone slow down, process questions, and look carefully at the details of a graph or word problem. This routine evolved from those experiences.

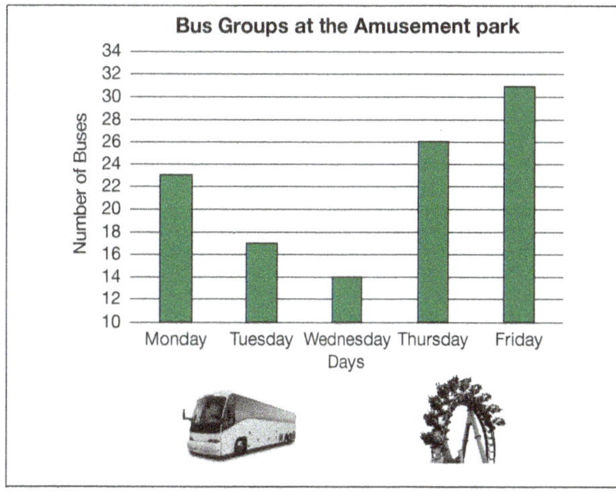

A How many buses came to the park on Monday?

B How many more buses came to the park on Friday than Tuesday?

C How many people were on the bus?

D How many buses came to the park in these 5 days?

Source: istockphoto.com/IlexImage and istockphoto.com/Lalin

This routine, Asked and Answered, takes aim at critical thinking about questions. In it, you provide a little context and a graph or table. You give students time to look closely at that information and briefly summarize what it is saying. Then, you pose a few questions. Students must determine whether the questions you pose can be asked *and answered* based on the information in the graph. Class discussion afterward exposes student

online resources All routines can be downloaded for your use at **https://companion.corwin.com/courses/jumpstartroutines-geometry**

reasoning and interpretation. Using the routine over time should help students begin to think more carefully about information, context, data, and questions they encounter with graphs and even word problems.

This routine is much more than a novel way to practice. At its core, this routine nurtures 21st-century skills including information literacy (Stauffer, 2022). It develops the thinking and reasoning students need to live in their world. It helps them learn to look at information critically. It provides opportunity to analyze viability and reliability of the questions and answers about quantity, data, and statistics.

HOW THIS ROUTINE HELPS

This routine deepens understanding of data by providing opportunities for students to

- take time to think about contexts, data within those contexts, and potential questions that could be asked about the context;
- determine whether a question can be answered with information presented;
- shift their approaches from grabbing numbers and computing to focusing on the information and the question;
- recognize that questions can't always be answered from the given information;
- identify important information presented in problems, graphs, or other data displays;
- practice ignoring unnecessary information in graphs and data;
- justify their thinking (MP3); and
- take ownership of interpreting, analyzing, and solving problems.

WHAT TO DO

1. Share an image for students to observe. Ask them what they know about the topic or the contexts. Ask them what types of things could be measured relative to the topic. In the example, you would show a tour bus and the roller coaster. Students might say you could count how many people can ride them or you can measure how fast they travel.
2. Display the data for students to observe for a few moments. Optional: Have students turn and talk about the information by having them describe or summarize the graph in their own words.
3. Pose three or four questions related to the data.
4. Have students think about which questions can be asked and answered with the data.
5. Have partners discuss their ideas about the questions.
6. Bring the class back together to discuss their selections. During discussion, any question that probes their thinking is a good question.

   For this example, some questions you could ask include the following:

   - How could a question with a number that isn't in the table be asked and answered? (question D)
   - How did you know that question B couldn't be asked and answered? What information would you use from the graph to answer question B?
   - Groups of people can ride a bus or a roller coaster. How did you know that question C couldn't be answered?
   - What more information would you need to answer question B?
   - Which questions might need an equation to answer? What would one of those equations be?
7. Optional: Have the group answer one of the questions from the set and discuss their solutions. Note: The point of this routine is not to solve questions. It is intended to focus

on questions that can be answered from given data sets. Finding exact solutions can distract students from the purpose. It is not suggested for initial experiences, and it is fine if an exact answer is never discussed for any of the questions.

8. Optional: After discussion, have students create new questions that can or can't be answered by the data. You can have each student generate one of each question type. Or you can have students pair with a classmate, with one partner creating a question that could be asked and answered and the other partner creating something that can't be answered. If time permits, some student creations could be shared. Alternatively, they can be written down and saved for the next day.

SOMETHING TO THINK ABOUT: IMAGES WITH DATA DISPLAYS

As you have noticed, each data display in this routine comes with a picture. That's true for all other displays throughout this book. You may have looked past them giving it little thought. Know that including the images is intentional and purposeful. In short, the image along with the title are "text features" that help students comprehend the topic or context. Teachers call attention to these when teaching reading and they have the same purpose in math. Images and titles are a big help with making sense of graphs and solving word problems for that matter (SanGiovanni, 2023). The images provide entry points for your students and play an important role for you as well because they help you gauge how familiar your students are with a topic. Of course, there are graphs and displays in your curriculum resources that don't come with images. That's OK. You don't always need to include an image but if you would like to, you're just a quick image search away from finding the solution. Coupling images with questions like, "What do you know about _____?" or "What do you wonder about ____?" helps in many different facets of learning and doing math, including sense-making, problem-solving, and even finding relevance.

ASKED AND ANSWERED (VARIATIONS): STUDENT CREATIVITY

Variations of routines throughout this book present ideas about how you can tap student creativity for new, engaging twists. Creating examples and problems gives students voice and agency. It promotes higher-order thinking. It can be hard! But be sure that you don't avoid giving them opportunities to create because of that. Instead, scaffold the creation process. Introduce examples first and be sure they understand how the activity works. Have them create examples with groups or partners before doing it independently. Share how you go about creating an example through a think aloud. Possibly the greatest benefit of having them create examples is that it lessens the burden on you. Take their examples, save them, and use them with the whole class another time.

Variation A: Single Category

This first variation shows how a picture graph can be used with this routine. It also speaks to some other things that may be overlooked by adults. The topic is playing cards and adults might assume that every student is familiar with them (even if we aren't). To offset this challenge, pose the image and nothing else. Have students tell you what they know about the image (e.g., those are cards for a game, they come in a pack, different cards have different values). Then, show some of the display and ask what they know or questions they have about it. If you notice the icon for cards, it doesn't look exactly like the logo. That difference seems minor, but it could be a significant misunderstanding for a student not familiar with the cards or one who is still learning about picture graphs. Even the labels in the graph can be confusing to someone who isn't an avid player or collector. Taking time to unpack the context will help you better determine how well students understand the math!

A1

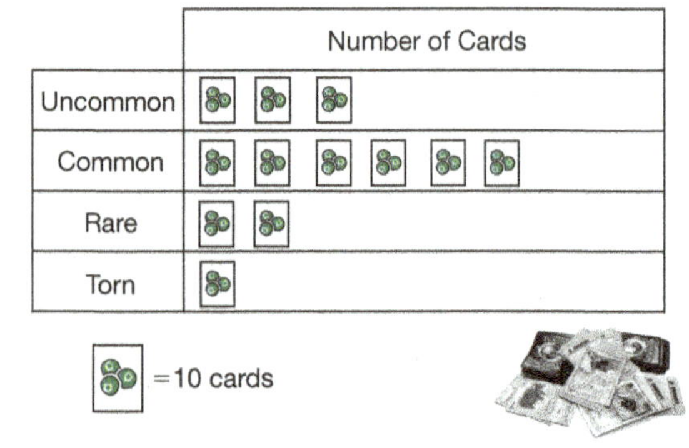

A2

Ⓐ Which types of cards have at least 20?

Ⓑ How many cards are there in total?

Ⓒ Which cards are the most valuable?

Ⓓ How many cards are torn?

Source: istockphoto.com/NoDerog

Variation B: Just Two Questions

Ideally, you would have students deal with about four questions when working with this routine. But at first, you might begin simply with two questions to limit distractors and potential confusion. The idea is to use this simplified variation as an introduction to the routine or with students who aren't ready yet to work with multiple questions. The example also uses a basic bar graph with just three categories (i.e., days). It's presented to remind you that this routine can be done with any grade and any graph regardless of complexity. In the example, question A can be answered but question B cannot. The graph is about the number of dogs not owners. Each dog might be there with one owner, but someone might have taken five dogs to the park. When using two questions, you don't have to use one question that can be answered and one that cannot. You can ask two of the same type of question, which leads us to the next variation.

B1

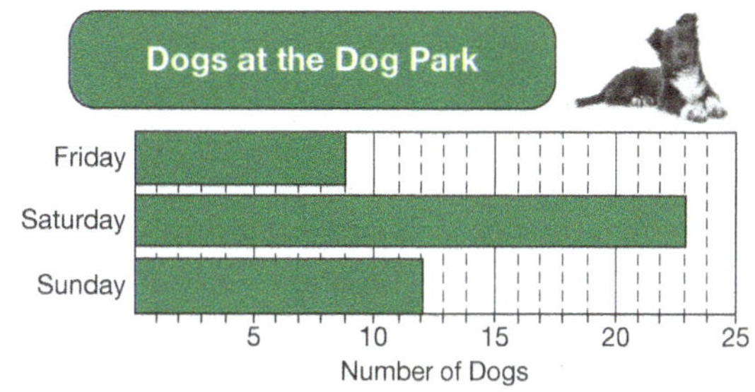

B2

A How many more dogs were at the park on Saturday than Friday?

B How many dog owners were at the park on Sunday?

Source: istock.com/Yellow Garnet Photography

Variation C: What Would You Need?

This variation shows how you can really go after your students' critical thinking. They will assume that at least one question will satisfy either condition. In other words, they will assume at least one can be asked answered and at least one cannot be answered. But in this instance, none of the questions can be answered. We offer it not for you to simply toy with your students. Instead, they must really grapple with each and potentially question their own thinking when they can't identify one that works. There's also a nice addition you can layer to this version and others. After students determine and explain which questions can't be answered, have them talk about what information would be needed in the graph, or in general, so that the question could be answered. For example, question A seems like it can be answered but the value of each X is unknown. It could represent one butterfly measured or more. To answer the question, a key that explains the value of each X is needed. D can't be answered because we don't know how many of the Xs represent adult butterflies. To know that, the display would have to use a different symbol for adult and juvenile butterflies.

C1

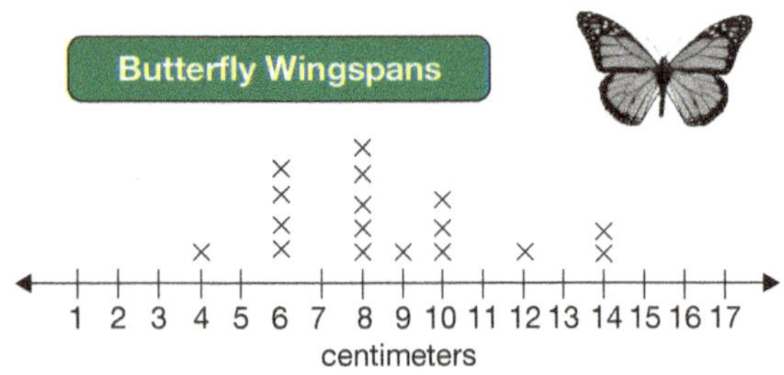

C2

- **A** How many butterflies were measured?
- **B** How many butterflies were females?
- **C** How many butterflies had the darkest wings?
- **D** How many adult butterflies had wingspans greater than 10 cm?

Source: istockphoto.com/Onfokus

Variation D: Student-Generated Questions

The blank set of questions is not a printing error. It's a talking point, or rather the point of this variation. There is great value in having students write problems and questions. It helps them think about how questions are phrased, how numbers go together, and how information might be gathered from a graph. As mentioned earlier, this is a great way to engage students while activating both their creativity and their agency. Though the image shows four options, it's probably better to have students write just two questions—one that can be answered and one that can't. Or, if you prefer, have them write one question. Then, have them group themselves into questions that can be answered and questions that can't be answered. Once grouped, students can compare their creations with others and determine whether they have grouped themselves correctly. Highlight a few examples from either group to reinforce understanding and close the experience.

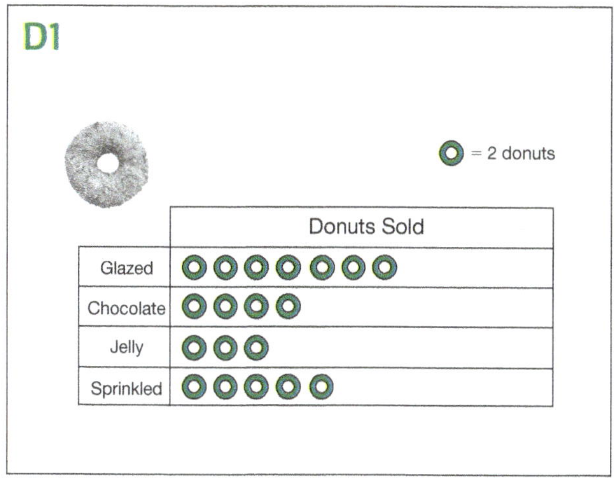

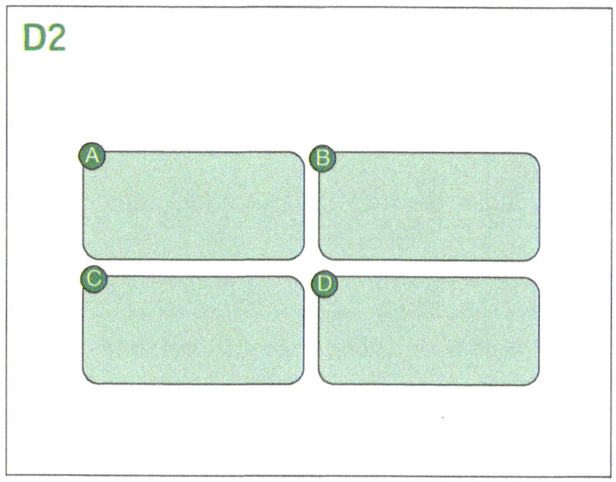

Source: istockphoto.com/Sergey Skleznev

Variation E: Data Tables and Statistical Questions

Data tables can be overlooked as displays like bar graphs and picture graphs, among others, are called out directly in curriculum standards. Though data tables may not seem to be in your standards, it's wise to include them in routines and to bundle them with other standards like solving word problem standards. This variation shows how a data table could be used with this routine. It's also offered for you to consider practice with another important concept about statistics and data. That concept is identifying statistical questions. Typically, this idea appears in middle school standards, but it is a reasonable question for young students to consider. You don't have to assess or grade their understanding. Just practice it. And for elementary students, you probably should avoid "statistical" and simply describe these as "questions about data" or "data questions."

Implement this variation of the routine as you would others. Share the title and have students talk about what the data might describe. Then, show the table with the peppers or with the days of the week. Ask students to discuss what information might be in the other row or column header. Discuss it briefly then reveal the data. Consider having students summarize the data or share observations (i.e., notice) and questions (i.e., wonder) about the information. At that point, you're ready to pose different questions for them to consider.

In the example, question A is a question about data. You can find out how many people in a group have a favorite pepper but that's not what this graph is about. Questions C and D are interesting questions, but they aren't about data (and statistics). Question B is a data question, and it can be answered with the information in the table.

E1

Weekend Produce Sales

	Fri	Sat	Sun
	17	25	16
	19	31	25
	14	28	16

E2

A. Which pepper do people like the most?

B. Which day had sold the most peppers in all?

C. Why are there different colored peppers?

D. Why do peppers have more than 20 seeds inside?

Source: istock.com/29mokara, istock.com/t_kumura, and istock.com/Josef Mohyla

Variation F: Different Content

Remember that the routines in this book are clustered around the topics of geometry, measurement, and data. Even though a routine is focused on a given topic, like data, doesn't mean that you can't tinker with it to use it for other skills and concepts. This variation is another example of how you might do that with this routine and many others in the book. Here, graphs have been swapped out for mass. There are three blocks or bricks presented on scales. Then, students identify which questions can be asked and answered about the blocks. Questions A and B can be asked and answered. Questions C and D can't be answered because the dimensions of the blocks are unknown. Other measurables, like length, volume, time, or money will also work well with this routine. Geometry will work, too, but the questions might be more foundational. For example, you might show some shapes and ask how many have four corners or how many have three sides. That can be answered. Coming up with questions that can't be answered about the shapes might be more challenging.

F1

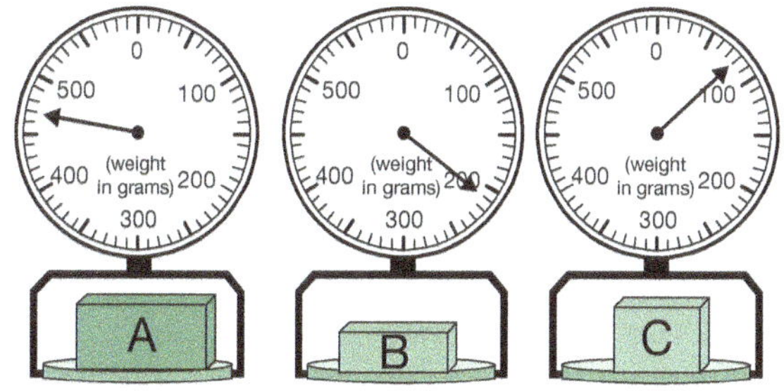

F2

- A: How much does block A weigh?
- B: How much more does block C weigh than block B?
- C: What is the volume of each block?
- D: Which block is the longest?

ROUTINE 18 SAME AND DIFFERENT

ABOUT THE ROUTINE

Comparing and contrasting is an effective way for learning about concepts. It is also a powerful thinking and reasoning strategy that works well with problem-solving (SanGiovanni, 2023) and interpreting data as shown in this routine. When students are challenged to make sense of data, you can ask them to think of a similar data set, a familiar context, or something that is the exact opposite of the current example. This routine, Same and Different, is an opportunity for students to analyze two similar, but different data sets. It helps them see that the same context can have different data points, that similar displays can represent different topics altogether, or that a given data set can be displayed in different ways.

In this example, you see that there are two different displays—a pictograph and a bar graph. You see that the contexts have similarities and that there are similarities in the data. However, there are differences too. For example, Lots of Wags Rescue had 24 dogs adopted in December whereas Happy Tails Rescue had 36 adoptions. To carry out the routine, you first share a display like the one on the left (Lots of Wags) and discuss it with your students. Ask them what they think the graph is communicating. Ask them to tell you facts about the data like, "How many dogs were adopted in September?" and how they know. Ask about what questions you can ask and answer along with what questions can't be answered (see Asked and Answered, Routine #17). And of course, be sure to have them point out certain features about the graph like the fact that each paw print represents eight dogs.

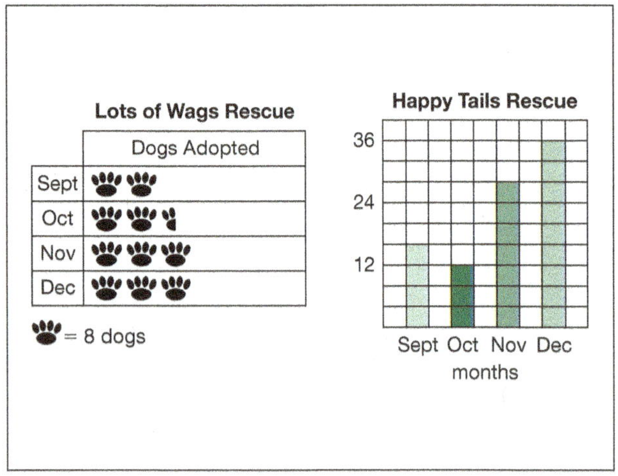

After you spend time with the first graph, present the second graph. Give students a few moments to study it and compare it to the first that you discussed. Then, ask similar questions about the second graph. Next, you want to spend time asking students to compare and contrast the data and the displays. Feel free to ask them which display they think is easier to read and why. Ask them which would be more efficient and how either might change with a different number of adoptions in a given month.

With clever variations, your students can compare important aspects of graphs. You can help them see how the same topic or context could be displayed in different ways. In other instances, you can opt for graphs that have a similar context but completely different numbers and contexts. You can have students notice that changing numbers can affect the displays even when everything else about a problem is identical. Using this routine consistently builds an essential "graph-attack"

online resources All routines can be downloaded for your use at **https://companion.corwin.com/courses/jumpstartroutines-geometry**

skill. But as you use it, be sure to close each time by asking students why looking at how graphs are the same and different can help them with a new, challenging, or confusing problem.

HOW THIS ROUTINE HELPS

This routine builds data literacy skills by providing opportunities for students to

- develop critical thinking skills about the architecture of data displays;
- focus on proven methods of thinking and reasoning to make sense of data and problems or questions posed about them (MP1);
- grow their confidence with graphs by developing an approach to analyzing them;
- help them generate an entry point with challenging or complex graphs;
- foster perseverance by teaching a strategy for helping one make sense of displays on their own (MP1); and
- reinforce an essential reasoning skill that can be transferred to other learning situations (MP1).

WHAT TO DO

1. Pose a graph to students.
2. Give students time to individually think about the graph. Ask them to ask themselves questions like the following:
    - What do I know about the graph? What is it about?
    - What's happening in the graph? What is it about?
    - What questions could I ask (and answer) with the data?
    - How would the graph change if ____?
3. Have partners share their ideas about the graph.
4. Bring the class together to discuss the graph. During discussion, be sure to highlight context, labels, data, and other important features about the graph.
5. Then, unveil a similar, but different graph.
6. Have students independently identify how the second graph is similar to and different from the first.
7. Have partners discuss their ideas and encourage them to speak to the context, the data, and other aspects of each graph (such as labels and other features).
8. Bring the class together again to talk about their ideas.
9. After the class discussion, ask students how comparing and contrasting two graphs can help them when they encounter new or unfamiliar graphs and data displays.

SOMETHING TO THINK ABOUT: SCAFFOLDING THE ROUTINE

Scaffolding a routine increases access to these important experiences. Remember that scaffolds should be temporary. However, there isn't a set number of experiences before you should take them away. The decision is based solely on your students' needs. It is likely a good idea to remove them when you notice that students are using them mindlessly, when the scaffold is becoming another procedure to complete, or when students go back to the scaffold after they have already made sense of the problem or even solved it. Charting student thinking is a good way to scaffold these routines as it documents ideas without causing students to keep too many thoughts in their working memory. With this routine, a traditional Venn diagram is a good tool to record and organize ideas. Other ways to scaffold this routine might be to first have students compare very familiar graphs with basic keys (e.g., one paw equals one dog) and more complicated keys (e.g., one paw equals two dogs). This helps students understand the process for examining, analyzing, and comparing two different graphs. Recording ideas on sticky notes or lap boards is a good move too. Having students do this first will help them remember it and focus their thoughts when they share.

SAME AND DIFFERENT (VARIATIONS): DIFFERENT POSSIBILITIES FOR MODIFYING

This routine is possibly the most important for you to modify. Simply, there are many different things you want students to consider when examining data. This example shows how a given context or situation can be displayed in two different ways. But you can change the contexts and keep the data or appearance of the graph identical. As you modify, think about what you've noticed about your students' work with data and graphs. Expose and explore missteps in this routine. If you see that they struggle when numbers or data sets become larger, pose two displays that are identical (context and graph) except that they use different number types (e.g., whole numbers on one line plot and fractions on another line plot). The following are just some of the ways that you can modify to harness the power of this routine.

Variation A: Same Data Display, Different Values

Students who show strength and understanding with a concept like line plots or word problems that have whole numbers, may struggle when the numbers change to fractions. A strategy to help them make sense of the situation is to substitute the more complicated number type (e.g., fractions) with something simpler (e.g., single digit whole numbers) (SanGiovanni, 2023). You can introduce this approach when working with data on line plots as shown in this variation of the routine. Here, you see plant heights centimeters in A1 and heights in inches in A2. There are clear similarities between the two line plots. Both are about measuring the height of plants, and both have the same number of plants measured and both even have the same number of tick marks on the number lines. Clearly there are differences too. The top has whole number measurements of plants in the garden whereas the greenhouse plants on the bottom are measured in fractions of inches. The location distinction is something to note. The line plots are designed to show similarities but the centimeter to inch conversions aren't exact. To compensate for this, we changed the plants being measured. Keep this in mind as you manipulate the data points, especially measurements, for your students.

A1

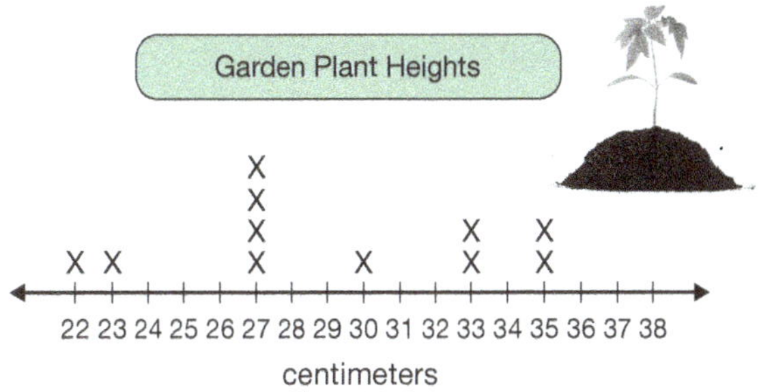

A2

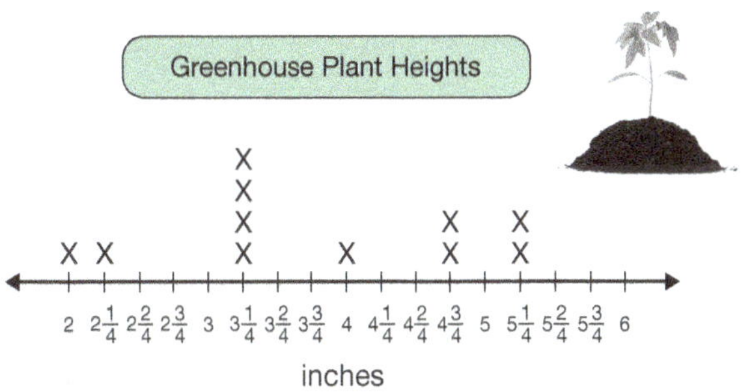

Source: istockphoto.com/Viorika

Variation B: Same Graph, Different Scales

Scales on graphs, like pictographs or bar graphs, change so that large quantities can be communicated practically and efficiently. These changing scales can present challenges to students who are learning to understand the display, to skip-count, and to attend to detail. In this simple variation, you present a display with one scale. Have students practice summarizing the data. Then, ask questions like, "How many more tons were recycled in the north part of the city than in the south part of the city?" or "How many tons were recycled in the west?" Record their answers to the questions and discuss their reasoning for each. After discussion, display the second graph with a different scale. Have students compare and contrast the graphs and then ask the exact same questions with the new graph. As they answer the questions, have them compare their new answers to the original answers. Ask them why the answers are changing. You can extend the experience by having them create a different scale for a third graph and then predict how their answers would change again. This variation is pretty easy to create. Take any data display in your resources and use that for the first scale and discussion. Then, simply change the scale for the second discussion.

B1

Paper Recycling in Parts of the City

North	♻ ♻ ♻ ♻ ♻
South	♻ ♻
East	♻ ♻ ♻ ♻ ♻ ♻ ♻
West	♻ ♻ ♻

♻ = 3 tons

B2

Paper Recycling in Parts of the City

North	♻ ♻ ♻ ♻ ♻
South	♻ ♻
East	♻ ♻ ♻ ♻ ♻ ♻ ♻
West	♻ ♻ ♻

♻ = 5 tons

Variation C: Same Graph, Different Context

If two graphs look the same, are they saying the same thing? Of course they don't. Situations and contexts change but the data within them might be similar. Take these examples. Both are about the number of students per grade. Each shows the same number of students per grade. But the one in C1 tells how many students were absent whereas the one in C2 is about the number of students in chorus by grade. This variation of the routine is a good way to help students focus in on the title and details of a graph to be sure they know what it is about. This is also a good way to talk about the questions that can (and can't be) answered through the graph. As questions are discussed, point out how they, too, are similar and different. For example, how many students were absent in Grade 1 is similar to how many students were in chorus in Grade 1. Both ask about the total for Grade 1 and both can be answered by reading the Grade 1 column. While this may not seem special to adults, these sorts of discussions go a long way toward solidifying young students' understanding of data displays. This variation is also pretty easy to make. Just use any data display in your resources and simply change the title. That's all!

C1

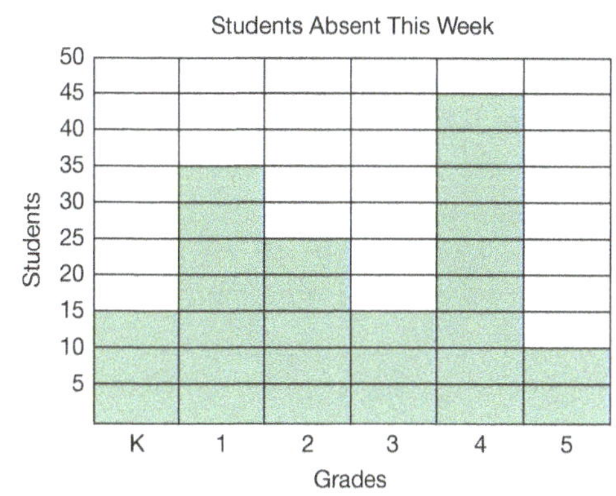

C2

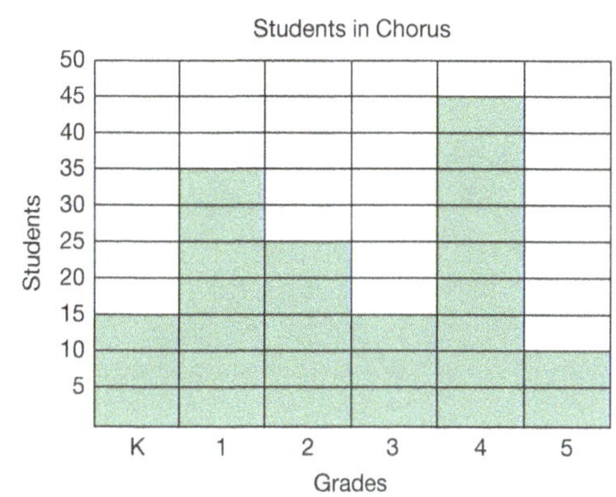

Variation D: Tables and Graphs

This variation is offered for a few reasons. First, it's an easy display to create. Find a line plot, bar graph, or pictograph. Then, create a table that mirrors the data. Have a good discussion about one of the displays, the graph or the table, then present the other for students to compare. It's a nice, easy way to compare displays. But it's also a good way to practice making a display from data collected. First, you present the table and then ask students to create an example of a corresponding display like a graph or line plot. Then, they share their ideas with a partner, and you hold a whole group discussion about what the display should look like. Then, you can present a display that you created. This can also be a good way to help students practice accuracy and precision. If you look closely at the examples in this variation, you'll notice that no data for 16 points was represented on the line plot. You can point this out to students, or you can wait for them to notice and ask about the missing data. Doing the latter will give you insight into how well they attend to the details within graphs, which is necessary for both creating and interpreting displays.

D

Scores on a Science Test

Points Scored	Number of Students
12 points	2
13 points	4
14 points	
15 points	1
16 points	3
17 points	6
18 points	2
19 points	1
20 points	1

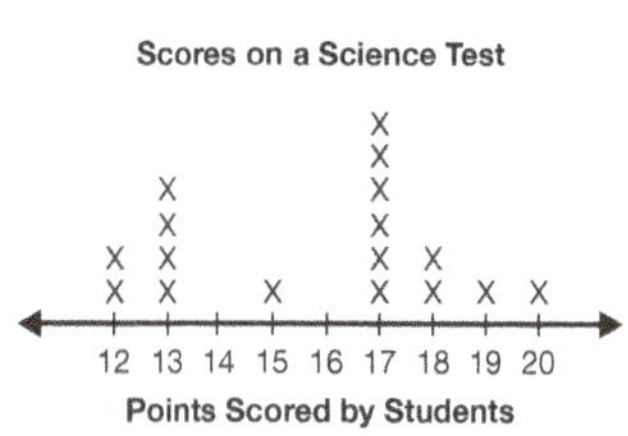

Variation E: Students Create Their Own Comparisons

It can be challenging to find and create data displays for lessons and routines. So why not have your students do some, if not most, of the work? This helps you and it really helps them practice constructing graphs. Keep in mind, a graph can't be made in the few minutes you dedicate to a routine. Instead, make it an independent work project or a small group activity during a lesson. Avoid a basic data set. Instead, use something with a variety of data points and topics like the example of snacks sold at a movie theater. This more complex set of data allows for many more data creations for students to compare and contrast within this routine. For example, a group might make a graph for popcorn sold whereas another might do drinks or nachos. They might both use a bar graph that will have similar features (e.g., days of the week) but with different data points. Some might make a double bar graph with two snacks shown that can be compared with a graph that has only one snack. The possibilities are endless because you are tapping into their insight, individualism, and creativity. Plus, the time it takes for them to create a graph is reclaimed by the many days of practice their creations can yield. And remember to pose the original, full data table to reference when you present two student-created graphs to compare.

But before you do this with your students take note of a few things. First, manipulate the data to make it manageable. Notice the data for each snack and day are a multiple of five. This is intentional for creating reasonable scales and graphs. Also know that your students might struggle to know what graph to make. That's OK! Let them choose. Provide some support, answer some questions, but don't feel like they all have to make the same graph. The different graphs will be a great chance for comparing and contrasting! Also, be on the lookout for errors. They will happen and it's OK. You can correct them at the moment of creation. Or you can let an error happen and then present it with a correct version of the same graph (likely made by you) so they can see precise and imprecise examples as mentioned in Variation D.

E

Snacks Sold at the Movie Theater

	Sun	Mon	Tues	Wed	Thur	Fri	Sat
Popcorn Tubs	145	75	80	35	55	165	180
Candy Boxes	70	55	20	30	25	75	95
Nachos	25	35	35	20	15	140	125
Drinks	155	70	100	45	25	205	225

Variation F: Area and Perimeter

Area and perimeter is an especially good example of how many other topics in this book would work well with this routine. Here, you see two rectangles with different dimensions. They both have the same perimeter of 28 units. However, the area of the two rectangles is different. The rectangle on the left has an area of 45 square units whereas the square on the right has an area of 49 square units. This serves as a good example because students sometimes believe that perimeter and area are static (i.e., if you know one you know the other). They sometimes believe that if one figure's area is larger its perimeter will be too. And in other cases, they rely on their sight to determine and compare area and perimeter of figures. But students might overlook the measurements and instead talk about the attributes of the figures as similarities including parallel sides and square corners. It's fine if they do. After that discussion, shift their focus to the dimensions.

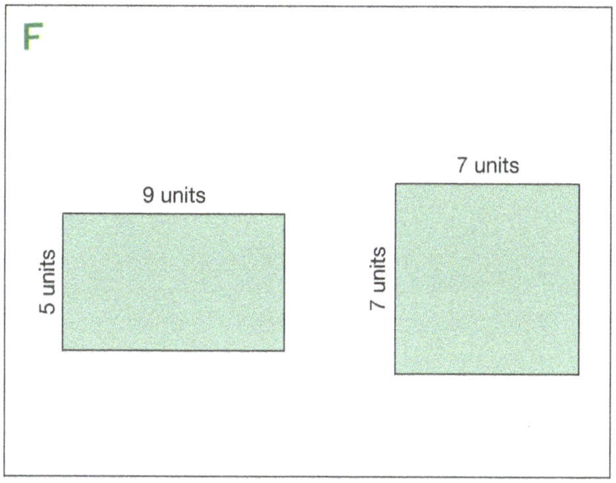

ROUTINE 19

MYSTERY DATA

ABOUT THE ROUTINE

Who doesn't love a mystery? You're likely familiar with number routines that have students determine a mystery number from given clues (SanGiovanni, 2020). These experiences ask students to think about the relative size of numbers, the place value of digits, how they compare to other numbers, and so on. They are perfect for engaging students in reasoning and discussion. They spark interest and curiosity. They help students consider possibilities, look for relationships, and consider differences. Mystery Data is a natural extension of this.

You begin by presenting a data display, a title, and some context like an image or a brief blurb. Ask students to think about and discuss what the data might be describing. In this example, you might expect students to talk about measuring fish caught by a scientist. Some might talk about a fishing tournament or something similar. Students might talk about the number of fish caught or the lengths of the different fish caught. After listening to some of their ideas, briefly share the context and prompt for the mystery data. In this example, you would share,

> "The line plot shows the lengths of fish caught at a fishing contest. Kendall caught one fish in the contest. Use the clues to figure out the length of his fish."

After sharing the prompt, present the first clue, "Kendall tied with one other participant." Note that *only* the first clue should be shared. If using slides, set them up so that each clue appears when you click forward on your computer or remote. Have students identify which measurement might be Kendall's and how they know that it is a possibility.

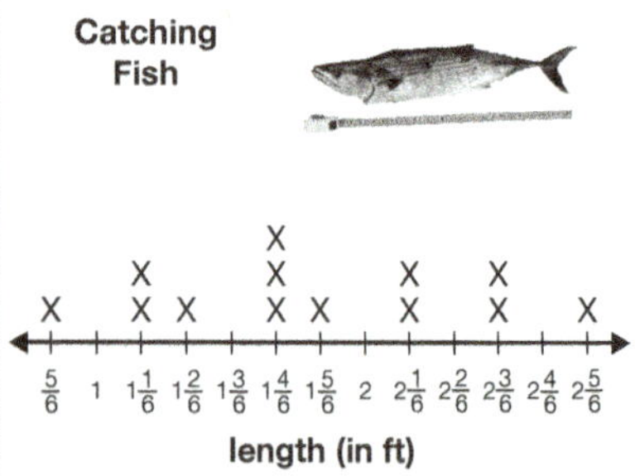

Clue 1: Kendall tied with one other participant.

Clue 2: His fish's length is > 2 feet.

Clue 3: His fish's length is not equivalent to $\frac{13}{6}$ feet.

Source: istockphoto.com/gece33

After a brief conversation, post the second clue, "His fish's length is greater than 2 feet." Again, hold a brief discussion and then move on to the third clue, "His fish's length is not equivalent to $\frac{13}{6}$ feet." The third clue narrows the mystery down to a single solution, which is $2\frac{3}{6}$. The mystery is solved! But you want to now revisit each clue to ensure that the solution does indeed match each of them. You can also take a moment to discuss why a certain data point didn't work for the clues.

Before you begin with this routine, you want to be sure that you have taught a lesson relative to the type of graph you feature in the routine. A single lesson, possibly two, is enough. Remember, this routine provides the quality practice experiences your students need. Also remember that students often answer simple questions about these data displays, such as "How many fish were $1\frac{4}{6}$ inches long?" or "Which length appeared the most?" This routine will offer work with those types of questions and much more.

online resources All routines can be downloaded for your use at https://companion.corwin.com/courses/jumpstartroutines-geometry

HOW THIS ROUTINE HELPS

This routine builds data literacy skills by providing opportunities for students to

- predict what a data display might be conveying;
- analyze and interpret data displays;
- reason about possible solutions (MP2);
- construct viable arguments (MP3);
- listen to strategies of others to acquire new strategies or refine their own (MP3); and
- give feedback to others about their ideas (MP3).

WHAT TO DO

1. Present a data display with a bit of context.
2. Ask students to make predictions about what the data is communicating and/or what you can learn from the graph. For example, you might ask the following:
   - What do you notice about the data?
   - What questions do you have?
   - What do you think the Xs on the line plot represent?
   - What do you think you can and can't tell about the situation from the line plot?
3. Explain what the data is communicating and pose the prompt. For this example, "The line plot shows the lengths of fish caught at a fishing contest. Kendall caught one fish in the contest. Use the clues to figure out the length of his fish."
4. Reveal a clue and ask students to think about what potential answers could satisfy the clue.
5. After discussion, reveal a second clue and then the third.
6. After the third clue, have students confirm how they know a given solution matches all three clues. Identify other possibilities and why those can't be solutions.

SOMETHING TO THINK ABOUT: USING FAMILIAR ROUTINES

Mystery Number routines and activities are familiar to teachers and students. With subtle adjustments, a familiar routine creates opportunities to work with all sorts of skills and concepts. The value in making these changes is that you don't have to teach an entirely new experience. Your students should be able to engage in this "new" routine with little direction. They should understand that the Mystery Number was about trying to determine a number, and in this routine, they're trying to determine a certain data point. They should be comfortable making predictions with the possibility of being wrong. They should have ideas about how to eliminate solutions or recognize that there can be more than one right answer to a given clue or prompt. Now imagine a group of students who work with Mystery Number in primary grades year after year. By the time those students get to third or fourth grade they'll be well-versed in what is expected in such a routine. So, when their teacher swaps out numbers for data, they should be able to transfer their thinking and understanding to the new content.

MYSTERY DATA (VARIATIONS): NEW MYSTERIES

Building off the idea of familiar routines, the following variations show how you can modify this routine for different number types (e.g., whole number line plots) or different data displays (e.g., bar graphs). The variations also show how you can change up this routine to practice other skills related to measurement. It would work well with geometry concepts, too, by creating a mystery shape or mystery figure experience. As mentioned with other routines, consider having students create the clues for any version of the routine regardless of the featured topic or content.

Variation A: Change the Number of Clues

Flexibility with routines is key! Changing things up keeps the experience fresh. It also allows for easy ways to differentiate an experience. This first variation shows that you can trim the clues to just two instead of the three clues shown in the first example. With just two clues, there will likely be more than one correct answer. In this variation, Bowser could weigh $2\frac{2}{8}$ or $2\frac{6}{8}$. Another option is to blend this variation with Variation D where students create all of the clues. To do this, provide the first two clues as shown then have students create a third and share their thinking with the class.

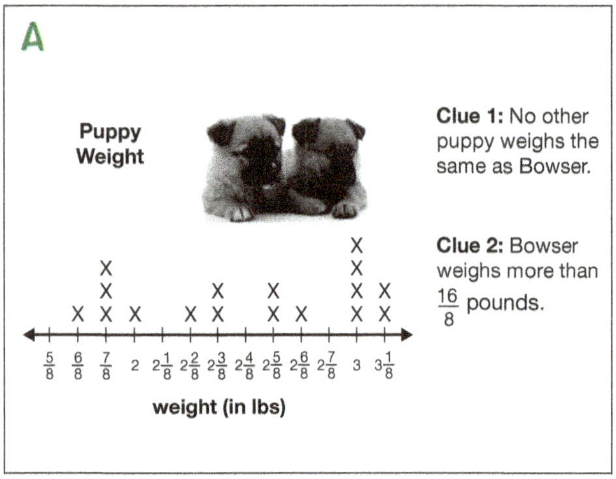

Source: istockphoto.com/Litvalifa

Variation B: Line Plots With Whole Numbers

At first glance, you notice how this variation changes the data from fractions to whole numbers. Using whole numbers on line plots will work well in most grades, especially second and third. But there is a bit more here than you might notice. First, this variation shows (yet again) how topics of measurement (time) and data (line plots) can be mingled so that students have opportunities to practice both in the same experience. In this example, the whole numbers represent minutes. Yet, the third clue references a fractional amount. So, students have to reason to find the number of minutes that $2\frac{1}{2}$ hours represent. The discussion they have can prove powerful for students who have difficulty with conversions. Here, a student might say that they thought about 1 hour as 60 minutes, doubling that and adding 30 more. Another student might share that they thought of a half-hour as 30 minutes and figured there would be 5 halves in $2\frac{1}{2}$.

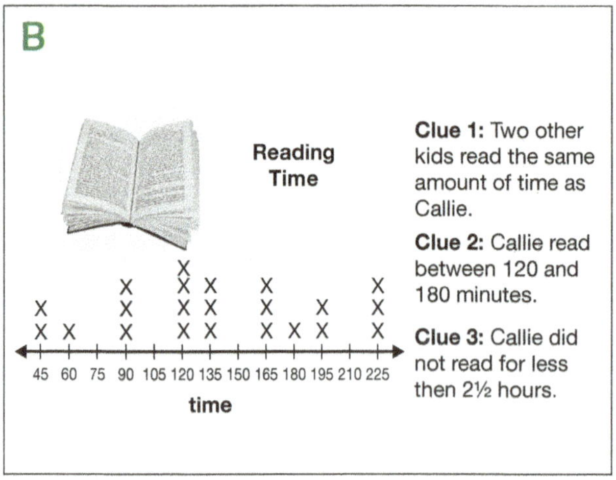

Source: istockphoto.com/VvoeVale

They then multiplied 30 x 5 to find 150 minutes. And there is also the opportunity to point out the 15-minute intervals on the line plot asking how many hours would be in 75, 105, or 150 minutes.

Variations C: Bar Graphs

This third variation of Mystery Data shows how you might use it with a different data display like a bar graph. Again, students are presented with some information like a title (Video Games) and some data along with missing elements such as the y- and x-axis labels. They'll use the clues to determine what those labels should be and in this case, which bar represents which character. Students share ideas about what the graph could be about. They might identify the numbers to be about the number of tries playing a certain game or the number of times a game has been played. They might share that the bars represent different games or possibly different players. Remember, you don't have to "fish" for the correct answers in this preliminary discussion. You simply want to have students talk about the data. After that discussion, you can present the clues. The first clue about Abby is presented. Have students discuss what they can tell and what they can't tell from that clue. Many students should be able to surmise that the graph is about the number of games different people have. Once this is shared, you can then ask what the scale and the bars represent. Students are also likely to point out that Abby must be one of the data points on the right. When they do, be sure to ask how they know (both bars are greater than 40). Then, repeat the process with each new clue. To extend the routine, you can then have students generate and share different clues that could have been used to identify the labels and bars in the graph.

C

Video Games

Abby: I have more than 40 video games.

Ben: I have 5 fewer video games than David.

Cara: Abby and I have a total of 70 video games.

David: I have less than 30 video games.

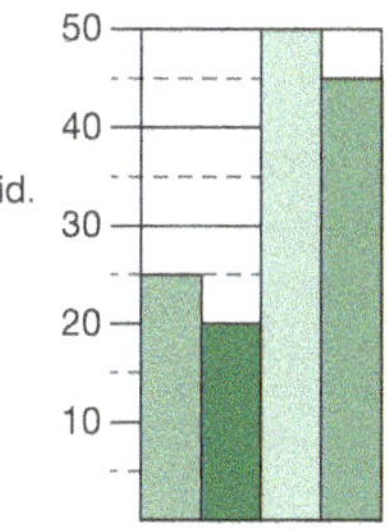

Variation D: Student Clues

This variation of Mystery Data is an option for sparking student creativity. Here, students create the three clues for the class to decipher. There is little context offered so be prepared for students to create it. Note that a key for the graph helps, along with a somewhat specific title. The openness of the experience might be tough for some students to grapple with. If so, talk with them beforehand about the graph and the context, and point out the key to help them get started. Instead of having them write the clues during the routine, you can have small groups collaboratively write their clues. Then, you can use their ideas with the same data display multiple times during the week.

D

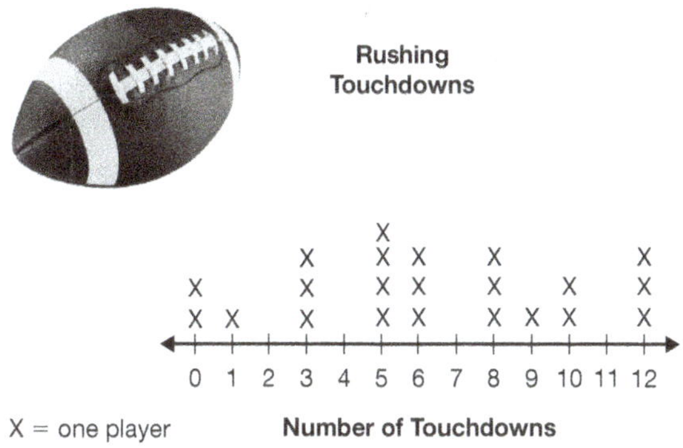

Source: istockphoto.com/AnthiaCumming

Variation E: Mystery Time

Telling time is a measurement standard that benefits from brief bursts of practice. This variation of Mystery Data challenges students to figure out what time the clock should be showing. You pose three or more clues about time, pausing after each one to ask students what the mystery time might be. Again, be sure to ask them why certain times aren't possibilities. For the first clue, something like 12:30 doesn't make sense because students are asleep at 12:30 AM and in school at 12:30 PM. Of course, someone will argue that they stayed up really late or that they're doing their homework in school. When that happens, acknowledge it and keep moving. To maximize this experience, you can have students draw hands on a clock and write the time (digital format) for each clue. To do this, create a blank analog clock and put it in a plastic sheet protector. Students can write on it with a dry erase marker and wipe off their ideas after each new clue is given.

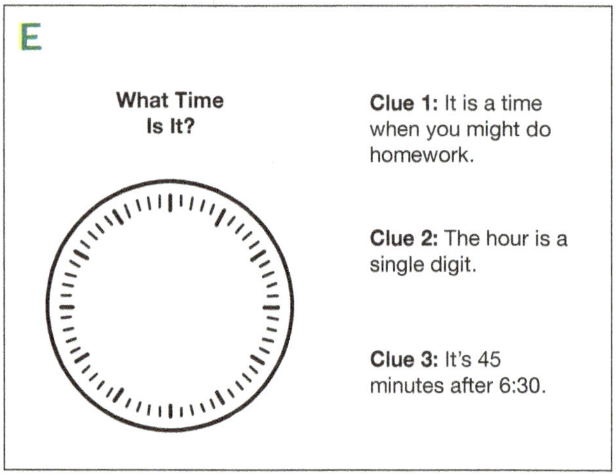

Source: istockphoto.com/JoyTasa

ROUTINE 20

NOT QUITE RIGHT

ABOUT THE ROUTINE

A challenge for students, regardless of mathematics content, is using and interpreting the language of mathematics. Part of the challenge is math-specific in terms of using academic vocabulary like *quotient*. Another part is that some vocabulary, like *sum* can sound like another word *some*, which is commonly used in contexts different than math. A third part of the challenge is that the grammar of mathematics and the English language are sometimes at odds. An example of this is when a student says, "4 divided by 32 is 8" to describe $32 \div 4 = 8$ or "3 minus 10 is 7" for $10 - 3 = 7$. Though this can be a symptom of conceptual misunderstanding it's often a simple matter of confused language. For example, when you ask students, "What is 5 less than 12?" or "How many 7s can you make with 28?", they may write expressions that match the grammar of the question, $5 - 12$ and $7 \div 28$, yet still perform the operations correctly to match the question! In other words, it isn't always the math that is the issue, it can also be the language of math.

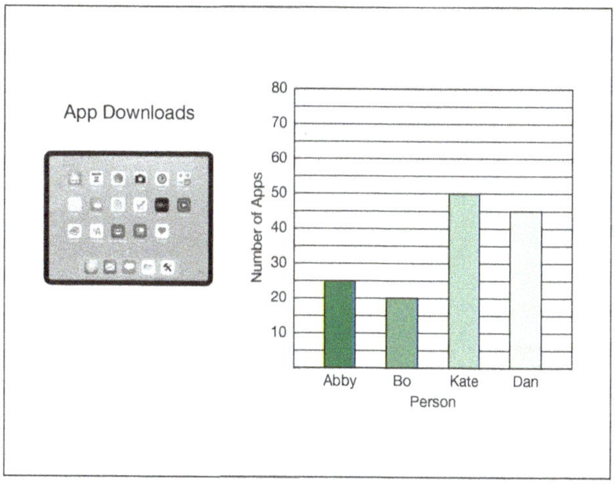

Source: istockphoto/grinvalds

Students can stumble with language the same way when trying to describe data displays. When talking about the bar graph in the example, a student may say, "Abby has twice as many apps as Kate", or when asked, "What is the difference between the number of apps Dan has and Kate has?", they may respond, "Dan's bar is shorter, but Kate's bar is taller." As you know, both of these are not quite right.

This routine is designed to help students build proficiency with interpreting both data displays as well as mathematical statements about those data displays. It builds on the work students did in other routines, such as I Would Say (Routine #16) where students summarize data and Asked and Answered (Routine #17) where students determine whether they can or cannot be answered. With this routine, you present students with a data display and a statement that is "not quite right," and students must identify what is incorrect about the statement and how they can change the statement so that it is correct. For the bar graph about app downloads, some not quite right statements to use could be

- Abby has 20 more apps than Dan.
- Kate has the tallest bar in the graph.
- Dan has more than Bo but less than Abby.

There is no right or wrong way to go about the routine. You can focus on imprecise statements

online resources — All routines can be downloaded for your use at https://companion.corwin.com/courses/jumpstartroutines-geometry

like the second one: "Kate has the tallest bar in the graph." You can make incorrect or incomplete comparisons like the first bulleted statement. You might summarize the data incorrectly like the second or third bulleted statements. You might use the wrong numbers to describe the data.

The routine is not relegated to early grades or primary grades. In all grades, you want your students to grapple with inaccuracy, be it their own or that of someone else. As graphs become more complex, it becomes even more important for them to interpret the data and question statements that are not quite right. Examples of not quite right statements for this fourth- or fifth-grade line plot could be

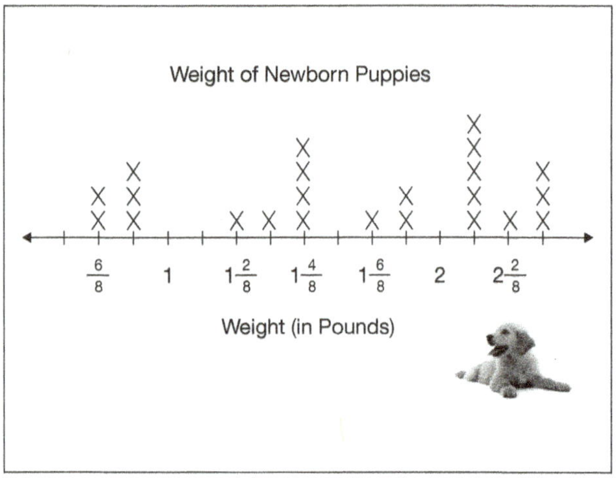

Source: istockphoto.com/101cats

- Most of the puppies weighed less than 1 pound.
- The same number of puppies weighed $\frac{7}{8}$ pounds as weighed $1\frac{7}{8}$ pounds.
- Twice as many puppies weighed $\frac{6}{8}$ pounds as weighed $1\frac{4}{8}$ pounds.

The first statement is not quite right because most of the puppies weighed more than 1 pound. For the second statement, the same number of puppies weighed $\frac{7}{8}$ of a pound and $2\frac{3}{8}$ pounds not $1\frac{7}{8}$ pounds. The last statement is reversed. Twice as many puppies weighed $1\frac{4}{8}$ pounds than those that weighed $\frac{6}{8}$ pounds.

This routine also helps students practice critical analysis of statements about data. It causes them to look carefully at data displays. It helps them think about what is incorrect about statements or data for that matter. You can begin with basic questions about reading the data display, like the first question about puppies in the example. You can work toward questions that require some degree of problem-solving like the third statement.

As mentioned, students should also tell how the not quite right statement should be revised to be accurate. They can also identify how the data would need to change so that the statement is true. For example, for the first statement to be true at least 14 more puppies would need to weigh less than a pound because 18 weigh more than a pound and 5 weigh less. For the second statement, 1 more puppy would need to weigh $1\frac{7}{8}$ pounds for there to be the same number as those weighing $\frac{7}{8}$.

HOW THIS ROUTINE HELPS

This routine builds data literacy skills by providing opportunities for students to

- make sense of information within data displays;
- retell or summarize a display in their own words (MP3);
- identify the important information in a data display (MP1);
- analyze statements about data (MP3);
- attend to precise statements about data (MP6);
- listen to how others interpret and describe data (MP3); and
- give feedback to others about their ideas (MP3).

WHAT TO DO

1. Prepare three or four statements that are close but not quite right or accurate about a data display.
2. Present the data display like a line plot as shown in the example or picture graphs and bar graphs as shown in the variations.
3. Give students a few moments to observe the information.
4. Optional: Have students summarize the data with a partner.
5. Present one of the not quite right statements about the data. Optional: You can tell students that there is something not quite right about the statement.
6. Have students read and determine what isn't right about the statement.
7. Ask students to share ideas with a partner about what isn't correct about the statement.
8. Bring the whole class together to share what is inaccurate about the statement.
9. Optional: Have students discuss how the statement should be revised so that it is accurate.
10. Repeat the process with the other statements.

SOMETHING TO THINK ABOUT: WHOLE SCHOOL AGREEMENTS

Whole school agreements are decisions that an entire school takes on for a cohesive, coherent mathematics experience that benefits each and every student (Karp et al., 2021). Schools need agreements about the language used, the "tricks" they won't teach, the shortcuts they'll avoid because they don't always work, the strategies for computation that students will learn, and what common notations and generalizations will be used and encouraged. Whole school agreements about problem-solving and problem-solving routines have great value as well.

Agreements about using routines consistently, even talking about which routines might be used in different grades is also helpful. Think about it. Students who learn how to engage with a routine one year are prepared to use it the following years. They have opportunity to deepen their understanding of the experience and are positioned to transfer their skills to new content. Imagine a second grader who works with this routine over the course of the year. Then, when they get to third grade, their teacher continues to use it with more complicated bar graphs before working in area and perimeter or some other content. In fourth grade, those students might use it with line plots as shown in the opening example and so on. Repeatedly analyzing statements about data or other content in the same way undoubtedly yields much more capable thinkers and doers.

NOT QUITE RIGHT (VARIATIONS): USING THEIR ERRORS

Descriptive feedback supports students' understanding of mathematics concepts and skills (Martin, 2021). Feedback can be provided in writing or through discussion. Routines provide a great opportunity for such feedback that affirms ideas and strategies or corrects misperceptions or errors. They can also serve to trigger certain points of feedback. For example, you might find that your students often overlook the scale in a bar or picture graph. If so, use those in your routines and in this routine include not quite right statements that contain errors relative to the scale of the graph. Manipulate routines and variations so that you can target areas of feedback to help your students advance their understanding of data or any other math content.

Variation A: Picture Graphs

Using the bakery sales data, not quite right statements could be

- $4\frac{1}{2}$ cakes were sold in December.
- A total of 80 cakes were sold in October and November.
- 15 fewer cakes were sold in December than in September.

Not Quite Right works well at any grade with any type of graph. You can use it with basic bar graphs, tally tables, or picture graphs. It can be a good tool for practicing scaled bar picture graphs. These graphs can present a challenge to students who rely on counting by 1s. Moreover, scales with 2 or 10, like the one shown, can be difficult when a half is represented like the months of October and December in the graph. The first statement takes aim at this misstep. There are 4 and half pictures of cakes. But, as you know, December sales were 45 not 4 and a half. Statements about combinations (middle statement) or comparisons (last statement) are great to include in this routine regardless of grade level, though you might first begin with simply reading a certain type of graph with or without a scale.

A

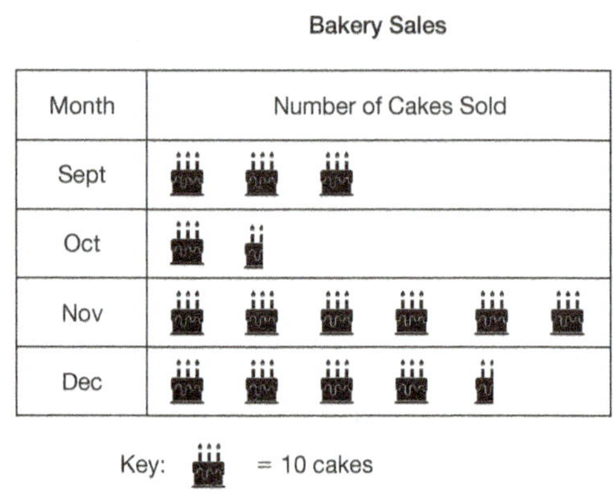

Source: istockphoto.com/Studiostockart

Variation B: Bar Graphs

Using the game controller sales data, not quite right statements could be

- 9 controllers were sold in October.
- 5 more controllers needed to be sold in December to equal November sales.
- November had the greatest sales of the year.

Like picture graphs, bar graphs also come with scales. The sales of game controllers is reported in groups of 5 rather than singles. When in a rush, students can overlook the scale and simply count the bars. That's why a little practice with this routine and not quite right statements like the first two have great value. The first statement isn't quite right, as 45 controllers were sold rather than 9. The second statement isn't right either because November sales were 25 controllers more than December sales, not 5. Focusing student attention on scales through these not quite right statements is a good idea. But all three questions don't have to focus on that misstep. The third is a nice alternative that students might struggle to answer. November does have the most sales of the three months in the graph but there are nine other months missing from the graph. The last statement needs a small adjustment to be accurate. This also reminds us that while this bar graph using three categories might be within the standard of your grade level, it doesn't mean you have to limit students to experiencing only three. A nice way to enrich, extend, or deepen their understanding is to use four or more categories like shown in the next example. And if you do use more categories, just be sure that you don't hold them accountable (i.e., grade or assess) on the more complex graphs.

B

Source: istockphoto/Chimpinski

Variation C: Student Statements Are Not Quite Right

Having students create situations, prompts, or examples has been suggested a few times throughout this book. It helps you create content to use with your class. Most importantly, it requires them to take a close look at situations, analyze them, decide what is true, and in this routine, come up with something that isn't correct. Though this routine typically features three or four incorrect statements for students to work with, you can ask your students to create just one statement. They can write them on sticky notes or index cards. You can have them write statements independently or collaboratively. Remember to keep your expectations in check. They might write tough statements to consider or simple ones like, "Orange has the greatest sales." They might write statements that seem to be answered with the data but aren't. For example, a statement like, "Lemon is the least favorite flavor" isn't quite right though it has the fewest sales. Maybe the first five sold were lemon and the seller ran out of the flavor. The graph tells what was sold not what was the favorite. And they might even write statements that aren't statistical or data-based statements as discussed in Asked and Answered (Routine #17).

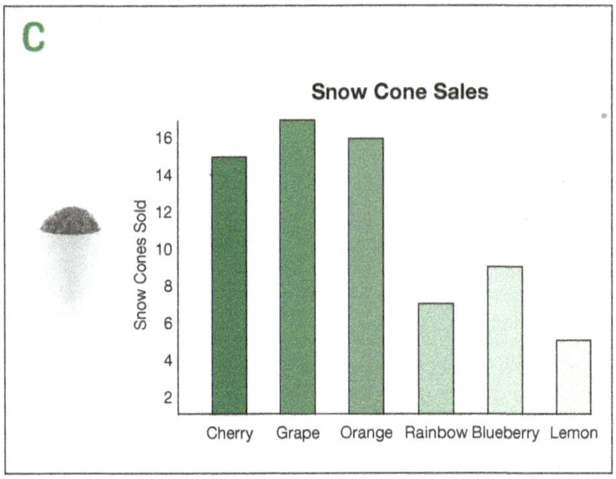

Source: istockphoto.com/duckycards

Variation D: Data With Infographics

Using the pumpkin data, not quite right statements could be

- The world records are shown every 10 years.
- 2011 was the largest pumpkin ever.
- The 1990 pumpkin was more than 1976 and 1981 combined.

Infographics were first mentioned in I Would Say (Routine #16). They would work great with this routine as well. Using these graphics with faulty statements should also provide the added benefit of causing students to ask questions about the data they encounter in these displays, among others. This notion pops with the first two statements especially. For the first statement, the world records aren't shown every 10 years but rather about every 10 years. That should spark the question, "why?" for your students. Was there no world record in 1971 or 1991? Were those years omitted because they were larger than other years? Look at the second statement. The year 2011 had the largest pumpkin ever according to the data presented. It can be assumed that it was the largest up to that point but maybe not. And 2011 was more than a decade ago. Have any larger pumpkins been grown since then?

Source: istockphoto/MariuszBlach

Variation E: Elapsed Time

Using the movie time information, not quite right statements could be

- Movie A is an hour and a half.
- Movie B is an hour and 15 minutes.
- Movie A is longer.

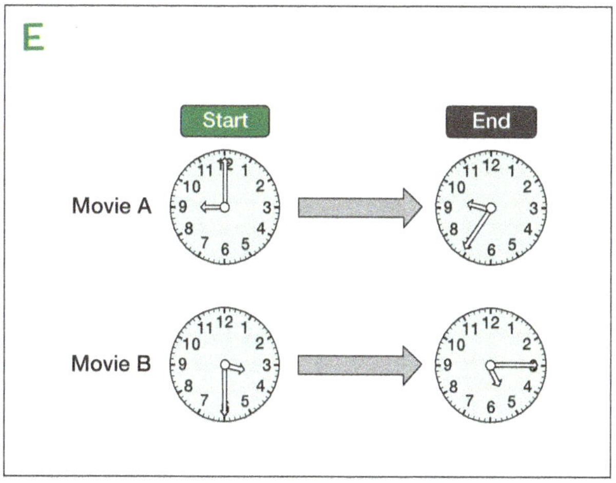

Elapsed time is an important and challenging measurement topic for students to practice. It will work well with other routines like See It, Build It (Routine #1). Here, you give two or more examples of elapsed time. Putting them in context, like lengths of a movie, can be helpful for posing questions. Students determine what isn't quite right about the statements that go with the information. In the example, movie A is an hour and 35 minutes. To make it a correct statement, students could say, "Movie A is more than a half hour." Movie B is an hour and 45 minutes not an hour and 15 minutes and movie B is longer. These two statements can be revised by simply making the information correct (i.e., movie B is longer). But to keep the experience fresh, and potentially more rigorous, ask students how the information might be changed so that the statements could be true. For example, movie B isn't an hour and 15 minutes. But if it was, how would the end time change if the start time is correct? Or how does the start time change if the end time of 5:15 is correct? In short, there is no one way to correct the statements.

Variation F: Area and Perimeter

Using figures A, B, C, and D, not quite right statements could be

- They all have the same area.
- Each figure has the same perimeter.
- Figure B has an area of 9.

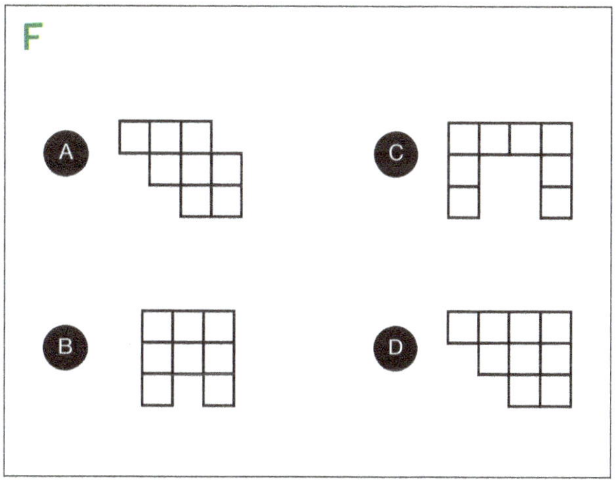

Area and perimeter are measurement topics that students sometimes confuse with each other and other times correlate. In other words, sometimes students see a static, unchanging relationship between area and perimeter. If a shape has an area of 12 and a perimeter of 16 then every shape with an area of 12 has a perimeter of 16. These students might think that as an area increases by 1 the perimeter increases by 1 and so on. That's why pentomino activities (See It, Build It, Routine #1, Variation E) have great value because they help students understand that figures with an area of 5 don't always have the same perimeter. Another way to practice this is to use a routine like this one where students compare the area and perimeter of different figures. These figures are good starting points because students can see the squares that make up each figure. In later experiences, or later grades for that matter, students would work with "open" figures with nothing more than the dimensions of each side provided. In this example, the first statement is not quite right because figure C has a different area. Figure D has a different perimeter, and figure B has an area of 8 making the middle and bottom statements incorrect, respectively.

Variation G: Money

For piggy banks A, B, C, and D, not quite right statements could be

- Piggy Bank B has the least amount of money.
- Piggy Bank A has less than 50¢.
- The total amount of money in all the piggy banks is over $5.00.

This routine offers a great opportunity to practice counting coins and comparing amounts of money. Students are presented with sets of coins and statements to evaluate. In this case, the coins represent money in four different piggy banks. The first statement is not true because piggy bank C has the least amount of money. The second statement is not quite right because bank A is just over 50¢. The third statement shows how you can incorporate all options into a statement. The banks do not total more than $5. Expect some students to count each coin in each bank to justify their thinking while others might reason that each of the four banks is less than $1 so in total they cannot be more than $5. This is more likely to happen when a statement, like the third, is offered after other banks have been discussed.

G

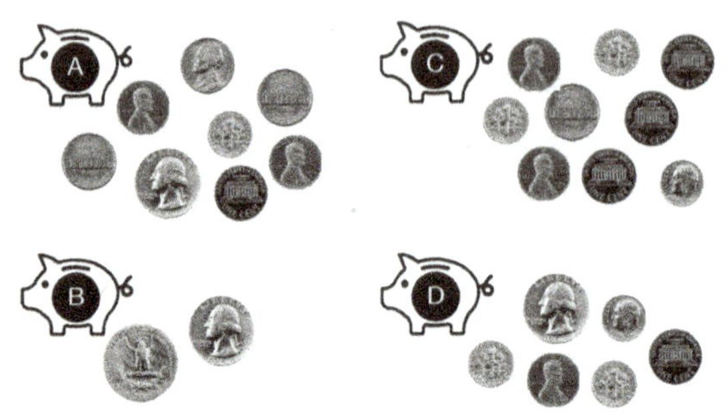

Coin credit: istockphoto.com/filo

Piggy bank credit: istockphoto.com/TymofiiMalynovskyi

PART 3

WHERE TO GO NEXT

You are now armed with understanding how routines can develop student skill with geometry, measurement, and data. You hopefully see how they can engage your students. You have examined a host of examples and modifications ready to implement in your classroom. So where do you go next?

MAKE A PLAN

Using routines in your mathematics classrooms might be considerably different from what has been done previously. To be successful, you need to craft a plan that addresses fundamental considerations. First, identify the big ideas you want to focus on with your students. Next, determine which routines you think will work best. Think about a rotation of routines and whether you will change routines out daily or if you will work with one routine for a few days before moving to the next. You can find success with either approach though the latter, sticking with the same routine for a week or so, is probably the better option. There are a few other details you need to think about to plan your routines with intention and purpose.

If you are a teacher who uses Number Talks or other number routines, you have to consider when and how you will use geometry, measurement, and data routines. You might decide to swap out a few of those experiences over the course of a month with these routines instead. Alternatively, you can add these routines as an experience after your opening number routine or situate them somewhere later in your instructional block. You should also consider which of your number routines or number content on the whole is in a good enough place for you to let go of for a bit.

Identify Content for Routines

Routines are not intended as first instruction. You want students to be engaging in rich discussion with content that they have been introduced to already. These routines are chances to practice geometry, measurement, and data. The topics that you select are relative to where your students are. Consider the content or topics that they learned about in earlier years. Think about the content you will be teaching and when. If the point is to practice these during the year to position students for success with standardized assessments, you'll have to teach some of that content earlier than what your scope and sequence might call for. And know that it is OK for classrooms in the same grade to be at different places. The goal is to advance all students' understanding and reasoning skills with this content from wherever they are currently.

Identify Routines

It's likely that you prefer certain representations, strategies, or instructional techniques in general. The same can probably be said about your preference of routines. It's also likely that your preferences are different from those of your colleagues. This collection of routines offers choice so that you can find the ones that suit you and your students best. Some may be simply more appealing than others. You have options. Do not feel compelled to use a specific sequence of routines or to "cover" or "complete" all of the routines.

Choose a few routines that you want to master first. You might make your selection based on students' interests or academic needs. You might choose See It, Build It (Routine #1) or Find It (Routine #4) because your students need practice with recognizing shapes. You might choose More or Less (Routine #14) or This or That? (Routine #15) because measurement conversions have proven difficult to your students. Or, you might choose I Would Say (Routine #16) or Not Quite Right (Routine #20) because you want your students to improve summarizing data and attending to precision within their statements.

Determine Your Rotation

Doing the same routine each day will become mundane quite quickly. Think about which routines you will rotate through including the order of them. It's OK to be unsure at first. It's OK to deviate from a planned sequence. You might find that you need to circle back to a certain routine before continuing on with your rotation.

It's important to realize that you don't have to dedicate a specific number of days or class periods to a routine before rotating to another. The time spent with two different routines may not be equivalent. You can plan the amount of time you spend with a routine based on students' needs, engagement, interest, and excitement for it. However, even if you spend a few extra days with a certain routine, you should plan to move on from it so that it doesn't become stale. You should be mindful of those routines that students truly enjoy and plan to come back to them throughout the year.

Give It Time

Thinking, reasoning, and discussion about geometry, measurement, data, or in general may be unchartered waters for some of your students. It's possible that many of your students haven't had many opportunities to work with these topics consistently. Some may not have had rigorous experiences with these topics either. Their lack of experience may mean that they are hesitant to share their thinking because they lack confidence or because they aren't sure how to talk about their thinking. Give them opportunity and time. When well nurtured, you will find that you can't stop them from sharing their ideas and insights.

This may be unchartered waters for you too. Many teachers have little training in effective geometry, measurement, and data instruction. They rely on their own experiences and perceive the goal of the activity to be getting the right answer. When students struggle, teachers can be compelled to stop the process and show them how to be successful. In short, your first routine, or two, may flop because of you and your students' unfamiliarity. That is fine. It should be expected. Be patient. Stick with it. Reflect on what happened, what surprised you, and how you might go about it differently. Try it again the next day and the next. Work to find a rhythm. But also know that some routines just might not work for you or your students. That's another reason why there are so many to choose from. If you find that one isn't hitting the mark after a few days of practice, toss it out and start with a new one.

Set Goals

You can offset the challenges with goals, but be sure to keep your goals reasonable. At first, you might set the goal of doing a routine three times a week or mastering a specific routine over the course of two weeks. You might set a goal to use three different routines over the course of a month or five different routines in a marking period.

You can think about setting goals for students as well. You might want to develop how well they summarize data. You might want them to work with justifying their thinking or decomposing shapes. You can measure those goals in all sorts of ways. One way might be to revisit a routine from early in the year with the exact same problems or numbers later in the year and compare student performance. In other situations, it might make sense to measure growing student proficiency on a brief written assessment. You can also measure student dispositions, behaviors, communication skills, and confidence. A simple set of survey questions like the following could be a good place to start.

- I can solve problems with geometry (measurement or data).
- I have ideas about how to solve new problems with geometry (measurement or data).
- I have different strategies for solving problems that I know how to use.
- I like solving problems.
- I like working with geometry (measurement or data).
- I know how to show problems.
- I can usually tell if my answer makes sense when I solve a problem.
- I know what questions to ask myself when I try to solve problems.

ADJUST TO THEIR REASONING

Throughout the day, you naturally respond to student thinking and reasoning. You ask questions to challenge student ideas. You push back on your students' strategies. You ask them to clarify. You'll need to leverage all of those same teacher moves during these problem-solving routines. You'll also need to keep in mind that as students work with routines, they'll begin to adjust their reasoning. They may begin to favor specific strategies or approaches. When they do, you'll need to respond by changing the numbers, skills, and/or the routine that you use.

FURTHER MODIFY ROUTINES

Each of the routines in this book are creations or adaptations of activities used in real classrooms. They have served real students very well. There are directions and procedures for implementing them; but those directions are not set in stone. In fact, many of the routines presented are variations of the first offerings. There are ideas for modifying presented throughout, but more can be changed. You should feel free to change how a routine is carried out. Change the starting point, the process, or how students interact. Modify these routines to make them their own.

DESIGN YOUR OWN ROUTINES

These routines are all built to go after the difficulties students have when they encounter geometry, measurement, or data content. Each routine is an opportunity for students to discuss and defend their reasoning. You can modify almost any instructional activity to become a routine. As you become more comfortable with routines, you can begin to develop your own based on games and activities you use during instruction. You can look for routines online. You might even investigate number sense routines or problem-solving routines and incorporate them in your instruction.

WORK COLLABORATIVELY AND SHARE THE LOAD

Sometimes your students' creative thinking will inspire new possibilities or new routines. Keep in mind that your colleagues are also an excellent creative source for generating examples. When teachers plan together, they learn about others' perspectives, experiences, and mathematical insights. They learn about how others think and reason about numbers and computation. The exchange of ideas with your colleagues can help you reinforce and grow your own ideas. It helps you prepare. It helps you facilitate student reasoning through discussion.

Leveraging insights from other teachers and students is also a great way to share the workload. For example, four teachers on a team could each create four sets of prompts for a routine. If those four teachers share their four, each teacher would have a routine planned for 16 days, or a little more than 3 weeks. Each of those teachers could also have students create examples of their routine. If so, they could select four student examples and rotate them as well. In doing so, a teacher who created four examples could wind up with 32 days ready to go.

USE JUMP-START ROUTINES FOR PROFESSIONAL LEARNING OR PLCS

Routines are the perfect focus for professional learning or a professional learning community (PLC). In fact, many of the routines offered in this book are the result of ongoing collaborative conversations, dabbling, and reflection. In a PLC about routines, you might first learn about what routines are, why they matter, and the instructional challenges they intend to solve. You and your colleagues can then begin to learn about specific routines, try them out, and share your experiences. The steps below are a helpful framework for investigating and learning about routines in a PLC.

1. **Learn About the Routine:** Colleagues select a routine that they all want to focus on. They read about it and discuss what it might look like or how it might be adjusted for their students.
2. **Identify Content for the Routine:** Colleagues discuss what problem situations and number types they would feature in the routine and why.
3. **Create Examples:** Colleagues select or create examples of the routine for use with their students. One way to do this is to make use of collaborative software, such as Google Slides, in which each teacher can craft some examples of the routine they intend to use with their students. A collaboration tool allows those teachers to have a record of their work for future use as well as providing a way to share examples between them. And, sharing examples also helps lessen the workload.
4. **Predict What Might Happen:** After making examples of the routine to use with students, colleagues anticipate what their students will do. They might share the strategies that students will use, the misconceptions they might show, or the questions that the teachers themselves might ask.
5. **Do Them:** Members of the PLC do the routines with their students.
6. **Reflect:** Individuals jot down notes or capture reflections about the routine. Those reflections are brought to the next meeting in which colleagues share their experiences and consider what went well and what they might do differently in the future.

These six steps are then started again with a new routine. There are no rules as to how this must proceed. There is logic exploring the same routines with your colleagues. However, the PLC can play out just as well if you and they select your own routines to use.

The work of the PLC might be strengthened through peer observation and feedback. To do this, you simply visit one another and look for how routines are being implemented. Then, you give and receive feedback from your colleagues about how things went. Peer observations can be supported with a "look-for" tool. It's possible that colleagues don't have the time to visit each other during the day. Another option might be for you to make a video of your routine for others to view and offer feedback.

Problem-Solving Look-For

A look-for tool helps guide a visit to a colleague's classroom as they do a routine. Some of those ideas are included here but the list is not exhaustive.

The classroom environment is conducive to a routine.

- Student proximity to the teacher is appropriate.
- Student arrangement promotes discussion between students and as a class.
- Respectful behaviors are established.
- Students are comfortable sharing ideas.

The routine is appropriate.

- The purpose of the routine is clear.
- The problem type is appropriate.
- The selected numbers are appropriate.
- The routine focuses on reasoning and sense making.

Multiple solutions/rationales are investigated/discussed.

- Student ideas and insights are solicited first before the teacher shares their ideas.
- Strategies are recorded and/or discussed.
- Thinking is recorded accurately.
- More than one solution pathway is investigated (as appropriate).

Communication is prevalent.

- Students share their reasoning.
- Students listen and react to the reasoning of others.
- Teachers react to student reasoning by asking questions.
- Representations (e.g., drawings, equations, etc.) are connected to the problem by the student and/or teacher.

Discussion promotes reasoning.

- More than one perspective is featured.
- Teacher asks students to justify their thinking and most attempt to do so.
- Teacher questions overly complicated or highly inefficient strategies.

JUMP-START MATHEMATICS ENGAGEMENT

A routine is an opportunity to jump-start engagement, problem-solving, and reasoning. They might work best at the beginning of a lesson (SanGiovanni, 2020) but can work well at any point during the math block. Routines are quality tasks for working with a wide range of content, concepts, and skills. They are opportunities for promoting engagement through novel prompts, interesting situations, and discussion. They are opportunities to play with geometry, measurement, and data. They are an opportunity for making student thinking and reasoning routine!

APPENDIX

Geometry, measurement, and data intersect with so much of what is learned and taught in mathematics. Some of those important considerations are unpacked throughout this book in the Something to Think About sections. These brief passages give you something to think about as mathematics comes to life in your classroom through your teaching. A brief overview of these sections are included in the following table.

ROUTINE	SOMETHING TO THINK ABOUT
Spatial Awareness (Routine 1: See It, Build It)	Spatial awareness is worth practicing as it supports reasoning and potentially student number sense.
Preparing Materials (Routine 2: Sorts)	Recruit student and parent volunteers to help prepare materials for hands-on, engaging experiences in math.
Routines as Formative Assessment (Routine 3: Venns)	Routines are the perfect opportunity for formative assessment. The insight you gather during a routine can help you decide if a topic needs to be retaught or practiced more.
Creating Examples (Routine 4: Find It)	Leverage your students' understanding and creativity to help with the burden of creating tasks and routines.
Doing It First (Routine 5: Dots)	Anticipating what students will do helps you think about the strategies you should look for and the missteps your students might make. It also helps you prepare to respond.
Lettering Options (Routine 6: The Truth)	Labeling with letters helps you facilitate a conversation.
Activities for Spatial Awareness and Reasoning (Routine 7: On the Move)	Classic games and puzzles that feature spatial awareness, reasoning, and problem-solving have a place in every mathematics class.
Differentiation (Routine 8: Views)	Directions, products, and other aspects of routines can be differentiated to increase access and support.
Slides, Document Camera, or Drawings (Routine 9: What's the Order?)	Presentation slides can be useful tools for routines or teaching in general. Be mindful of how you use them. Relying on them can undermine responsiveness.
The Importance of Estimation (Routine 10: That's a Fact)	Estimation is critically important as it helps students determine if their strategies *and* solutions are reasonable.
Using Centers to Reinforce (Routine 11: Volume Quick Images)	Skills and concepts you practice through routines can be further supported by centers and homework experiences that are related to the routine.
Manipulatives During Routines (Routine 12: Close, Far, Between, and More)	Manipulatives can support student engagement and reasoning during geometry routines.
Routines in the Building Thinking Classroom (BTC) (Routine 13: It's About)	Routines are a natural complement to instruction aligned to Building Thinking Classrooms.
Anchor Charts (Routine 14: More or Less)	Anchor charts support engagement, accuracy, retention, and conversation.

ROUTINE	SOMETHING TO THINK ABOUT
Why So Many Routines? (Routine 15: This or That?)	There are different skills to practice, and they need to be practiced in different ways. A variety of routines promote transfer of skills while aligning to preferences and strengths of students and teachers.
Graphic Organizers (Routine 16: I Would Say)	Graphic organizers help students summarize and communicate.
Images With Data Displays (Routine 17: Asked and Answered)	Including images with data displays supports comprehension and sense-making.
Scaffolding (Routine 18: Same and Different)	Scaffolding a routine promotes student access and equity.
Using Familiar Routines (Routine 19: Mystery Data)	Geometry, measurement, and data routines can be developed from familiar number routines.
Whole School Agreements (Routine 20: Not Quite Right)	Approaches to teaching problem-solving should be consistent across grades and schools.

REFERENCES

Anderson, L. W., & Krathwohl, D. R. (Eds.). (2001). *A taxonomy for learning, teaching, and assessing: A revision of Bloom's taxonomy of educational objectives*. Longman.

Bargagliotti, A., Franklin, C., Arnold, P., Gould, R., Johnson, S., Perez, L., & Spangler, D. (2020). *Pre-K–12 guidelines for assessment and instruction in statistics education (GAISE) Report II*. American Statistical Association & National Council of Teachers of Mathematics.

Bay-Williams, J. M., & Fletcher, G. (2017). A bottom-up hundreds chart? *Teaching Children Mathematics, 24*(3), 153–160.

Bay-Williams, J. M., & SanGiovanni, J. J. (2021). *Figuring out fluency in mathematics teaching and learning, Grades K–8*. Corwin.

Beckmann, S. (2013). *Mathematics for elementary teachers with activities*. Pearson.

Berry, R. (2018). *Thinking about instructional routines in mathematics teaching and learning*. National Council of Teachers of Mathematics. https://www.nctm.org/News-and-Calendar/Messages-from-the-President/Archive/Robert-Q_-Berry-III/Thinking-about-Instructional-Routines-in-Mathematics-Teaching-and-Learning/

Clements, D. H. (2003). Teaching and learning geometry. In J. Kilpatrick, W. G. Martin, & D. Schifter (Eds.), *A research companion to Principles and Standards for School Mathematics* (pp. 151–178). National Council of Teachers of Mathematics.

Cohen, R. L. (1999). *Spatial reasoning and its relation to cognitive development*. Cambridge University Press.

Common Core Standards Writing Team. (2013). *Progressions for the common core state standards in mathematics (Grade 8)*. Institute for Mathematics and Education, University of Arizona

Dietiker, L. C., Gonulates, F., & Smith, J. P. (2011). Understanding linear measure. *Teaching Children Mathematics, 18*(4), 252–259.

Dinsmoor, K. (2022). Math manipulatives. In S. L. Mason (Ed.), *Student-centered approaches in K–12 and higher education.* EdTech Books. https://edtechbooks.org/student_centered/math_manipulatives

Dweck, C. (2006). *Mindset: The new psychology of success*. Penguin Random House.

Egan, M. (1999). Reflections on effective use of graphic organizers. *Journal of Adolescent & Adult Literacy*, 42, 641–645.

Fennell, F. M., Kobett, B. M., & Wray, J. A. (2017). *The formative 5: Everyday assessment techniques for every math classroom*. Corwin Mathematics/National Council of Teachers of Mathematics.

Gay, A. S., Haistings, J., & Rucker, J. L. (2022). Bodies in motion: Exploring dynamic angles. *Mathematics Teacher Learning and Teaching PK-12, 115*(8), 559–565. https://doi.org/10.5951/mtlt.2022.0073

Gladwell, M. (2008). *Outliers: The story of success*. Little, Brown and Company.

Grouws, D. A., & Cebulla, K. J. (2000). The impact of the van Hiele model on instruction and learning. In D. A. Grouws (Ed.), *Handbook of Research on Mathematics Teaching and Learning* (pp. 120–138). Macmillan.

Kablan, Z., & Uğur, S. S. (2020). The relationship between routine and non-routine problem solving and learning styles. *Educational Studies, 47*(3), 328–343. https://doi.org/10.1080/03055698.2019.1701993

Kandaga, T., Rosjanuardi, R., & Juandi, D. (2022). Epistemological obstacle in transformation geometry based on van Hiele's level. *Eurasia Journal of Mathematics Science and Technology Education, 18*(4), em2096. https://doi.org/10.29333/ejmste/11914

Karp, K. S., Dougherty, B. J., & Bush, S. B. (2021). *The math pact, elementary: Achieving instructional coherence within and across grades*. Corwin.

Klaxoon. (n.d.). *Who invented the Venn diagram?* Klaxoon. Retrieved December 15, 2024, from https://klaxoon.com/insight/who-invented-the-venn-diagram

Krasa, N. (2010). *Number sense and number nonsense: Understanding the challenges of learning math*. Paul H. Brookes Publishing Co.

Liljedahl, P. (2020). *Building thinking classrooms in mathematics: 14 teaching practices for enhancing learning*. Corwin.

Liljedahl, P. (2016). Building thinking classrooms: Conditions for problem-solving. In P. Felmer, E. Pehkonen, & J. Kilpatrick (Eds.), *Posing and Solving Mathematical Problems* (pp. 361–386). https://doi.org/10.1007/978-3-319-28023-3_21

Martin, C. (2021). Using feedback to support students' critical learning. *Mathematics Teacher: Learning and Teaching PK-12, 114*(4), 266–268. https://doi.org/10.5951/MTLT.2021.0015

Metoyer, S. K., Bednarz, S. W., & Bednarz, R. S. (2015). Spatial thinking in education: Concepts, development, and assessment. In O. Muñiz Solari, A. Demirci, & J. van der Schee (Eds.), *Geospatial technologies and geography education in a changing world* (pp. 21–33). Springer.

Miller, E. K., & O'Connell, J. D.. (2004). *The development of spatial reasoning in childhood and adolescence. Psychology Press.*

National Council of Teachers of Mathematics. (2024). *Data science: Position statement*. https://www.nctm.org/Standards-and-Positions/Position-Statements/Data-Science/

National Governors Association Center for Best Practices & Council of Chief State School Officers. (2010). *Common core state standards for mathematics*. http://www.corestandards.org

Parrish, S. (2010). *Number talks: Helping children build mental math and computation strategies*. Math Solutions.

SanGiovanni, J., Bay-Williams, J., & Katt, S. (2024). *Figuring out fluency—ten foundations for reasoning strategies with whole numbers*. Corwin.

SanGiovanni, J., Katt, S., Rivera, G., & Knighten, L. (2023). *Answers to your biggest questions about teaching elementary math*. Corwin.

SanGiovanni, J. J. (2023). *Daily routines to jump-start problem solving K–8*. Corwin.

SanGiovanni, J., Katt, S., & Dykema, K. (2020). *Productive math struggle: A six-point action plan for fostering perseverance*. Corwin.

SanGiovanni, J. J. (2020). *Daily routines to jump-start math class: Elementary school*. Corwin.

SanGiovanni, J. J. & Milou, E. (2018). *Daily routines to jump-start math class: Middle school*. Corwin.

Smith, M. S., & Stein, M. K. (2018). *5 practices for orchestrating productive mathematics discussions* (2nd ed). National Council of Teachers of Mathematics.

Stauffer, B. (2022, March 17). *What are 21st century skills?* AES. Retrieved April 22, 2022, from https://www.aeseducation.com/blog/what-are-21st-century-skills

Tall D. O., & Vinner S. (1981). *Concept image and concept definition in mathematics, with special reference to limits and continuity*. Educational Studies in Mathematics, 12, 151–169.

Vojkuvkova, I. (2012). The van Hiele model of geometric thinking. In J. Šafránková & Jiří Pavlů (Eds.), *WDS '12 Proceedings of Contributed Papers, Part I* (pp. 72–75). https://physics.mff.cuni.cz/wds/proc/pdf12/WDS12_112_m8_Vojkuvkova.pdf

Van de Walle, J. A., Karp, K. S., & Bay-Williams, J. M. (2023). *Elementary and middle school mathematics: Teaching developmentally* (11th ed.). Pearson Education, Inc.

van Hiele Model of Geometric Thinking. (2024). Ohio Department of Education and Workforce. https://education.ohio.gov/getattachment/Topics/Learning-in-Ohio/Mathematics/Model-Curricula-in-Mathematics/Van-Hiele-Model-of-Geometric-Thinking.pdf

Young Mathematicians. (n.d.). *About quick images*. Retrieved December 16, 2024, from https://youngmathematicians.edc.org/math_games/quick-images/

INDEX

JENNIFER M. BAY-WILLIAMS, JOHN J. SANGIOVANNI, ROSALBA SERRANO, SHERRI MARTINIE, JENNIFER SUH, C. DAVID WALTERS, SUSIE KATT

Because fluency is so much more than basic facts and algorithms.

Grades K–8

MARIA DEL ROSARIO ZAVALA, JULIA MARIA AGUIRRE

Discover innovative equity-based culturally responsive mathematics instruction that unlocks the mathematical heart of each student.

Grades K–8

IVANNIA SOTO, THEODORE RUIZ SAGUN, MICHAEL BEIERSDORF

Focus on the literacy opportunities that multilingual students can achieve when language scaffolds are taught alongside rigorous math and science content.

Grades K–8

JOHN J. SANGIOVANNI, SUSIE KATT, LATRENDA D. KNIGHTEN, GEORGINA RIVERA, FREDERICK L. DILLON, AYANNA D. PERRY, ANDREA CHENG, JENNIFER OUTZS, KAREN MESMER, ENYA GRANDOS, KEVIN GANT, LAURA SHAFER

Actionable answers to your most pressing questions about teaching elementary math, secondary math, and secondary science.

Elementary, Secondary

CHRISTA JACKSON, KRISTIN L. COOK, SARAH B. BUSH, MARGARET MOHR-SCHROEDER, CATHRINE MAIORCA, THOMAS ROBERTS

Help educators create integrated STEM learning experiences that are inclusive for all students and allow them to experience STEM as scientists, innovators, mathematicians, creators, engineers, and technology experts!

Grades PreK–5 and Grades 6–12

CORWIN